HOW
TO
READ
NOW

HOW
TO
READ
NOW

ESSAYS

ELAINE
CASTILLO

VIKING

VIKING
An imprint of Penguin Random House LLC
penguinrandomhouse.com

LIBRARY OF CONGRESS CATALOGING-IN-PUBLICATION DATA
Names: Castillo, Elaine, author.
Title: How to read now : essays / Elaine Castillo.
Description: [New York] : Viking, [2022] | Includes bibliographical references.
Identifiers: LCCN 2022002699 | ISBN 9780593489635 (hardcover) |
ISBN 9780593489642 (ebook)
Subjects: LCSH: Reading. | Literature and society. | Literature and race. |
Imperialism in literature. | Books and reading—Sociological aspects.
Classification: LCC PN83 .C37 2022 | DDC 418/.4—dc23/eng/20220509
LC record available at https://lccn.loc.gov/2022002699

Printed in the United States of America
1st Printing

Book design by Daniel Lagin

I said, "All along I have been wondering how you got to be the way you are. Just how it was that you got to be the way you are."

JAMAICA KINCAID, *LUCY*

CONTENTS

HOW
TO
READ
NOW

AUTHOR'S NOTE,
OR A VIRGO
CLARIFIES THINGS

In the years since my debut novel came out, I've been thinking a lot about how to read. Not about how to write—I wouldn't trust a book about how to write by a debut novelist, any more than I would trust a book about how to swim by someone who'd accomplished the exceptional achievement of not having drowned, once. But reading? Most days when I look back at my childhood, it feels like first I became a reader; then I became a person. And in the postdebut years of touring, and traveling—in hotel rooms in Auckland and East Lansing, on festival stages in Manila and Rome, in bookstores in London, and in the renovated community library of my hometown, Milpitas—a thought came back to me, again and again; a ghost with unfinished business, a song I couldn't get out of my head: we need to change how we read.

The *we* I'm talking about here is generally American, since that's the particular cosmic sports team I've found myself on, through the mysteries of fate and colonial genocide—but in truth, it's a more capacious *we* than that, too. A *we* of the reading world, perhaps. By readers I don't just mean the literate, a community I don't particularly issue from myself, although I am, in spite of everything, among its fiercest spear-bearers. I mean something more expansive and yet more humble: the *we* that is in the world, and thinks about it, and then lives in it. That's the kind of reader I am, and love—and that's the reading practice I'm most interested in, and most alive to myself.

The second thought that has come to my house and still won't grab its coat and leave is this: the way we read now is simply not good enough, and it is failing not only our writers—especially, but not limited to, our most marginalized writers—but failing our readers, which is to say, ourselves.

When I talk about reading, I don't just mean books, though of course as a writer, books remain kin to me in ways that other art forms—even ones I may have come to love with an easier enthusiasm, in recent years—aren't. At heart, reading has never just been the province of books, or the literate. Reading doesn't bring us to books; or at least, that's not the trajectory that really matters. Sure, some of us are made readers—usually because of the gift (and privilege) of a literate parent, a friendly librarian, a caring kindergarten teacher—and as readers, we then come to discover the world of books. But the point of reading is not to fetishize books, however alluring they might look on an Instagram flat lay. Books, as world-encompassing as they are, aren't the destination; they're a waypoint. Reading doesn't bring us to books—books bring us to reading. They're one of the places we go to help us to become readers in the world. I know that growing up, film and TV were as important to my formation as a critical thinker—to the ways in which I engaged with "representation" in any real sense—so I can't imagine not writing about them, even in a book supposedly about reading.

When I talk about how to read now, I'm not just talking about how to read books now; I'm talking about how to read our world now. How to read films, TV shows, our history, each other. How to dismantle the forms of interpretation we've inherited; how those ways of interpreting are everywhere and unseen. How to understand that it's meaningful when Wes Anderson's characters throw Filipinx bodies off an onscreen boat like they're nothing; how to understand that bearing witness to that scene means nothing if we can't *read* it—if we don't have the tools to understand its context, meaning, and effect in the world. That it's meaningful to have seen HBO's *Watchmen* and been moved and challenged by its subversive reckoning with the kinds of superhero tropes many kids, including myself, grew up on. Books will always have a certain historical pride of place in my life—but it's also because of books that *reading* can have a more expansive meaning in that life, both practically and politically.

In a more personal sense, as a first-generation American from a working-class / fragilely middle-class upbringing, most of the people in my life simply don't read: aren't sufficiently confident in their English, or don't have the leisure time, or have long found books and reading culture intimidating and foreclosed to them (for all my love of independent bookstores, I've also been glared at like a potential shoplifter in enough of the white-owned ones to temper that love). I don't want a book called *How to Read Now* to speak only to the type of people who read books and attend literary festivals—and in the same vein, I don't want it to let off the hook people who think they don't read at all. I can't write a book about reading that tells people there's only one type of reading that counts—but equally, just because you don't read books at all doesn't mean you're not reading, or being read in the world. Of course, *How to Read Now* runs off the tongue a little easier than *How to Dismantle Your Entire Critical Apparatus.*

I've been an inveterate reader all my life, and yet I'm writing this book at the time in my life when I have the least faith I've ever had in books, or indeed reading culture in general. (The fact that this sentiment coincides with having become a published author doesn't escape me.) For my sins, I haven't lost faith in the capacity of books to save us, remake us, take us by the scruff and show us who we were, who we are, and who we might become; that conviction has been unkillable in me for too long. But I have in some crucial way lost my faith in our capacity to truly be commensurate to the work that reading asks of us; in our ability to make our reading culture live up to the world we're reading in—and for.

When I first began writing this book, I was in Aotearoa, also known as New Zealand, as a guest at the Auckland Writers Festival. Much happened in between those stolen, heady moments of writing on hotel room couches in the spring of 2019 and the (not quite) postpandemic world we now find ourselves in—worrying about the nurses in my family still working on the front lines; supporting loved ones who'd lost their jobs; mourning loved ones who'd lost their lives; joining the many marches here in the Bay to protest the anti-Black police brutality that took the lives of George Floyd, Breonna Taylor, among so many others, as well as the rise in anti-Asian hate, fueled by Trump's virulently racist coronavirus rhetoric. I'd also rolled into lockdown after already being essentially confined at home in convalescence for over two months: in December 2019, just before Christmas, I'd been hospitalized for emergency surgery due to the internal hemorrhaging caused by an ectopic pregnancy, in which my left fallopian tube was surgically removed in a unilateral salpingectomy. This was my second pregnancy loss, after complications with a D&C for a miscarriage at twelve weeks left me in and out of King's College Hospital over the summer of 2017, back when I was still living in London and editing my first novel, *America Is Not the Heart*.

All this to say, when I look back at the inception of this book, I can't help but feel that I'm looking at it from an entirely different world. In 2018 and 2019, the things I'd witnessed and experienced in the publishing industry during those early first-novel book tours and festivals made it distressingly clear to me that there was also something profoundly wrong with our reading culture, and particularly the ways in which writers of color were expected to exist in it: the roles they were meant to play, the audiences they were meant to educate and console, the problems their books were meant to solve. It started to feel like it would be impossible to continue working in this industry if I didn't somehow put down in writing the deep-seated unease I had around this framing.

I wanted to write about the reading culture I was seeing: the way it instrumentalized the books of writers of color to do the work that white readers should have always been doing themselves; the way our reading culture pats itself on the back for producing "important" and "relevant" stories that often ultimately reduce communities of color to their most traumatic episodes, thus creating a dynamic in which predominantly white American readers expect books by writers of color to "teach" them specific lessons—about historical trauma, far-flung wars, their own sins—while the work of predominantly white writers gets to float, palely, in the culture, unnamed, unmarked, universal as oxygen. None of these are particularly new issues; Toni Morrison's landmark, indispensable *Playing in the Dark* remains the urtext on the insidious racial backbone of our reading culture. But I was occasionally alarmed during book tour events when I would make reference to *Playing in the Dark*, and realize that many in the audience had not read it and, indeed, seemingly hadn't ever had a substantial reckoning with the politics, especially racial politics, of their reading practices.

That was then. I still believe in reading, and I still very much want to write this book; I have written it, after all. But there was the intellectual idea of writing a book called *How to Read Now*, in a critical attempt to contend with the racial politics and ethics of how we read our books, our history, and each other—and there was the actual lived practice of writing that book, in the midst of the historic social upheaval brought to us by a global pandemic whose grotesquely racist coverage and criminally incompetent mismanagement under Trump's America has not only utterly upended the daily lives of everyone I know, but has laid bare the outrageous truths many of us have always known, in particular regarding the true value of Black and Brown lives in this country, where systemic injustice and government neglect has meant predominantly poorer Black and Brown communities have borne the brunt of COVID-19's destruction.

When I was working on this book in 2019, there were things I believed stridently about the politics of reading and writing. I know the twenty-first-century pose of literary personality in late capitalism is usually one of excoriating self-doubt and anxiety, but I am a bossy Virgo bitch, and I have generally always been irritatingly sure of myself and my convictions, occasionally to my detriment, certainly to the chagrin of those who have chosen to love me. But I would be lying if I said that the events of 2020 and 2021 hadn't profoundly affected me, and begun to permanently transform how I think about the world, and how to make art in it. I think most of all it's become clear to me that when I named the book *How to Read Now*, I must have subconsciously meant the title both as a bossy Virgo directive and as an inquiry: a question, open-ended. I, too, want to know how to read now.

But what I thought then, and what I still think now, is this: the way we read now is, by and large, morally bankrupt and indefensible, and must change immediately, because we are indeed failing not just our writers and ourselves, but more pressingly our future—which will never look any different from our current daily feed of apocalypse if we don't figure out a different way to read the world we live in. I'll paraphrase the hackneyed quote by the equally hackneyed George Santayana (who was often a pretty piss-poor reader of the world himself, and who believed, for example, that intermarriage between superior races—his own—and inferior races—hi—should be prevented): if we don't figure out a different way to read our world, we'll be doomed to keep living in it.

I don't know about you, but I find that prospect unbearable. Anyone who is perfectly comfortable with keeping the world just as it is now and reading it the way they've always read it—is, frankly, a fed, cannot be trusted, and is probably wiretapping your phone.

HOW TO READ NOW

White supremacy makes for terrible readers, I find. The thing is, often when people talk about racists, they talk in terms of ignorance. *They're just ignorant*, they say. *Such ignorant people. I'm sorry, my grandpa's really ignorant. That was an ignorant thing to say. What an ignorant comment.* We're besieged on all sides by the comforting logic and pathos of ignorance. It's a logic that excuses people—bad readers—from their actions; from the living effect of their bad reading.

Most people are not, in fact, all that ignorant, i.e., lacking knowledge, or simply unaware. Bad reading isn't a question of people undereducated in a more equitable and progressive understanding of what it means to be a person among other people. Most people are vastly *overeducated*: overeducated in white supremacy, in patriarchy, in heteronormativity. Most people are in fact highly advanced in their education in these economies, economies that say, very plainly, that cis straight white lives are inherently more valuable, interesting, and noble than the lives of everyone else; that they deserve to be set in stone, centered in every narrative. It's not a question of bringing people out of their ignorance—*if only someone had told me that Filipinos were human, I wouldn't have massacred all of them!*—but a question of bringing people out of their deliberately extensive education.

When I say that white supremacy makes for terrible readers, I mean that white supremacy is, among its myriad ills, a formative collection of fundamentally shitty reading techniques that impoverishes you as a reader, a thinker, and a feeling person; it's an education that promises that whole swaths of the world and their liveliness will be diminished in meaning to you. Illegible, intangible, forever unreal as cardboard figures in a diorama. *They don't know how to read us*, I've heard fellow writer friends of color complain, usually after a particularly frustrating Q&A in which a white person has either taken offense to something in our books or in the discussion (usually the mention of whiteness at all will be enough to offend these particularly thin-skinned readers), or said something well-meaning but ultimately self-serving, usually about how their story made them *feel terrible about your country.*

White supremacy is a comprehensive cultural education whose primary function is to prevent people from reading—engaging with, understanding—the lives of people outside its scope. This is even more apparent in the kind of reading most enthusiastically trafficked by the white liberal literary community that has such an outsize influence, intellectually and

economically, on the publishing industry today. The unfortunate
influence of this style of reading has dictated that we go to
writers of color for the gooey heart-porn of the ethnographic: to
learn about forgotten history, harrowing tragedy, community-
destroying political upheaval, genocide, trauma; that we expect those writers to provide those intellectual commodities the
way their ancestors once provided spices, minerals, precious
stones, and unprecious bodies.

Writers like me often do carry the weight of forgotten history, harrowing tragedy, community-destroying political upheaval, genocide, and trauma. But how then are we read? And
equally as important, how then are we edited? How is our work
circulated in a marketplace that struggles not just to see all of
its writers as equals, but to pay them as equals? For if our
stories primarily serve to educate, console, and productively
scold a comfortable white readership, then those stories will
have failed their readers, and those readers will have failed
those stories. All the "representation matters" rhetoric in the
world means nothing if we do not address the fundamentally
fucked-up relationship between writers of color and white audiences that persists in our contemporary reading culture.

I have no desire to write yet another instruction manual
for the sociocultural betterment of white readers. I don't know
any writer who, if asked what they wanted their work to do in
the world, would reply: "Make better white people." Equally, I
don't see a sustainable way to continue in my industry without
reckoning with the rot at its core, which is that, by and large,

the English-language publishing industry centers the perspective and comfort of its overwhelmingly white employee base and audience, leaving writers of color to be positioned along that firmly established structure: as flavors of the month, as heroic saviors, as direly important educators, as necessary interventions ("classic American story / genre / historical episode, but now populated with brown people!" continues to be one of the most dominant and palatable gateways for white audiences to become accustomed to seeing Black and Brown bodies on their screens and in their pages), as vessels of sensational trauma—but rarely as artists due the same depth and breadth of critical engagement as their white colleagues; rarely as artists whose works are approached not just as sources of history or educational potential but specific and sublime sensual immersion: sites of wonder, laughter, opulence, precision; a place to sink into the particular weather of a particular town; a place to pang at the love of strangers, thwarted or salvaged.

At heart, my issue with how we read is as much an existential grievance as it is a labor dispute: the industry is simply not serving its employees equally. And it asks, repeatedly, for uncompensated overtime from writers of color who, often in lieu of engaging in detail about the actual book they've actually written, find themselves instead managing the limited critical capacity of mostly white readers, here offended by the appearance of a non-English word, there alienated by a conversation not translated for their benefit. Writers of color often find themselves doing the second, unspoken and unsalaried job of not just being a professional writer but a Professional Person of Color, in the most performative sense—handy to have on hand for panels or journal issues about race or power or revolution, so the festival or literary journal doesn't appear *totally* racist; handy to praise publicly and singularly, so as to draw less attention to the white audience, rapt in the seats too expensive for local readers of color. Running the gauntlet of book promotion for my first novel, it became patently obvious that much of our literary industry functions as little more than a quaint pastime for its adherents, like Marie-Antoinette in the Petit Trianon's Hameau de la Reine: a place to merely cosplay diversity, empathy, education. Not a place to truly be diverted from oneself; not a place to be made humble in one's vulnerability; not a place to be laid bare in one's unknowing.

IT WAS MY FATHER WHO FIRST INTRODUCED ME TO BOOKS. I grew up in what was once a small town—the tech boom of the Bay Area ensures it will never be a small town again—in which I was never a visible, singled-out minority. Instead, I was part of an exceedingly invisible and thus banal majority: what's often called, usually with a faintly lurid dash of fearmongering, a "majority-minority town."

I emphasize the demographic makeup of the community I came out of primarily because I've found that so much of our contemporary imaginings of minority lives, especially immigrant lives, always seem to posit the idea of the Only One: the only Asian, in the white town. The one minority, beset on all sides by white people. That narrative is often sold as the pre-eminent narrative of minority experience in America, and the people who sell this story often frame it as a story of typical American hardship: the difficulty of being the only Asian kid in a white class.

That this dominant narrative bears zero resemblance to my own experience doesn't make it untrue, of course; I know there are plenty of people who grew up as the only kid of color in a white town. But it's the way that narrative is deployed that matters here. It successfully centers whiteness in a minoritized person's story—making their narrative about adapting or not adapting to "America," which is always a code for adapting to whiteness. It also mistakes difference for oppression, which is not the same thing: to be the only Asian person in an otherwise white town is just as much an indicator of privilege as it is of oppression, because most economically disadvantaged minorities do not live in majority-white towns. In a place like the Bay Area, they more typically live, as I did, in the satellite suburban towns that house a larger urbanized area's lower-income support workers—my town was made up mostly of Filipinx, Vietnamese, and Mexican working-class immigrant families (with pockets of wealthier immigrant families here and there) whose jobs as security guards, nurses, cooks, domestic workers, and subcontracted landscapers serviced the larger, whiter towns to which we all commuted, for work or school.

I've very often seen successful people of color framing

their experiences of being the only person of color in their classrooms as narratives about struggle, rather than *also* being narratives about class and power; I emphasize *often*, because it seems to me that in fact many successful people of color in our mainstream media happen to be precisely the sort of people who grew up the only person of color in white towns. It is precisely *because* they grew up adjacent to whiteness and its social and economic privilege, precisely *because* they were well versed at an early age on how to adapt to and accommodate whiteness that they could thus use those skills as professional adults, living under white supremacy.

Like many other Filipinx people of a similarly working-class, middle-class aspirational background, I grew up surrounded by a wide and diverse (it should not be a revelation that a minority community can itself be diverse) Filipinx community. It meant that I grew up with the assumed sense of my own centeredness, if not necessarily centrality or importance. I was not visibly particularly different, special, or unique from most anyone else I grew up with. And while there were of course conflicts mainly across class and colorist lines, whiteness was not the reference point or framework in my community, and so I did not learn early on to prioritize it in my psychic, intellectual, or sociopolitical life. That includes the way I read—the way, more specifically, my father taught me to read.

My parents had a mixed-class marriage, although on paper, by the time I was born, it wouldn't have read as such. By then, my father was a security guard at a computer chip company and my mother was a nurse holding down at least two, sometimes three, different jobs at various hospitals and nursing homes. My mother came from abject rural poverty of the kind that has made her literacy shaky, not just in English but in Tagalog, the controversial lingua franca of the Philippines (her first language—and mine, now lost—being Pangasinan). Like many first-generation kids, I spend a lot of my time as my mother's English safety net, language-checking everything from legal documents to her Facebook statuses.

My father, on the other hand, born in 1930 (and so twenty-two years older than my mother), came from a comfortable upper-middle-class Ilocano background—a dark-skinned boy descended from a mix of the indigenous northerners of Luzon and the merchant Chinese class—in which literacy and literary education were a given. He circulated with people who read widely in English, who discussed the literary and philosophical merits of Philippine national hero José Rizal (the only national hero I can think of who was also a novelist). It's because of this that my reading life can never be disentangled from questions of class and power, as readership has always been not just a gift but a privilege: Would I have become the reader I became if I'd had a different father? He was making me read Plato's *Symposium* when I was in middle school, a fact that none of my white teachers believed, and in fact actively and aggressively tried to disprove—another lesson familiar to many kids of color I know.

One of the first places I ever learned about bad readers was from white teachers in the Catholic schools I attended. (Catholic schools are the nearest thing to affordable private schools for working-class immigrant parents—not to mention the fact that my mother was and remains a devout if irreverent and syncretic Catholic, and wanted her children educated in the faith. In my case, my parents only had enough gas in them to send one kid to such a school—which means my younger brother had a largely public education. That, among other things, has created a palpable class difference that still affects us today.) Some people have great teachers growing up, and I truly envy them, but my great ones were very, very rare; for the most part, my memories of education are of sneering, condescension, and neglect. Teachers in the Mountain View / Los Altos region of the Bay Area where I attended junior high and high school— significantly whiter and wealthier than the Milpitas schools I attended throughout elementary school—often seemed threatened, occasionally enraged, by the idea of a smart, bookish, and vocally irreverent Filipinx kid. It was understood that if kids who looked like me were ever to succeed, we were meant to do so docilely, gratefully, quietly. Not confidently. Not proudly. And when I look back now, despite the casual cruelty of those days, that educational neglect also meant I never really got a successful education in the profoundly incurious way those teachers read books, the world, and me.

Instead, I got my father's kind of reading. In the world of books that I lived in with him, I was in Plato's world, playing in the cave; there was no difference between me and James Joyce,

and darling, I should really read *Finnegans Wake* to experience
what some people called modernism; ditto Rizal, and Bertrand
Russell, and Kant, and Virginia Woolf, and buckets and buckets of Greek mythology, which I fell in love with and nearly
became a classicist for in college, during my I-want-to-be-the-
Pinay-Anne-Carson stage.

We read a lot of white people. But we didn't read them
with a white-centering view; we didn't read them like those
books and the worlds in them were the only ones that existed,
or mattered. We read them like they were just books, and they
had things to say, and they were sometimes very powerful and
fragile and beautiful; just like I was a person, and I had things
to say, and I was sometimes very powerful and fragile and
beautiful. It was, I realize now, a deeply weird, genreless, free-
wheeling way of reading. It wasn't decolonial exactly—I mean,
we were still reading the jerks, and Kant obviously didn't think
we were human beings—but the motley, secular, antihierar-
chical, unacademic way we read this wide swath of books bore
the seeds of the decolonial. Reading with my father taught me
to read across borders, and to read in translation (he loved
Thomas Mann and Goethe, and he loved that I loved Japanese
and Latin American writers like Banana Yoshimoto or Manuel
Puig). Our practice taught me most of all to read like a free,
mysterious person who was encountering free, mysterious
things; to value the profound privacy and irregularity of my
own thinking; to spend time in my head and the heads of oth-

ers, and to see myself shimmer in many worlds—to let many worlds shimmer, lively, in me.

So much of why that reading was truly liberating and life-forming was that it went hand in hand with my father's (and to a slightly lesser extent, my mother's; lesser not in terms of intensity but only in terms of volume, since she worked so much that she simply wasn't actually around to do this kind of ideological child-raising) frankly ferocious commitment to instilling in me what I know now to be a furnace of immutable and indestructible pride—its life-giving warmth buried so deep in my bones it must have belonged to someone much, much older than either of us, much older even than either of the countries we came from. An ancient life-source, evergreen.

My father died in 2006, after a long—too long, in his opinion—fight with lymphoma. When it became clear we'd do anything to keep him alive, even if that meant repeated trips to the ICU, repeated nights sleeping in hospital waiting rooms waiting for morning visiting hours to begin, he took the decision out of our hands: he took his oxygen mask off in the middle of the night, hours after insisting on seeing me, for what I didn't realize was the last time I would ever see him fully conscious. He let himself go first, so we would have to let him go, too.

My father died penniless and indebted, and I inherited nothing from him—nothing but my entire life: the frequency at which my attention to the world resonates, and most of all, that bone-deep, soul-shaped pride, which to this day I feel move in me, like a chord that will not go silent.

Pride is not always one of the best qualities to be abundant in, and it got me into a lot of trouble as a kid; if you're proud, but treated a little or a lot like shit by either boys in your class, or lighter-skinned wealthier Filipinx friends, or white teachers, you have a tendency to be constitutionally programmed to start rumbling the first person who blinks at you funny. I got into a lot—*a lot*—of fights as a kid, and the family mythos of my child self is one that alternates near-death fragility (I was also a physically sickly child) and a pugnacity bordering on the feral.

The only thing that prevented that pride from becoming my villain origin story—well, for now—was its steadfast companion, which was the gift of the town I grew up in: the unshakable knowledge of my own smallness, in both a terrestrial and a cosmic sense. I was never the Only One: not singular, not special, not different. My community showed me that I was not best understood by being contextualized against whiteness; I did not have to translate myself for its understanding or approval, which I had little experience with and was never told I needed. I did not have to perform or deform myself for the right to be myself. Growing up in a town like Milpitas taught me that my ordinariness to myself was a gift, and a root; that this ordinariness, uninterpreted, was enough. It did not have to be distilled or bleached to have value.

That I, too, am a full person who deserved respect in my

wholeness seems now like such a basic lesson, and yet the enduring force and redemption of that lesson make it one that I've gone back to again and again, in my life and in my work. My father in the years I knew him—late in the long book of his life; that last, uneven, American chapter—was mostly a quiet, melancholy, and deeply internal person, who nevertheless had an indomitable sense of his own worth; a worth that was singular, unwreckable, and mysterious, like a diamond core inside a rock-shelter. It was a worth that resisted being misread, but was not diminished when misreading came knocking. He was, of course, misread every single day of his life in America. Old Pinoy security guard at a computer chip company, moreno, poor, taciturn, lives in the town near Newby Landfill, the one that famously smells like shit. What stories could he have to tell?

But the way he lived blotted out that misreading. He might have been foreign or exotic to others, but he was never foreign to himself—mysterious, yes, in the way that we are all mysterious to ourselves—but not foreign. His ordinariness to himself was a treasure, its precious scroll all there to read, for the people who could read it. And then he passed that treasure down to me, so I could read it, too. Moreover, so I could expect to *be* read like that, in my own life: like a scroll of worth poured out of me, and it was all mine—not something to be bartered or made palatable so I would one day have value in the world. But a gift; glorious, banal, and whole unto itself.

When I describe the way my reading life is inextricable from the way I was raised—built, really, to be a person in the world—and how my reading life now is committed not just to reading books, but to the world that those books helped me to bear witness to, what I'm really saying is that my reading life was also an inheritance; one that came in the form of an ongoing act of love.

Post-2020, it feels impossibly hard and incalculably stupid to say that you love the world. Why bother? Why does reading matter? Why does truly trying to know the world we live in, the history that makes us, matter? It feels impossibly hard and incalculably stupid to commit to that love, to bear it and be borne by it, but that is what I feel—it is the wellspring that reading leads me to, every time. Loving this world, loving being alive in it, means living up to that world; living up to that love. I can't say I love this world or living in it if I don't bother to know it; indeed, be known by it. It's that mutual promise of knowing that reading holds us in—an inheritance that belongs to us, whether we accept it or not. Whether we read its pages or not. This book remains just one small part of that work: that inheritance, and that love.

READING TEACHES
US EMPATHY,
AND OTHER FICTIONS

People often say that art builds our empathy. Reading, in particular. It's one of those feel-good lines that gets trotted out at literary readings, writing festivals, panel discussions on diversity in fiction, in classrooms, on book jackets, book reviews, book blurbs, not to mention in uncomfortably long discussions with white people who've read your book and want you to know !!!for sure!!! that they're not racist. When we read books about immigration, our exposure to the toil of good, hardworking immigrants makes us more empathetic to their plight—and so on, for books about queer people, and books about slavery, et cetera. Diverse books are empathy machines, or so the received wisdom would have us believe. Like Trinity in *The Matrix*, we can upload a book's world into ourselves and feel our empathy skills powering up, juicing through the veins. I use the impoverished term "diverse books" deliberately here, because it's the books that fall under the rubric of diversity that are the ones most often prescribed to us as empathy boosters; books built for purpose.

But the idea that fiction builds empathy is one of incomplete politics, left hanging by probably good intentions. The concept of instrumentalizing fiction or art as a kind of ethical protein shake, such that reading more and more diversely will somehow build the muscles in us that will help us see other people as human, makes a kind of superficial sense—and produces a superficial effect. The problem with this type of reading is that in its practical application, usually readers are encouraged— by well-meaning teachers and lazy publishing copy—to read writers of a demographic minority in order to *learn* things; which is to say, as a supplement for their empathy muscles, a metabolic exchange that turns writers of color into little more than ethnographers—personal trainers, to continue the metaphor. The result is that we largely end up going to writers of color to learn the specific—and go to white writers to feel the universal.

The problem is, if we need fiction to teach us empathy, we don't really have empathy, because empathy is not a one-stop destination; it's a practice, ongoing, which requires work from us in our daily lives, for our daily lives—not just when we're confronted with the visibly and legibly Other. Not just when a particularly gifted author has managed to make a community's story come alive for the reader who's come for a quick zoo visit, always remaining on her side of the cage.

———

HOWEVER, THE ANNOYING PROBLEM WITH PUSHING BACK against the self-serving platitudes of fiction-as-empathy machine is that sometimes you run into people who disdain the value of empathy in art for entirely different, but equally self-serving reasons: the art-for-art's-sake gang, here to rout out political correctness, save literature, and make sure we all have the right to keep reading the same white Europeans forevermore.

This squad has no time for diverse books as empathy machines, either—not because the practice bowdlerizes the work of minoritized writers, about whom the art-for-art's-sake gang could generally care less, but because to this regime of thought, any consideration of identity or empathy, or indeed being in any way consciously political in one's art making and one's art consumption, necessarily diminishes and cheapens our relationship to that art. This particularly strident Hogwarts house protests against the relationship between fiction and empathy not because of the unequal distribution of burden it places on writers of color vs. white writers, but because prioritizing empathy through fiction gets in the way of a reader's supposedly pure relationship to that author's art; its apparently sacred nonpolitical storytelling force.

I'm reminded of a *New York Times* opinion piece by Bret Stephens, written after the controversial awarding of the Nobel Prize to casually fascist stylist Peter Handke, the Austrian writer known both for his spare epigrammatic texts and for his fervently pro-Serbian stance with regard to the violent collapse of the former Yugoslavia and his denial of the genocide of Bosnian Muslims at the hands of Serbian forces—showing his support by, among other things, famously attending the funeral of Serbian president Slobodan Milošević, the first sitting head of state to be charged for war crimes. The *New York Times* piece defended those who would continue to read the Austrian's work, with the passion typical of people whose commitment to art is such that it compels them to defend white fascists and their apologists:

> What's the alternative? Those who think that a core task of art is political instruction or moral uplift will wind up with some version of socialist realism or religious dogma. And those who think that the worth of art must be judged according to the moral and political commitments of its creator ultimately consign all art to the dustbin, since even the most avant-garde artists are creatures of their time.

This is the white liberal argument that characterizes much of our reading culture: that there is a fundamental binary between political art and the Real Art that transcends such dogma, such instruction, such moralizing. The panic here is that Art, True Art, our tragic and ever-far Dulcinea, may be under siege from the contaminating force of the polity and its concerns; that indeed we risk losing *all* art—throw it straight into the garbage bin!—if we ever dare to ask art to be more than it is; to do more than what it ought to do.

The problem is, this panicked defensiveness rarely seems to actually know what it wants the art to be; what it wants art to do. This paranoid Testudo formation rarely seems to have a handle on what reading, and in particular critical reading, actually consists of. Sure, critical reading is an intellectual exercise, an aesthetic exercise, and a profoundly private, emotional, and visceral undertaking—while also being an ethical act; a civic act. It is all these things at once. Books ask us to live this multiplicity every single time we open them. But there's often a conservative, reactionary resistance to the expansive multiplicity (and specifically, inclusivity) of critical reading, which encompasses postcolonial readings, queer readings, what's sometimes pejoratively called "anachronistic" readings. The argument usually goes something along the lines of: we can't apply contemporary political worldviews onto older texts, because "the world was different then."

Sure, it was—but it also wasn't, is the thing. The lives of the characters in Jane Austen's novels will always be entwined with Britain's empire and slave economy: that was always the case. Slavery and the capitalist extraction of resources from Caribbean colonies were banal and foundational facts of life in Austen's era, and that ubiquity does not erase the world-rending evil those practices represented, nor does it invalidate the minutely drawn humanity of the specific parts of her world Austen *was* able to recognize and bring to life. Although, as Montclair State University professor and scholar of British abolitionist literature Patricia Matthews has deftly pointed out, both in her *Atlantic* article "On Teaching, but Not Loving, Jane Austen" and her webinar " 'I Hope White Hands': Wedgwood, Abolition, and the Female Consumer," the canonization of Austen ("whose fiction played with, but ultimately conformed to, the social conventions of [her] time") throws into relief the fact that many of Austen's less-passionately-remembered contemporaries did, in fact, write about race and interracial marriages ("that were not tucked away in Charlotte Brontë's attic"). Rejecting contemporary discussions of race when it comes to Austen's work also masks the fact that political debates about abolition among wealthy educated whites, especially the white women who were both Austen's subject and audience, were by no means exceptional: Austen's (not to mention Elizabeth Bennet's) contemporaries were known to have "circulated petitions, raised funds for the cause and boycotted sugar from the West Indies." Even Wedgwood (famed purveyor of teacups to many a well-heeled character from Austen to *Bridgerton*, as well as any self-respecting cottagecore picnic bitch influencer) produced teapots and cameo medallions and sugar bowls decorated with abolitionist artwork and slogans, due to founder Josiah Wedgwood's membership in the Society for the Abolition of the Slave Trade—while, of course, also producing tea services that celebrated Britain's naval might and seafaring heroes, demurely declining to elaborate just to what purpose and laden with what cargo those great ships, immortalized in bone china and creamware, once sailed. In fine-combing the political nuances and limitations of the era's gendered economies, Matthews draws our attention to a dynamic that echoes Toni Morrison's diagnosis of the way white selfhood was necessarily illuminated by casting Blackness as its shadow: the Regency construction of white womanhood (the deliberate signals sent by its purchasing tastes, the nobility of its humanitarian and protofeminist endeavors) necessitated—literally served up—a subaltern Black object for the liberal white woman to save, consume, and ultimately absorb into the drama of her own political enlightenment. (TLDR: A contemporary Austen character would wear that Dior feminist slogan T-shirt.)

Thus the complicated political substance of an abolitionist teapot cannot be divorced from its time period (although Matthews notes that one antislavery teapot she was looking for in the Birmingham Museum was missing, conspicuously kept separate from both the museum's transatlantic slavery and abolitionist section, as well as its creamware and pottery section; where are such things categorized, then?). Most of all, the Regency teapot cannot be divorced from its users, largely women, who not only cast themselves as righteous protagonists in the political theater accessorized by these objects (the better word here may be *props*), but also, crucially: *delighted* in the objects and the rituals they enshrined—in the complex seductions and pleasures of their material objecthood. Fundamentally, these objects were meant to be enjoyed as aesthetically beautiful, commercially desirable, and morally edifying, all at once. Not unlike some books. (When I lived in London, I once brought my visiting mother to afternoon tea at an upscale hotel, where towers of scones, sandwiches, cakes were served to us, as well as a great pot of lapsang souchong that came in a beautiful Wedgwood tea service I seriously considered buying—and still sometimes consider buying—had not the teapot alone cost one hundred and fifty-five pounds; marked up to three hundred and twenty-five dollars if bought here, unrepublicanly, in America.)

All this to say, continuing to read Austen's work does not require the zero-sum feat of intellectual gymnastics that the art-for-art's-sake gang seems to fear: acknowledging the truth of colonialism and the slave trade in Austen's era is no vandalizing act of literary deletion, but an act of literary expansion and restoration, not to mention the barest concession to reality (if anything, it's quite a politically radical reading to argue that race did not exist as a subject of contemplation in Austen's world; as bizarre as arguing that it does not exist as a subject of contemplation in ours). To suggest that literary critique of Regency-era literature must, in order to evade the specter of anachronism, segregate the spheres of the domestic and the political, is simply to misread the Regency era, not to mention the domestic and the political; to have never seen a Wedgwood patch box circa 1800 with a supplicating Black figure in chains illustrated upon it, pleading, "Am I not a man and a brother?" If Austen's contemporaries could bear storing rouge in these boxes and spooning sugar out of these pots, we can certainly bear talking about the fact that they existed—and what that existence might mean for us.

The museum Jane Austen's House in the English village of Chawton recently announced plans, according to *The New York Times*, to "include details about Austen and her family's ties to the slave trade, including the fact that her father was a trustee of a sugar plantation on the Caribbean island of Antigua," thus contextualizing the broader sociopolitical reality in which Austen lived and worked. Incidentally, the Chawton House features pieces from the Wedgwood dinner service set belonging to Austen's family.

The ensuing fervor was predictable: cries of revisionism and "woke madness," much fretting about cancel culture. But the binary presumed here is absurd. Being capable of engaging with both Austen's work *and* the historical realities of its time period is not a mutually exclusive exercise, but a mutually formative one, the very stuff of being a reader in the first place. To insist otherwise only reinforces the false universalizing of our art that Morrison once called tantamount to a lobotomizing of our art. The people who think that upholding a heavily edited and whitewashed truth about an author's historical context is the only viable way to truly protect and honor that author's work, are in fact protecting and honoring something else entirely.

In any case, turns out historically minded Austenites and their vandal comrades have the will of the people on their side: "Record numbers join the National Trust despite claims of 'anti-woke' critics," announced an October 2021 article in *The Guardian*, detailing that "the history and heritage charity . . . accused by the campaign group Restore Trust of losing members as a result of issues including a 'woke' rebrand" in fact broke subscription records, "with 159,732 new signups in August, the third highest-ever month. In October, one member joined every 23 seconds."

"FOR MYSELF," STEPHENS CONTINUES IN HIS *NEW YORK TIMES* article, "I plan to add one or two of Handke's books to my shelf, at least the non-political ones. They'll sit alongside Pinter, Saramago, Grass and, of course, Dahl—writers to whom I will always feel grateful, not least because they did not choose politics as their vocation."

This sanctimonious caping for the depoliticization of our art is a fundamental misunderstanding of the relationship between art, politics, and vocation—not to mention a clear indication of just which demographic of writers, judging by the white European men listed, this particular article is so at pains to defend. It's not without some irony that I look around and note that the writers and artists who are the most disdainful of art's edifying function, the people who seem most openly suspicious of—and threatened by—the idea of politics in fiction, or indeed empathy-building in fiction, are also the people who have historically benefited the most from the universal goodwill and empathy that is afforded someone living in a cis, white, middle-class body. Because what more powerful empathy machine do we have than heteropatriarchal white supremacy? I didn't even have to grow up in a town with actual white people for my indoctrination into American civic life, on every level, to feel like a never-ending empathy drill for white supremacy: the main characters in nearly every book we were assigned, in nearly every prime-time show on television, in nearly every movie in the local movie theater, in nearly every state and federal government position.

But no one ever told us that we were being shown these books and movies to build *our* empathy. This was just the inherited status quo of consumption and interpretation that came with a twenty-four-hour cycle of saturation in white-centered imaginative, intellectual, and moral narrative life—the genre I still jokingly call "white people having feelings." So much of the handwringing around reading and censorship in the contemporary age asks us to believe that we're all coming to art as both equal consumers of art *and* equal subjects of art: that it is the same thing to tell writers of color that they cannot identify with white characters (a common pressure point that those terrified by political correctness often jab at like a panic button) as it is to tell white writers that they cannot write characters of color (ditto). But no one ever told me my heart couldn't throb in tune with Maggie's, in George Eliot's *The Mill on the Floss*. Western education is *precisely* about asking everyone to make this imaginative leap, in the name of art—a leap almost always into unnamed and transcendent whiteness. It is not remotely a risky defense of our art to protect that leap, or to maintain a status quo that ensures the leap will always be unidirectional. So when the works of authors like Handke, Pinter, Saramago, and Grass are seen and interpreted as dealing with a universally legible and graciously apolitical soulfulness—and resolutely *not* seen and interpreted as also being the identity-politics-driven work of a specific white milieu—what we're really offering them is that precious empathy, which white supremacy levies from us every day and never has to name.

AS A HIGH SCHOOLER, I READ MORE THAN "ONE OR TWO OF Handke's non-political books." I spent much of my formative reading life reading in translation, thus leaving weird, uneven gaps in my knowledge of the English-language canon that has persisted into adulthood (although I do recommend reading George Eliot's *The Mill on the Floss* only after reaching one's thirties; books about childhood always break you best when you're an adult). My father read and recommended a lot of German literature, and on my own zigzagging path to filial piety, I swerved away from my father's Hesse and Mann and Goethe to their neighbors: neighbors like the Austrians Thomas Bernhard, Ludwig Wittgenstein—and, yes, Peter Handke. At the time, I was intrigued by these writers and their profoundly internal, often speechless fiction (especially as a high schooler who was annoyed by the twang of speech in most of the largely white American fiction that was assigned to us; a twang that was always implicitly and sentimentally sold to students as *the* American voice); the knife-edge of clarity and madness that many of these books balanced upon; most of all the singularity of their brutally lonely, often suicidal characters.

Back then I'd never been to Austria, and didn't know a thing about it. I didn't know that I would eventually elope with someone who'd grown up mostly in Bavaria, Germany, Austria's neighbor and cultural cousin (with all the sublimated hostility that cultural neighborliness often implies). I didn't know that I'd eventually visit Salzburg, or learn to love its little Mozartkugeln, great foil-wrapped lumps of pistachio marzipan and nougat covered in chocolate, which I discovered in my love's hometown of Munich. I didn't know that once, in my mid-twenties, I would board a train from Munich to Salzburg that was standing room only, and that I would fume loudly in English when I saw an elderly Chinese couple, shabbily dressed, sitting on the floor because none of the younger, able-bodied, all-white passengers had given up their seats for them. I didn't know yet that when a single seat opened up before me, I would jump on it viciously, then wave the couple over—and now, looking back, I can't remember how they sat down: if the wife sat down right away, or if the husband stood in front of the seat, shyly, and gestured for his wife to sit down. At the time of my reading Handke for the first time, all I knew of Austria was whatever I found in those youthful pages: seeing myself shimmer in other worlds; seeing them shimmer in me.

One of those strange, early shimmers I think about now came from reading Handke's *Across*. Like many of Handke's books, it's slim and dense, as were many of the books I admired at that time in my life (if you'd told the seventeen-year-old me that she'd write a four-hundred-page novel about three generations of Filipinx women, she'd probably have hit you; probably with a thin Lispector or Bioy Casares novel). The protagonist of *Across* is Andreas Loser, and predictably there's much philosophical rumination on this name, how common it is in German languages, its obvious double entendre in English. He's a classics teacher living in Salzburg, whose supposedly quiet, uneventful life is disrupted when he glimpses a tree defaced by a swastika, immediately chases down the vandal, and throws a stone at him, thereby murdering him.

Most of the book reviews of this 1983 novel (Ralph Manheim's English translation was published in 1986) have focused primarily on its protagonist's existential drama; in a *New York Times* review titled "Personal Growth Through Murder," Lawrence Graver writes of the murder: "With this action Loser crosses what may be the most significant threshold of his life, and the rest of the novel is a gripping, resonant account of the practical consequences and their meanings." And when the reviews are critical of the book's shortcomings, like the *Kirkus*

Reviews piece below, those critiques focus mainly on its willful obscurity and excessive restraint:

> This [murder]—more surprising and palpable than what usually "happens" in a Handke novel—promises to deepen the book into a rumination upon freedom from solipsism. But that never quite happens. One descriptive if oxymoronic paragraph follows another, the latter a metaphor for the former; and though there are discernible themes—change and conciliation—and though much of the writing is surreally beautiful, a droning sameness of tone—which is Handke's mode in general—pulls the electricity out of the book after the murder.

The general critical reception of *Across* paints a portrait of a slightly failed existential novel, one whose greatest flaw is that it falls short of truly dramatizing the way in which a sudden, abrupt act of violence can bring a person from one life into another one entirely; the emphasis in this school of reading tends to focus on Loser's admitted obsession with thresholds (and crossing them), thus the book's title itself.

But the German title of *Across* is not *Hinüber*, as it would be if *Across* were a direct translation. The original title of Handke's novel is *Der Chinese des Schmerzes*, loosely translated as *The Chinaman of Suffering*, or *The Suffering Chinese Man*. Presumably Handke's English-language translators thought a literal translation here would yield a less commercial title for their markets. (Its title in the comparatively bolder French and Spanish translations is, respectively, *Le chinois de douleur* and *El chino del dolor*.) Strange, then; this mysterious suffering Chinaman to whom the book owes its original title. Who is he? Where is he?

Every English-language review I read of Handke's *Der Chinese des Schmerzes* focuses on Loser's singular act of violence against an act of neo-Nazi vandalism. Yet few of the reviews seem concerned with pointing out to the reader that Loser's act of violence isn't singular at all; isn't a turning point that leads its protagonist to a "freedom from solipsism"; isn't even the first time that he's acted out violently against someone. In the early pages of the book, Loser describes knocking down a random man in the street, who, in overtaking Loser, had accidentally jostled him, "with the result that we collided. To tell the truth, though, it wasn't a collision, because I could have stepped aside. I pushed the man intentionally, and it wasn't just a push, but more like a punch, a sudden impulse, so actually it's wrong to speak of intention."

Then, Loser goes on to detail his history of youthful violence:

In my decades as an adult, I have twice struck someone: once, on the night of a dance, I hit my girlfriend, who had just kissed someone else before my eyes and in public; and a few years before that—actually I was an adolescent at the time—a boy from one of the lower grades, whose study hall I had been appointed to supervise. It's true that as we left the dance the girl herself had asked me to hit her, and my own blow, which came as a surprise to me and which I did not repeat though she asked me to, was in itself a solution. At the time, my act gave me real satisfaction. Come to think of it, it wasn't an act, but more like a reaction, occurring at the only possible moment, comparable to the jump or throw of an athlete who for once knows with certainty: now or never. So my conscience wasn't troubled and there was no question of reproach. Violent as my blow was, it inflicted no pain—of that I'm sure—but only made both of us smart. That was the turning point. We both recovered from our paralysis. In that instance, I'm innocent. But the slap in the study hall, brought on by some trifling provocation, is still on my mind. Up until then, I had been a man like other men; that slap showed me up as a criminal. The look on the boy's face—though my blow hadn't struck home—has said to me down through the years: Now I know you, now I know what kind of man you are, and I won't forget it.

A random man on the street; a girlfriend; a fellow adolescent. What all of these acts of violence share is the way Loser deliberately and repeatedly obfuscates, how slippery his hold on right and wrong: alternately defiant, recriminating, justifying, downplaying, self-aggrandizing. For the man in the street, he could have stepped aside but didn't; instead, he punched him—but it was an impulse (like killing the man with a rock?), and therefore not intentional. His cheating girlfriend *asked* him to hit her, so he did, and he was noble enough not to do it twice, and he's sure it didn't hurt her—and here again it isn't an action, but a reaction: "In that instance, I'm innocent." Only slapping the young boy, for a "trifling provocation"—the earliest and thus perhaps most formative of these acts of violence against others—has stayed with Loser, and the look in that boy's eyes is one he sees in the man he knocks down on the street: "its intention seemed to be to make me impossible, not to others but to myself. That eye, I sense, is right, and I sense that I, too, am right." *I am impossible, not to others, but to myself* sounds like the exact kind of edgelord narcissism that dudes who hit their girlfriends and kill animals use to justify their mysterious grimdark ways, but go off, I guess.

We know, then, that Loser's murder of the neo-Nazi vandal isn't a unique eruption that transcends the thresholds of life itself, but part of an easily trackable pattern of impulsive, self-justified acts of violence—violence that he disavows responsibility for, again and again. That someone who is violent to a girlfriend or a classmate may well be violent to a stranger on the street isn't a particularly novel revelation; the pattern brings to mind similarly chilling statistics on the connection between domestic violence and police brutality, such that police officers in the United States are fifteen times more likely to be domestic abusers, with 40 percent of cops having reported being involved in acts of domestic violence, as Alex Roslin, the author of *Police Wife: The Secret Epidemic of Police Domestic Violence*, points out. But the way that pattern goes largely unremarked (indeed, willfully unread) in reviews of Handke's novella feels of a piece with the culture of silence that would protect an abusive police officer and his job, or indeed, a fascist apologist and his Nobel Prize.

When Loser eventually commits the book's fateful murder, the description of the murder in English is deliberately detached and passive, with no sense of a specific subject committing a specific crime:

> But then the stone was thrown and the enemy lay literally crushed on the ground, as unexpectedly as once in my childhood a rooster, which unintentionally to be sure, I had hit on the head with a pebble thrown from a distance—with the sole difference that the rooster, just as surprisingly, stood up and ran off as if nothing had happened.

"But then the stone was thrown." It's a deliberate and telling choice of words, and correctly translates the original German, "Doch dann war der Stein geworfen," taking advantage of the German-language grammatical structure that often puts verbs at the end of sentences (*geworfen*, thrown), so that the description of action is deferred, as in the sentence describing the murder. But Loser tellingly doesn't say, "Doch dann habe ich den Stein geworfen," which would be translated as "But then *I* threw the stone."

For Loser, violence is a quasi-metaphysical force of nature, something that has no fixed perpetrator, something that merely works through him—not something he commits, with his own hand, again and again. "I felt an unaccustomed impersonal strength, which however, did not emanate from the stone in my hand." And sure, that's one way of reading Loser's crime; it's certainly the way Handke's narrative choices throughout the novel, along with much of the critical response, expect you to read it: nonpolitically, to use Stephens's term. We're asked to engage with Loser's act as something almost primordial, a singular, inexplicable mystery that asks us to question the nature of violence itself—not as a deliberate act committed by a white man with a proven history of violence. Convenient, then, this nonpolitical practice of reading: the way its commitment to deferring responsibility and, god forbid, judgment, seems to allow certain kinds of characters to, quite literally, get away with murder.

Another aspect that many of the reviews of *Der Chinese des Schmerzes* share is their admiration—sometimes reluctant—of Handke's deft ability to portray Loser as a consummate observer, someone whose internal life of *noticing* is laid bare to the reader, in often overwhelming detail. Yet rarely do they mention the fact that one thing Loser notices, fairly often, is foreigners: often immigrants, often people of color. In the city, old peat-cutters' huts that have fallen into decay are occupied by foreigners. Here, there's "an Asian in an orange plastic cape [who] came in with a bundle of newspapers fresh off the press;

a moment later, he had vanished; no one was in a reading mood just then." There, he sees "a black-eyed, brown-skinned adolescent [who] came in with a child who looked like him, and went to the bar, where he exchanged a large empty wine bottle for a full one. He introduced the child as his uncle," Handke's narrator says, pseudo-anthropologically, as if sharing this detail about immigrant family life were innocent, and not deliberately lurid.

The boy "went to the local public school; the special class that had been organized for foreigners was known as 'the color class,' not because of the crayons . . . but because of the different skin colorations represented. The principal, said the boy, is proud of this class; he had even arranged for it to have a special entrance, and the hours are different from those of the Austrian classes. . . . Most of the [children's] drawings were about war: Turks against Greeks, Iranians against Iraqis, Yugoslavs against Albanians."

Walking back to his housing development, Loser thinks: "The asphalt under my feet was home ground; this was in every sense *my* territory. Hadn't I once wanted to shout at a noisy group of foreigners in the Old City: 'Quiet—this is Austria!'?"

It's important to point out that Loser never once describes anyone as white; notices anyone as white—least of all himself, but more on that soon.

Loser doesn't just notice marginal immigrant workers or foreign students being taught in segregated classes. Foreigners— and their foreign*ness*—also appear as symbolic figures functioning only to heighten narrative dread, without any real agency or substance of their own. As Loser runs through the Old City to chase after the vandal, the stone figures atop the steeples of Salzburg's Kollegienkirche "became grimacing Indian idols." After he kills the man, the scene of the crime resembles "the ruins of a temple in the jungles of Central America." And in one particularly gruesome description of a nightmare, Loser dreams of being in the lobby of an air terminal building, where

a stairway led down to a restaurant that was jam-packed with Chinese. It was a sinister den, dimly lit and low-ceilinged. In the middle there was a platform—this was the place of slaughter. Naked men with long, curved, two-handed swords flung themselves on other naked but unarmed men. There was no struggle. Nor did the unarmed men run away. They buckled like apes overtaken by a pursuing lion, bared their teeth, and hissed (or rather squeaked) their last cries of terror at the butchers. The soles of the victims' feet seemed also to buckle and formed high, loudly creaking arches on the platform. A moment later, the whole body was gone. Not only had it been cut into little pieces, but almost simultaneously it had been devoured by the people in the room below. What an instant before had been part of a gesticulating human being was now a chunk of meat vanishing into someone's gullet. The mouths with these unceasingly active gullets marked, as it were, the innermost core of the Chinese quarter, which at one time had been the hub of all world happening. The slaughter would never end.

A paranoid fantasy of inevitable and endless slaughter at the hands of foreign hordes; perhaps Stephen Miller read *Der Chinese des Schmerzes* as a primer to his immigration policy. Is this where we finally locate our elusive suffering Chinese man, at least? No. Besides this dream, there are no speaking Chinese characters in the book.

Instead, what the readers come to realize is that *Loser* is the one who identifies as the Chinese man. He identifies throughout the book as an outsider, a foreigner—even as the slaughtered people in this dream. He recalls encountering a child coming toward him in the street who shouted to their mother, "'Look, an Indian!'" When he gets off the bus home as the last passenger, "I took elaborate leave of the driver, becoming more verbose from step to step. 'Good night, Mr. Chinaman,' said the driver."

When a woman he sleeps with toward the end of the novel, in a particularly cringe-inducing example of literary sex writing ("In passion, our bodies did not diverge but remained together. They consummated the act, which was not a frenzied struggle but a mighty game, the 'game of games'"), tells him she doesn't trust him, the way she explains it is this:

> "You don't seem to be wholly present; you breathe discontent. You're kind of run-down. I desire you but I don't trust you. You have something on your conscience; not

theft, or you'd be on the run. It's plain that you are outside ordinary law, and it makes you suffer in a way. I
don't trust you, and I do. You are like the man in the
doorway. Though very ill, he went to see a good friend.
In leaving, he stopped at length in the doorway and tried
to smile; his tensed eyes became slits, framed in their
sockets as by sharply ground lenses. 'Goodbye, my suffering Chinaman,' said his friend."

Besides being an Olympic-level example of lampshading
in literature (not to mention this gem: the character's "tensed
eyes became slits" before he is called a Chinaman), this paper-
thin female character's primary functions in the scene are to
(1) fuck our protagonist, because, sure, and (2) further em-
broider the edgelord philosophy that Loser self-flagellates to
throughout the book: *outside ordinary law*, *suffering*, *desirable
but not trustworthy*. But what does the woman's story mean,
Loser asks. The woman simply laughs.

Unsurprisingly, Loser interprets that wordless laugh however he likes. Closing his eyes, he "heard a sort of answer after
all: In the end, the friend said to the friend, 'At last, a Chinese—
at last a Chinese face among so many native faces.'"

Loser the Indian, Loser the suffering, alienated Chinese—
Handke's aim here is to show us the ways in which *Loser* is the
foreigner, Loser the outsider, Loser the one estranged from
society. And its portrait of an aggrieved white man with a victim complex, beset by a hostile modernizing world, feels dis-

tinctly contemporary; there's a through line from Loser to the kinds of people who say things like "reverse racism." After his subdued impulse to yell at a group of foreigners to be quiet, *this is Austria*, Loser sinks into a weary rumination of Austria itself: "My country: an enamel sign in a provincial railroad station showing a pointing hand, with the words: 'To the well.' My country, indeed. A man's own country meant refuge, he could defend himself. 'But would you also defend this country of yours?' 'Perhaps not the parliament building' would be my answer to such a question, 'but this barn and that vintner's hut, definitely.' For I can say of myself: 'I am sick with my country.'"

In a *New York Times* article covering Handke's Nobel win, journalist and Handke biographer Malte Herwig describes the author's Austrian upbringing, as the child of a Slovenian mother and German father: "He grew up in very poor conditions, in a remote provincial region. It was dirt hard. He was the only one who went to college and so on. He still has this air about him . . . If you look at his fingernails, there's usually dirt underneath them." In his childhood, Herwig says Handke "was a highly sensitive kid . . . nervous, easily aroused with anger, or easily startled" and "totally a square peg in a round hole."

When Loser describes Austria, his admission of weary provincial shame-pride, his dismissal of larger civic institutions, and his unmistakably banked furnace of fury, frustration, self-victimization, and defensiveness all ring very familiar today, to someone who has lived under what people often call Trump's America, which, in the end, is just America; the America that was always there, but which Trump's election gold-plated and armed with assault rifles.

(My mom also grew up in abjectly poor, "dirt hard" conditions in the provinces in the Philippines, and regularly worked sixteen-hour days in her American life—yet her working-class American story is rarely awarded the same importance or frenzied sympathy that white working-class stories like Handke's, or the totemic ones that crop up around presidential elections, tend to enjoy. My mom, mysteriously, also didn't turn out to be a genocide denier, or a Trump voter. She also hasn't—yet!—won a Nobel Prize.)

Loser thinks of himself as the lone man against the world, the vigilante meting out justice by impulse, not even by choice, compelled by something greater than himself, something far beyond himself, there beyond right or wrong. But Loser is also Loser the white Austrian classics teacher, who murders a man in cold blood, hits his girlfriend, hits his classmate, punches a man in the street, throws rocks at a rooster. He's also Loser the white suburban Austrian, who despairs of his country, its noisy foreigners, and their complicated families. He's also Loser the white European who thinks of himself as an Indian or a Chinaman but has never, seemingly, known one. He's also Loser the white middle-class Westerner for whom both indigenous people and Chinese people are simply symbols, metaphors, vehicles through which to express his own tortured sense of self.

But the fact that Loser murdered a neo-Nazi—surely that means Loser was on the right side of history, seeking his own brand of frontier justice in return for an act that symbolized a global historical wrong, and its persistence in the modern day. Loser, avenging angel? But when Loser sees the swastika, he doesn't think of the Jewish people's systematic genocide by the Nazi regime. He thinks, crucially, of himself:

> this sign, this negative image, symbolized the cause of all my melancholy—of all melancholy, ill humor, and false laughter in this country. And this accursed mark had not just been daubed on out of caprice or thoughtlessness; it had been traced with malignant precision and black determination, laid on thickly and thoroughly; the exaggerated hooks were intended to threaten evil, to hit the viewer full in the face; and indeed, they hit me full in the face. Me? I? One great burst of passion.

What bothers Loser is not what the swastika actually means to the people who were crushed by those killing in its name; he's not angered by hate speech, or antisemitism in the specific. No, he's angered by what the swastika signifies to him about Austria, a vague miasma of "melancholy, ill humor, and false laughter." The hooks of it "threaten evil," but this evil is never named or contextualized, and their primary target is not those exterminated by the SS but, rather, Loser himself: "they hit me full in the face. Me? I?" He's angered by the swastika's history, but only in the sense that he's ashamed by what it *reminds* him of, what it digs up in him, what it doesn't let him forget. He's angered that the swastika was put up deliberately, not thoughtlessly (how much better is a thoughtless swastika?), and he's angered by what the swastika does to him: incriminates him, and the rest of Austria with him. Loser drags his victim's body to a cliff edge, then "let[s] the dead man fall" into the gully. The stone Loser uses to kill the man is the same stone he uses to then scratch out any trace of the swastika. Afterward, he rejoices, breathlessly, at his initiation into the society of criminals: "no nation is more dispersed and isolated." As the corpse tumbles off the cliff, Loser triumphs: "And my obituary was as follows: 'At last, you have lost your right to exist!'"

For Loser, erasure is the ideal form of reparations: scratching out one's history, dumping the incriminating bodies off a cliff, snuffing out that history's right to exist (rather than doing the more daily and difficult work of contending with its legacies in ordinary, ongoing life). Loser is angered the way people get angry when you point out racism, claiming that pointing out racism is itself racist, when in actuality what angers them is having racism named at all. He's angered by the personal and national reflection that the sight of the swastika flashes back at him, and when he murders the man and dumps his body, what he's doing is what all countries do when they don't want to face the living reality of their history: burying the evidence. What Loser does isn't vigilante justice; it isn't even justice. For Austria—and for this American reader, too—it's just the same old, same old.

Here, then, is Handke's nonpolitical writing: the whiteman blues, with a goose-step beat. The last line of the book, before its epilogue, is about storytelling, the kind of storytelling Handke himself traffics in: "The storyteller is the threshold. He must therefore stop and collect himself." *Der Chinese des Schmerzes* thrives on the threshold, precisely because it wants to have it both ways: it wants Loser to be both the victim and the murderer, the wronged and the outlaw, the foreign Chinaman and the besieged white Austrian. The obfuscating and narrative obscurity Handke has often been associated with (sometimes accused of) throughout his career has a purpose: in *Der Chinese des Schmerzes*, it means Handke never has to really commit to the story he's actually telling. He points in long, loping sentences to ideas, actions, feelings, but neither author nor character ever lingers long enough in those ideas or actions to take responsibility for them—or indeed, ever truly be implicated in them. Eventually those long, loping sentences begin to sound familiar to anyone who's heard a bullshitter spin a long, complicated yarn to conceal shorter, less mysterious truths. In the wake of Handke's Nobel win, Norwegian writer Karl Ove Knausgaard once defended the Austrian author's work, saying: "The world and the people in it never are black, never are white, never are good, never are bad . . . but all these things combined."

That description should be true of any remotely decent book for adult humans; if this is the standard by which Nobel Prize winners are judged, the bar is the floor. Increasingly, crying "human mystery, human mystery!" sounds like a deus ex machina not just for characters but for their authors. It is, in-deed, mysterious that this literary recourse to the nonpolitical seems, again and again, to protect only certain authors and their right to artistic impunity, excusing readers from having to fully engage with the words that are on the pages of these books—which, as far as I can remember, is what reading is supposed to actually do.

It's a romantic idea: storytellers being thresholds. It might even be true. But the convenience of the threshold philosophy of storytelling is kindred with the nonpolitical philosophy of storytelling: it's how a story about a violent white middle-class Austrian gets to be reviewed as a largely existential drama, not *also* a political one—how Loser's long history of violence is ob-scured, and his major crime transmuted into an overarching story about the universal condition of mankind; the literary version of a headline that describes a white rapist as an up-standing athlete.

It's how a writer like Handke becomes someone known as a gifted stylist, a chronicler of oblique European historical malaise, rather than *also* as someone whose books often point to white male violence and its relationship to postwar defeat. Writers like Handke might be lionized by articles like the *New York Times* one "because they did not choose politics as their vocation," but the idea that some of us can simply opt out of politics—the idea that politics is something one *chooses* as a vo-cation, rather than something we have whether we choose it or not; something that encompasses the inevitable material realities that shape every atom of our lives: where we live, how we work, our relationship to justice—is a fantasy of epic proportions. This kind of nonpolitical storytelling—and the stunted readership it demands—asks us to uphold the lie that certain bodies, certain characters, certain stories, remain depoliticized, neutral, and universal. It asks us to keep those bodies, characters, stories, forever safe from politics—forever safe, period. At the end of the novel, Loser walks free.

Let's say an Austrian writer of color had written *Der Chinese des Schmerzes*; let's say Loser had been, in fact, a Chinese man, a classics teacher, not particularly identifying as political, prone to violence in the street, disgruntled with Austria, who kills a man for defacing trees with swastikas. I guarantee you every single review of that book would be about: immigration, political violence, hate crime, discrimination. It would be a different book, sure. But the point is that *Der Chinese des Schmerzes* itself is already a different book from the *Across* that Handke's *New York Times* readers think they're reading. The people who are reading Handke's work assuming it is nonpolitical are simply *not reading Handke*.

The very last line of *Der Chinese des Schmerzes* returns us to the thick quiet of Loser's city: "from the medieval figures over the doors of the Old City churches—flow peace, mischief, quietness, gravity, slowness and patience." For some readers, that line might indicate a return to the eternal, quasi-holy importance of narrative—nonpolitical storytelling, in its tiny banal details. But I've found that line has always felt absolutely—and yes, politically—chilling. Speaking from my own experience: anyone else who's ever been a person of color walking around in towns like Salzburg, from Austria to America, knows intimately the heaviness of the supposed peace, quietness—and *Geduld*, patience—of a town where you are visibly, materially (not just, like Loser, metaphorically) foreign. It's a last line fit for a murderer with a clear conscience.

AT THE SWEDISH ACADEMY'S PRESS CONFERENCE FOR HANDKE'S Nobel win, Handke addressed the journalists attending the event, who'd asked the author about his history of genocide denial. Handke declared, "My people are readers, not you."

Only someone who believes that readers must necessarily practice the kind of resolutely nonpolitical critical thinking that would absolve and protect him from deeper scrutiny would make this pointed distinction (are journalists not readers?). It's a tellingly autocratic vision of the relationship between an author and a readership; that we as readers are an author's people, and that to be someone's people is to gaze upon them with a blurry, benevolent eye—ever receptive, ever docile. What Handke really seems to mean is that his readers are *fans*; enablers, sycophants. For that's all the depth of readership that this level of sensitivity to critique can withstand.

I'm the last person who would ask us to read less (although I do often think it would serve us to read fewer books, and more slowly, to dispense with a practice of reading that serves as yet another anxious rite to keep cultural FOMO at bay), to remove authors, even ones like Handke, from our shelves—but we have to push back against the idea that engaging with our art in ways that look beyond the aesthetic is a cheapening of our engagement. Not least of all because the people who are so eager to police the borders of our critical engagement *are* reading politically: it's a political choice to protect and continue to narrowly read certain writers, while willfully ignoring choice parts of their oeuvre (reading Handke's books, "at least the non-political ones"). It's a political choice to declare that not reading writers like Handke or protesting the Nobel's legitimizing of his work is tantamount to a foreclosure of readerly curiosity and openness—and *not*, for example, consider that it might be equally incurious of a reader to vociferously defend the right to read supposedly nonpolitical white European men, and not seek out the chance to make space on one's shelf for the apparently-inherently-politicized Everyone Else. It's a political choice to say that certain artists make Real Art That Must Be Protected, and other artists (seemingly always writers of color, queer writers, minoritized writers) make only socialist realism or sentimentalist dogma.

In the end, we can't say we believe in things like diversity in fiction or decolonizing our art (our screen, our pages, our readerliness) if we don't think *something* of value—something which is not solely aesthetic, and which bears something beyond the literal political value of a vote—occurs when we encounter a work of art. Either we think that art can effect some extra-political and extra-aesthetic change in the world—how we live in it, how we are alive to it, how we know ourselves and each other—or we don't.

Because it *is* empathy-building to defend Handke's narrative universe from closer scrutiny. It *is* empathy-building to ask us to look at his characters universally, not specifically—in the benevolent macro, and not the more sharply defined micro. But writers like Handke don't think of their readers as deliberately practicing the very specific kind of empathy-building that protects these very specific kinds of writers. To them, this is what readership, as they've always known it and expected it, is supposed to do.

RECENTLY I'VE BEEN THINKING OF SOMEONE I'VE BEEN CALL-ing the unexpected reader. Sometimes it's the unexpected listener, the unexpected audience member. I've been thinking of the unexpected reader whenever there's yet another scandal with some Hollywood type whose misogynist abuse has been discovered; some comedian whose homophobic tweets have been unearthed; some writer whose racist depictions have been condemned.

Every reader, in principle, should be unexpected: it's a minor miracle, to create a work of art that reaches another person; to write something that then finds someone willing enough to take it on, engage with it—*read* it. But the older I get, the more I realize that certain artists don't, actually, have any relationship to their unexpected reader. When artists bemoan the rise of political correctness in our cultural discourse, what they're really bemoaning is the rise of this unexpected reader. They're bemoaning the arrival of someone who does not read them the way they expect—often demand—to be read; often someone who has been framed in their work and in their lives as an object, not as a subject.

A book like *American Dirt*, for example, can only be written if literally every single person involved in its making never once considered the possibility of a Chicanx reader—or indeed, any reader who might find something problematic about a white woman monetizing border trauma to hawk at predominantly white suburban readers, using barbed-wire-themed imagery as part of the marketing "aesthetic," describing characters in the book as a "faceless brown mass," and in a now-notorious author's note, saying of the book that she "wished someone slightly browner than me would write it." A book for an invented, incurious marketplace, where the sensationalized trauma of communities of color is commodified—barbed-wire decorations!—to produce the ethno-porn that spoon-feeds empathy to a readership that is expected to do little more than swallow. In her review of the book, *New York Times* book critic Parul Sehgal writes:

> But does the book's shallowness paradoxically explain the excitement surrounding it? The tortured sentences aside, "American Dirt" is enviably easy to read. It is determinedly

apolitical. The deep roots of these forced migrations are never interrogated; the American reader can read without fear of uncomfortable self-reproach. It asks only for us to accept that "these people are people," while giving us the saintly to root for and the barbarous to deplore— and then congratulating us for caring.

There is only so much space I can make for this controversy, both in these pages and in my life; controversies like this go beyond racial microaggressions—they've become predictable and occasionally lucrative trauma engines, and continually asking writers of color to produce a comment from the hot-take jukebox on the latest fuckup perpetrated by a dementedly racist and tone-deaf publishing industry is asking those writers to wipe a shit they did not take. What I'm much more curious about is what these fuckups reveal about readership: who we expect our readers to be, what we expect our readers to do, and how this might change.

I've been an unexpected reader all my life, from the very first biblical children's story or watered-down Greek myth picture book my father handed me from the local Goodwill or Milpitas Library. By unexpected reader I mean someone who was not remotely imagined—maybe not even imagin*able*—by the creator of that artwork or anyone in its scope; someone who was not included as the "people" of a certain book or certain author, in Handke's phrasing. I'm always reminded of it when I read a book or watch a television show and someone, in passing, mentions "Filipino houseboys"; inevitably, there's always the sense that those people and their expected reader or viewer are talking among themselves, that I am walking in on a conversation I wasn't meant to witness, that they never really expected an actual Filipinx person to hear them.

But I realize now that being an unexpected reader has turned out to be the most valuable gift of my intellectual life. The fact that I was an unexpected reader—an interloper, in so many worlds—meant that I was very rarely in any assumed complicity with a writer or the world she created. It meant that I was almost always lost, and always foreign, and always had to make my way through with the only tool I had: continuing to read. It meant growing up I never felt targeted by a book; comforted, addressed, like I was the one the book was speaking to. It meant I rarely felt comfortable in anyone's dialogue or descriptions; no one ever wrote about the California I lived in, even (especially) the supposedly great California chroniclers like Steinbeck and Didion. It meant no one ever held my hand, or spoon-fed me a book's morals, or handed me a map to Argentina; I just had to keep reading Manuel Puig's *Kiss of the Spider Woman* and *Betrayed by Rita Hayworth*.

It meant I was exposed early to the moments in books where I would glimpse women like me, Filipina women who appeared as characters (barely), by authors who very clearly had never really imagined them as readers—books like Handke's fellow Nobel Prize winner J. M. Coetzee's *Diary of a Bad Year*, or Phillip Lopate's *The Stoic's Marriage* (both, curiously, about older, self-important white men getting scammed by thinly written younger Filipina seductresses; u ok boomer?). It meant I was inured to uncomfortable moments in storytelling, moments that were plainly not written for me, for my comfort, or even for my understanding; that was true of nearly everything I read, so I had to get used to it. It meant, moreover, that I took books fucking seriously, because I loved them, and because the stakes in them were often high, knowing every book meant I had no guarantee of explanation or safe passage; I had no light to guide me but the light that books themselves throw off, with every page.

When white readers claim to be made uncomfortable—as many I heard from claimed—by the presence of something like untranslated words in fiction, what they're really saying is: *I have always been the expected reader.* A reader like this is used to the practice of reading being one that may performatively challenge them, much the way a safari guides a tourist through the "wilderness"—but ultimately always prioritizes their comfort and understanding. This tourism dynamic means that even when writers of color tell their own stories, those stories must cater to the needs and wishes of that expected, and expectant, reader: translations, glossaries, indexes, maps, rest stops along the way. When intellectuals bristle at their white liberal politics being parsed and critiqued by BIPOC readers, when they get tetchy at their white feminism (that overused stage name, meant to obscure its legal name: Ye Olde Garden-Variety White Supremacy—Now Available in Girlboss) being exposed for its transphobia, what they're really saying is: *I'm the only reader I have ever been expecting.*

That art should not serve to make us comfortable is such a basic argument I'm loathe to even repeat it. Yet the arguments about the comforts or disruptions of art cannot be held in good faith if we don't address the fact that a white supremacist reading culture means we are conditioned to accept that some of our work is in fact routinely expected to comfort; that the work of writers of color must often in some way console, educate, provide new definitions, great epiphanies, and, most of all— that buzzword of both the commercial marketplace and political theater—be relevant. Whereas the work of white writers must be free to: offend, transgress, be exempt, be beyond politics, beyond identity—to delight, in other words, in the myriad fruits of its political immunity. And their readers must, in turn, always extend empathy toward that lucrative and culturally rewarded immunity—which is, after all, great art.

Committing to being an unexpected reader means committing to the knowledge that what bonds us together is neither the sham empathy that comes from predigested ethnographic sound bites passing as art in late capitalism, nor the vague gestures at free speech that flatter the tenured powerful and scold their freelance critics—but the visceral shock, and ultimately relief, of our own interwoven togetherness and connection. Readers do half the work of a book's life; that means we must do half the heavy lifting of its project. I write books about Filipinx people because that is part of my work, and there is no part of my work that is not intertwined with yours—there is no part of being a person, with history, on this planet, that is not in some way intertwined with another's. There is no way of writing about Filipinx Americans that is not also writing about America; there is no way of writing about Americans (or indeed, Austrians, or New Zealanders) that is not also about its many genocides and empires. Sure, I write stories about the neither-black-nor-white experience of Being a Person—at least by Knausgaard's not overly demanding intellectual standards—but I don't hide behind that argument to avoid having to politicize my own work (and thus bear the responsibility of the politics latent in it), the way white writers given the benefit of universality and the aegis of free speech are able to.

Some might call it a privilege, the power such writers have to write—and be read—apolitically. But increasingly I think that privilege is in fact a curse: a curse to never know yourself as an author, or be truly known by your reader.

Because readers are not an author's people, in the sense of a head of state—or a crowned Nobel winner—looking down from a press conference dais at the citizens he governs and from whom he expects subservience. If readers are an author's people, it's only in the barest, deepest, most contrary, and least convenient communal sense (the same with any community): readers are the people that an author comes from, embedded deep in the genetic code of readerliness (which is not the same thing as literacy)—and vice versa.

It's not easy to have a people; to come from a people. It's

not easy to not just be a super-special, historically unique sub-ject railing against the world (Loser, indeed) but someone in-stead pinned by context, easy to trace—someone who shows up in the census. I don't just mean the people you're born to, although that's one way of having a people. And your people are not always the ones who keep you safe or sane, and some-times you need to run from them—certainly I've belonged to a few peoples in my time, and I've run away from one or two of mine. And I don't imagine it's easy to go your entire life being the expected universal reader, and then to suddenly be named as the specific, contextualized, white middle-class reader. But we can only be each other's people if we actually do the work of *being each other's people*: looking our shared history in the face and really reading it. An expected reader always expects to be led by the hand; the unexpected reader knows we get lost in each other.

IN "WHY I STOPPED HATING SHAKESPEARE," JAMES BALDWIN wrote about Shakespeare's poetry in a passage that feels here like a wholesale rebuke to the Handke way of thinking about writers and their people. It's also a bracingly germane argu-ment for the future of literature (American or otherwise)—if indeed literature is to have a future:

> The greatest poet in the English language found his po-etry where poetry is found: in the lives of the people. He

could have done this only through love—by knowing, which is not the same thing as understanding, that whatever was happening to anyone was happening to him. It is said his time was easier than ours, but I doubt it—no time can be easy if one is living through it. I think it is simply that he walked his streets and saw them, and tried not to lie about what he saw: his public streets and his private streets, which are always so mysteriously and inexorably connected; but he trusted that connection. And though I, and many of us, have bitterly bewailed (and will again) the lot of an American writer—to be part of a people who have ears to hear and hear not, who have eyes to see and see not—I am sure that Shakespeare did the same. Only, he saw, as I think we must, that the people who produce the poet are not responsible to him: he is responsible to them.

Writers like Handke and their defenders have no working concept of this responsibility: that responsibility which, to paraphrase the words of our queer (allegedly!) First Lady Eleanor Roosevelt, comes with freedom. No, what they are defending is their comfort, and what they are preserving is their power—neither of which is the same thing as freedom, as those of us who have known lives without either can attest.

It is this supposedly nonpolitical writing that, paradoxically, tells us the most about empathy, because it is this writing that benefits the most from it. It does not need the people it nevertheless imperiously lays claim to; it prefers the reliable comforts of empathy to the human risk of intimacy. It does not want to practice that labor of love that Baldwin, sharply and tenderly, called *knowing*: it neither wants to know nor be known, because both require vulnerability, at the cost of power. It does not bend; it will not learn. It awaits the silence—and empathy—of the reader it expects.

THERE IS PERHAPS NO WORD MORE BELOVED NOR MORE BORING in the American lexicon than *freedom*: here in the land of the free, where freedom rings, over freedom fries. Most of us already know that the fantasy of American freedom has always been just that—the stuff of fantasy: a fever dream of lone pioneer individualism, built on the back of slave labor and the theft of indigenous land; a Photoshopped image of ruggedly independent, usually male interiority à la Henry David Thoreau, subsidized by the mother who does the laundry and brings the sandwiches, like a nineteenth-century Instagram Boyfriend.

I'm far more interested in inheritance. In not being a person or a nation sui generis; not some manifest destiny American settler colonial who, in the noxious words of equally noxious Rick Santorum, thinks we "created a blank slate; we birthed a nation from nothing." Understanding who we are from the perspective of inheritance, not freedom or exceptionalism, means knowing ourselves as fundamentally made possible by—and fundamentally reliant upon—other people, both living and dead, some we may know intimately and some we may never know.

The kind of art (and the kind of artist) that would refuse entirely this reliance and inheritance is the kind of art (and artist) that is afraid to know the ways in which its making—its freedoms, its universality, its predominance—is made possible by webs of connections, violences, erasures, and enclosures. This art(ist) doesn't want to know how it is made possible, because it wants to neither be *made* nor *possible*: it wants to just be. Unquestioned, singular. This art(ist) doesn't want to be marked, because it thinks of being marked as something beneath itself, something for Others (this is why white people in an audience get very uncomfortable when you repeatedly call them white, as I have found to my bemusement). It wants to remind everyone of its uniqueness; it doesn't want to be reminded of its debts.

But what if our artistic practices were founded not on the presumption of artistic freedom—certainly, at least, not the individualistic, late capitalist brand of American freedom? What if we as artists didn't fight tooth and nail to safeguard the freedom to do whatever we wanted in our art—in fact, what if we didn't come to art to practice the trite choreography of that freedom at all?

What if art was the space not for us to enjoy our freedom, but for us to encounter our bondages—and our bondedness? That in our art making and our art consumption, we paid attention not just to the things that made us feel free, expansive, containing multitudes, but to the things that remind us we are not just free but delimited—the things that make us feel our smallness, our ordinariness, our contingency, our vulnerability and reliance? The things that make us feel not neutral but *named*—actually known by the world, so that we might be truly in it, and of it?

Many of us already come to our art that way, and always have—never having tasted the sugared privilege of that neutral freedom in the first place; having always been already marked, delimited, named, othered. Perhaps it seems strange to suggest that taking a communal, structural—relatively dispassionate, even—view of racism and white supremacy and its effects in our reading and intellectual culture would actually be a greater act of intimacy than the incomplete empathy we traffic in today. But what could be more intimate, as a civic person, than finally, fully seeing oneself *not* as one sole, free actor in the world—such that it would be enough to achieve justice by simply not being overtly racist, or by being satisfied with paternalistic overtures of charitable feeling, or by thinking that one's defense of a fascist could be apolitical as long as it focused only on his *art*, or by hoping that one's patently obvious exploitation of free speech to protect oneself from legitimate critique by marginalized voices would go unremarked—but instead, to know oneself as one small flawed part of a whole? To know that the contours of our lives are drawn by each other; that the history that made us is the history that makes us? That we are implicated, in the full sense of the word? Implicated like perpetrators, witnesses, and inheritors of a great crime, the other word for which might be our history. And *implicated*—like pages bookmarked by someone who wanted to remember what was written there: we are folded, inseparably, into each other.

Because none of this work is meant to be done alone. Reparatively critical reading is not meant to be work performed solely by readers and writers of color. But the logic of empathy would have us believe so: it would have us believe that other people tell stories, which are there to make us feel things, the line between the two neatly delineated. The logic of empathy says "I feel your pain"—but the logic of inheritance knows this transaction has always been corrupt at its core. The story I'm telling is not just something for you to feel sympathy for, rage against, be educated by: *it's a story about you, too.* This work has left a will, and we are all of us named in it: the inheritances therein belong to every reader, every writer, every citizen. So, too, the world we get to make from it.

HONOR THE TREATY

Relax. Wash hair with tears. Condition with Kumarika oil, coconut oil, olive oil of the ancient Greek kind. Relax. Egg whites for a hot glossy shine. Gasoline for a hot glossy shine. Light a match for an edgy new cut. Distressed is in. Relax. Buy a box of Nordic blond every full moon but never use it. This is imperative. Rinse thoroughly with intergenerational trauma and pink water. Blow-dry straight with a 1950s gold soft-paddle brush made from the hair of the finest palomino ponies. Now take a step back and relax. Admire your silky manageable mane.

TAYI TIBBLE, "POŪKAHANGATUS: AN ESSAY
ABOUT INDIGENOUS HAIR DOS AND DON'TS"

n 2019, about a week and a half into my first visit to Aotearoa—also known by its settler colonial name, New Zealand—I thought I'd discovered a new species of white person. Or at least, new to me. The possibility that I might be encountering a new species was something that occurred to me the first couple of days I arrived there, like a baby botanist in a forest who's glimpsed, maybe, the appearance of a long-extinct—or perhaps entirely, excitingly new—species. I wasn't sure if what I was seeing truly was unique, but I certainly hadn't come across it in my (fairly extensive, for a girl from Milpitas) travels or studies before. I had no labs or archives behind me, I had no team of wayward researchers or hopeful anthropologists, but if there's one enduring lesson I've retained from the settler colonials that destroyed and thereby defined the California I was born in: when you see something new, absolutely zero problems arise from just saying you discovered it. Ergo: I decided I had indeed discovered a new species of white person.

WHEN I WAS IN NEW ZEALAND, I REMEMBER BEING STRUCK BY how much of the civic language of the country was bilingual—I don't think it would be an exaggeration to say nearly all of it. During the Auckland Writers Festival pōwhiri, or traditional Māori welcome, huge parts of the ceremony were recited in Māori with absolutely no translation—with both white and Māori New Zealanders addressing the crowd in a mix of Māori and English, moving between the two languages without waiting for us to catch up. I could not help but think about having written a book in English that used multiple untranslated Filipinx languages, and the occasional but vociferous resistance I encountered from some white readers who were affronted by the lack of translation; think about what it might be like for those people to grow up in a world like the New Zealand I was witnessing, where translation was not only absent but unnecessary.

I thought of the small-town America I grew up in: Milpitas is built on Muwekma Ohlone and specifically Tamyen land—and yet none of the several Ohlone/Costanoan languages (both names, notably, derived from colonial sources; the name Costanoan was invented by early Spanish settlers, to denote the people's proximity to the coast), including Tamyen, are among the major languages currently spoken in Milpitas. None of the signs are in indigenous languages, and certainly none of the local civic leaders I grew up with—the majority of them Southeast

Asian immigrants—spoke or indeed gave any indication of ever having heard of any Native language. The States does not even perform what in Australia is called the "welcome to country," a rite I've seen only in Australia, Canada, and New Zealand, in which speakers before any size of gathering make a traditional acknowledgment that the people in that space are standing on occupied land, naming specifically the indigenous group whose land they are standing upon; the Gadigal people, in Sydney, for example.

I mentioned being moved by this gesture to Winnie Dunn, a brilliant young Tongan Australian writer and activist who also runs an important Western Sydney–based collective for women writers of color, indigenous and immigrant, called Sweatshop. We met at the Sydney Writers' Festival, and as part of my participation in the festival, I was invited to lead a writing workshop for the members of Sweatshop. I said to Winnie over pizza that while I knew the land acknowledgment was only a symbolic act, it was still one that felt charged with meaning to my American eyes. Winnie, in her characteristic incisiveness and generosity, was kind enough to firmly remind me that in Australia, at least—unlike both the States and New Zealand—the Aboriginal people have no treaty, and Australia is indeed the only Commonwealth country to not have a treaty with its indigenous people. So that symbolic "welcome to country," at least in Australia, is *solely* symbolic—and most would exchange it in a heartbeat for an actual treaty, with actual rights, land, and sovereignty; the Gadigal people in Sydney have never relinquished their sovereignty, the welcome to country clearly states.

A week later, in Auckland, I met a white New Zealander musician and activist named Steve Abel, who took me and a group of other Auckland Writers Festival participants on a day trip through the Waitākere Ranges and to the black-sand Karekare Beach, where Jane Campion filmed scenes for *The Piano*. Steve pointed out that New Zealand's own treaty, which is to say its founding document, was an agreement called Te Tiriti o Waitangi, or the Treaty of Waitangi, written in both te reo Māori and English, made between the British Crown and over five hundred Māori rangatira, or chiefs. It was signed on February 6, 1840—comparatively late for a founding colonial document. It was signed at a time, Steve suggested mildly, by which the British had perhaps learned a tiny, tiny something from the horrors of their own empire, and the colonial management—and mismanagement—therein.

Obviously, this document cannot be in any way romanticized: the treaty was still a document of imperial contact and occupation; it was still one that the British later betrayed multiple times; it was still originally written by British subjects, and translated into te reo Māori by British missionaries; the translation was disputed and the meaning of true Māori sovereignty over lands whose governance and ownership was ceded to the British produced major, ongoing conflict. It is of course by no means the Thanksgiving fantasy that most Americans grow up with, and white supremacy and institutional racism flourish in New Zealand as they do everywhere. And yet equally it remains a joint political document that sets out the founding of a bicultural nation-state and government. Much of the graffiti that you see around New Zealand, Steve said, and much of the language of indigenous protest, consists of these words: HONOUR THE TREATY. Which is to say, honor the founding promise that this nation was based on—the founding sovereignty and rights that its indigenous people are owed.

It would be impossible for me, as an outsider, to calculate the half-life of the Treaty of Waitangi; to fully describe how its failures, lacunae, betrayals, and hypocrisies have shaped, in manifold ways, Aotearoa's past, present, and future. I know that New Zealand's statistics around race and wealth, race and the carceral state, look much like those of the United States: Māori prisoners make up more than half the incarcerated population in New Zealand, while only making up 16 percent of the total population. "It was never a good thing, a positive thing being Māori growing up," according to Bic Runga, a New Zealand singer of Chinese and Ngati Kahungunu descent who "shot to international fame in her 20s with the 1997 album *Drive*," and who is "part of a wave of popular musicians who have not only embraced te reo Māori, the indigenous language of New Zealand, [but] have propelled it on to the world stage"—especially poignant, given that in 1999, when Dame Hinewehi Mohi sang the New Zealand national anthem for that year's Rugby World Cup final, "she was met with a wave of anger" for taking the nation by surprise and singing in Māori. "[The backlash] was devastating at the time," says Mohi, now "one of the driving forces behind *Waiata/Anthems*, a compilation project released in 2019 that worked with artists . . . to reimagine their songs in te reo Māori."

I can only speak to what I felt when Steve told us this story, which was that I, as a reader, was listening to an entirely different origin story from any I had ever heard in a settler colonial society. Origin stories tell us who we think a people are—who we think *we* are, and why. The American origin story is written in Native genocide, transatlantic slavery, and imperial subjugation overseas. That is its originating fact, and so to write the next chapter of that story means contending with this prologue, which most Americans find themselves constitutionally unable and unwilling to do. And so we remain willfully illiterate to ourselves.

But here was a different kind of origin story, with a different, still-becoming, outcome. An origin story that was followed with harrowing chapters, of course; and written and read in blood, of course; and followed by much-needed and still-ongoing protest, resistance, and revision, of course. But also, an origin story that was bilingual; an origin story that was a mutual (which is not to say equal) pact. I imagined the average Bay Area citizen having a working facility of their specific region's indigenous languages, or civic discourse that regularly acknowledged the Anglo-American and Spanish destruction of the Native land we live on as Californians; imagined taking for granted the fact that signs in our public spaces in our country ought to be bilingual, even multilingual, that those languages should include the indigenous languages of the region, and that non-Native people, like the white people I met in Queenstown and Auckland, should have at least some working familiarity with those languages themselves.

I imagined that country, but don't know it, can't recognize it, have never visited it, not yet—though its arrival may not be entirely impossible. "Here in California, we actually do not have treaties," points out Dr. Cutcha Risling Baldy, Hoopa Valley Tribe / Yurok / Karuk, and assistant professor and department chair of Native American studies at Humboldt State University, in the *Vox* article "6 Native Leaders on What It Would Look Like If the US Kept Its Promises":

> Well, we do have treaties, but those treaties were not ratified. There were 18 in total that were made with California Indians in the 1800s, but at the time, Congress decided not to ratify them and then put them under an injunction of secrecy.... Treaties are foundational agreements the United States made with Native nations. Nobody fooled the US into entering into treaties, nobody tricked Benjamin Franklin (or whatever founding father) into building a nation that also had many other nations within it. This is the nation they built; these are the agreements they made. If we honor the Constitution, we have to honor the treaties. If we are truly going to honor

the treaties, we have to center Indigenous histories, support self-determination, and build decolonized futures by given back stolen land.

In July 2020, after having been stripped of their ancestral land 250 years prior, the Esselen Tribe in Northern California regained 1,200 acres near Big Sur, not far from where I live in the South Bay Area, on Muwekma Ohlone land, in a $4.5 million purchase made with a grant from the California Natural Resources Agency and negotiated by the Western Rivers Conservancy, an environmental group based in Portland. According to Tom Little Bear Nason, chairman of the Esselen Tribe of Monterey County, the 214-strong tribe will share the land with other Central Coast tribes that were also dispossessed during the Spanish missionary era, including the Ohlone, Amah Mutsun, and Rumsen people. "We're the original stewards of the land," Nason said, using the language of land acknowledgment I'd often heard in the public spaces of Australia and New Zealand, but which still so rarely comes up in American civic discourse (had I ever heard a president recite a land acknowledgment in the State of the Union?). "Now we've returned. We are going to conserve it and pass it on to our children and grandchildren and beyond."

ONE WEEK DURING MY TRAVELS I WAS IN TĀHUNA, ALSO KNOWN as Queenstown, a resort town on the South Island of New Zealand. My first day in Queenstown, my partner and I thought we'd start off with an easy hike—we'd come straight off the plane from the Sydney Writers' Festival and I was still fighting off the residual adrenaline and subsequent crash that usually follows festival life: the stimulation and conversation and the ebullient writerly kinship that only comes when people who spend most of the year locked in small rooms are suddenly thrust into that foreign territory, Social Life. We planned to climb the Tiki Trail, a supposedly short hike that takes people up through a mostly fir and beech forest, emerging onto a summit where you'll find an alpine lodge, complete with restaurants, a luge, and most importantly, a gondola you could have taken to get up there in the first place.

During the hike, we were surrounded by Douglas firs, a tree familiar to me as a North American and a Californian specifically, where they are abundant and native. Here in Queenstown, those firs were originally planted by European settler colonials, who thought the South Island's vast and relatively treeless mountain landscape should look like the Alps and Highlands they knew back home.

Today the trees' rapid growth cycle, due to the climate and their lack of natural competitors—as they would have back in Europe or California where they are from—is wiping out native plants and wildlife, a process described to me by a very kind sustainability guide, who was also one of the few people of color I met on the South Island, which is noticeably whiter and more Anglo than the North Island. The relative lack of birdsong during hikes is eerie and telling; later, a tourist bus driver to Piopiotahi, otherwise known as Milford Sound, a fjord system sometimes called the eighth wonder of the world, told us how the wide variety of native birds in New Zealand were essentially hunted or driven to extinction through human settlement in the islands, but particularly by the accelerated exploitation of the land that European settlement introduced. Europeans also introduced rabbits, stoats, ferrets, and rats to the islands, and these have become pandemic-level pests, whose destructive presence only exacerbates the country's at-risk biodiversity. *All because one bored Englishman wanted rabbit pie*, the driver, a white New Zealander, told us grimly. The Englishman brought six rabbits over for himself. But the rabbits bred as rabbits do, and so it goes.

The trees, the rabbits, the ferrets, the ghost of birdsong: all were troubling and revelatory glimpses of the ways in which contemporary issues of climate change and sustainability (even concepts of natural beauty; many people think, of course, that the Douglas fir forests are beautiful, and aren't concerned with their origin or their impact on the country's environmental future) are still inextricably connected to the politics of coloniality.

My own home state of California has been regularly ravaged by wildfires, in a hideous collaboration between human-wrought climate disaster and equally human-wrought corporate negligence: investigations have shown that electric company PG&E caused over 1,500 wildfires in the past seven years. In

2019, the Kincade Fire burned nearly 78,000 acres in Sonoma County, with nearly 180,000 people forced to evacuate their homes and millions left without electricity, often for days. According to a report in *Business Insider*, a jumper cable had broken on a PG&E transmission tower in the area, just before the fire began; the California Department of Forestry and Fire Protection identified the cable before PG&E personnel even arrived at the scene. PG&E's history of prioritizing corporate profits over safety (not just of the environment, but of the people who live there) has been well established:

> After a PG&E pipeline exploded in 2010, killing eight people, state regulators started investigating the company. They found that PG&E had collected $224 million more than it was authorized to collect in oil and gas revenue in the decade before the explosion. At the same time, it spent millions less than it was supposed to on maintenance and generally fell short of industry safety standards.
>
> "There was very much a focus on the bottom line over everything: 'What are the earnings we can report this quarter?'" Mike Florio, who was a California utilities commissioner from 2011 to 2016, told *The New York Times*. "And things really got squeezed on the maintenance side."

The people who bear the brunt of this avoidable disaster are, overwhelmingly, minorities. A 2018 *New York Times* article on wildfires cites a study published in the journal *PloS One*, by Ian Davies and others, suggesting that "people of color, especially Native Americans, face more risk from wildfires than whites. It is another example of how the kinds of disasters exacerbated by climate change often hit minorities and the poor the hardest." The article continues:

> They found that 29 million people in the United States live in high-risk locations. Most of them are white and not poor. But the researchers then used census data to identify 12 million people with characteristics that made them especially vulnerable to the effects of wildfires. Mr. Davies called those socioeconomic circumstances "adaptive capacity."
>
> "They are things that would make someone more vulnerable and less able to adapt to a wildfire if it occurred," he said.

During the Kincade Fire, I recall how so much of the coverage in the news focused on the loss of Sonoma County's famous vineyards, with most of the articles lamenting that loss written by white middle-class survivors of the fire. But when I lived in Santa Rosa, Sonoma County, just after graduating from college—the only place in California I have ever seen trucks waving Confederate flags just above their gun lockers—what I remember most clearly is the large population of Mexican and Central American workers, whose labor was the unspoken foundation of the region's entire economy. The sight of day laborers waiting on the street to be picked up by white contractors was a daily occurrence. There were fewer articles in the wake of the Kincade Fire addressing the loss of livelihood for these laborers, people who worked but did not own the land that was destroyed by fire, and yet were disproportionately affected by its aftermath nonetheless. According to *The New York Times*,

> In 2017, as three fires raged across California's Napa County, most emergency messages were delivered in English even though 30 percent of Napa's population identifies as Hispanic. . . .
>
> "What is interesting about wildfires is that the wealthy often put themselves in harm's way—the second home in the woods phenomenon," Dr. [Bob] Bolin [professor of environmental social science at Arizona State University] wrote. "The difference between the wealthy and the poor is the wealthy can afford losses, they have insurance, health insurance, secure jobs (typically somewhere else) and the poor don't."
>
> Mr. Davies found that Native Americans living on federal reservations were six times more likely to live in both the most vulnerable and the most fire-prone areas.
>
> Part of the reason is the historical legacy of the reservations, which have created persistent economic inequity. And the reservations are often located on grasslands or abutting forests that have a high potential for wild-

fires. But the century-old rules that were designed to reduce forest fires through fire suppression, and that made
it illegal to set fires on public forest lands, essentially
banned many tribes from using controlled fires to reduce
wildfire risk.

It's impossible to untangle our disastrous climate present
from our disastrous colonial past. "European colonization of
the Americas resulted in the killing of so many native people
that it transformed the environment and caused the Earth's
climate to cool," revealed a January 2019 article in *The Guardian*, based on research by University College London scientists, on the period in the late 1500s and early 1600s also known
as the Little Ice Age.

Here is our unfinished climate disaster movie, over four
hundred years in the making, its sequel yet to be written: the
dispossession of land from its indigenous people and the exploitation of that land for maximum capital extraction; the
white supremacist policies that saw those people and their
descendants shunted to some of the most environmentally
vulnerable areas in the country (in a practice that would then
be repeated centuries later on subsequent communities of
color), and then forbade the historical practices of land stew-
ardship that had previously helped these very communities
avoid the worst consequences of seasonal wildfires; the settler
colonial hunting practices and introduction of European
fauna that ravaged biodiversity across the globe; and most of

all the repeated historical pattern of poor and marginalized BIPOC communities bearing the weight of these biopolitical catastrophes.

The pattern sees itself mirrored in New Zealand, in the United States—and of course, in the Philippines of my parents, so regularly visited by disastrous typhoons and volcanic eruptions whose destruction, exacerbated by the corporate profiteering that remains a holdover from the colonial era, has always come knocking first on the door of the rural and indigenous poor. In his landmark book *Suspended Apocalypse: White Supremacy, Genocide, and the Filipino Condition*, Dylan Rodríguez describes the notorious eruption of Mount Pinatubo in 1991 and the disaster's pronounced displacement of the indigenous Aeta (or Ayta—sometimes pejoratively called Negrito, another inheritance from the Spanish colonial era) tribe who live in the region, comparing the state's failure to protect its indigenous people with the anti-Black indifference that left so many vulnerable after Hurricane Katrina in 2005, and the Aeta suspicion of the Philippine state's role in the crisis, quoting their testimonials after the disaster:

> "Since long ago our ancestors have taken care of the mountain. But perhaps in time, our leaders' minds had been tainted with a destructive nature. Thus, they allowed the Philippine National Oil Company, which had no right to disturb the mountain, to get in. . . . Not everyone thought it was wise to drill into Pinatubo. The

93

Ayta leaders thought that these operations would affect our way of living, the environment, the water, and our resources. . . . We didn't want PNOC to endanger these basic needs. But we were betrayed. . . . That was when Pinatubo started to emit smoke."

As Rodríguez points out, "this series of reflections from displaced Aetas implicates a structure of planned social obsolescence," a deliberate process that echoes the state machinations by which Native Americans were deliberately displaced onto environmentally precarious land and Black Americans were left to fend for themselves in the wake of Katrina.

This is how the Aeta retrospective on the Philippine neo-liberal state's tampering with the ecology of the mountain politically resonates with the common, longstanding suspicion shared among black Louisianans (and many others) that the U.S. state was largely responsible for manufacturing and (urban) planning the human casualties of Katrina (e.g., the decades of refusal to address the obsolescence of levees adjoining the Lower Ninth Ward, and the generalized withholding of response/relief capacities as the atrocity unfolded).

The stakes of this fight remind us that intergenerational justice means thinking about intergenerational inheritances, down to the trees and the birds—not least of all because the

fact that environmental justice is linked to the legacy of coloniality necessarily means that environmental justice is racial
justice. This is colonial business, and it requires decolonial
work. Back in New Zealand, many are fighting to renativize
the landscape and protect it from invasive species, like the
Douglas fir. The New Zealand Biodiversity Strategy 2000–
2020, a government initiative led by the Department of Conservation, "establishes a framework for action to halt the decline
of indigenous biodiversity."

New Zealand was one of the last large land areas on earth
to be settled by humans. The settlers, and the exotic species they brought with them, had a dramatic impact on
our indigenous biodiversity. . . .

This means managing biodiversity in ways that are
of benefit to all. It requires us to think "over the fence."
We cannot continue to think of protected and produc-
tive places separately. Natural systems do not recog-
nise human boundaries. As well as protecting our most
important places for indigenous biodiversity, we have
to manage this biodiversity as best we can in farming
and forestry environments and alongside marine industries, while ensuring a sustainable return from these
activities. . . .

Māori have a holistic view of the environment and
biodiversity that derives from a cosmogony (belief system) that links people and all living and non-living

things. Descended from the union of Ranginui (the sky father) and Papatuanuku (the earth mother), and their offspring, the atua kaitiaki (spiritual guardians)—Tane (atua of forests), Tumatauenga (atua of war and ceremony), Rongo (atua of cultivation), Tangaroa (atua of seas), Tawhirimatea (atua of wind and storms) and Haumietiketike (atua of land and forest foods)—humans share a common whakapapa (ancestry) with other animals and plants. People are therefore part of nature and biodiversity.

All components of ecosystems, both living and non-living, possess the spiritual qualities of tapu, mauri, mana, and wairua. Māori, as tangata whenua, are the kaitiaki (guardians) of these ecosystems and have a responsibility to protect and enhance them. This responsibility of people to other living things is expressed in the concept of kaitiakitanga—or guardianship.

Learning about this conservation work, it seemed to me a powerful living metaphor, and an inspiring example of what decolonial work might look like on an institutional level; how that work is fundamentally cooperative. It will require the descendants of settler colonials—who continue to enjoy the wealth and safety reaped by their ancestors—to face our history and materially transform our land management, in reparative collaboration with the indigenous people whose lives today remain striated with the damage that very history has wrought. It's not difficult to make a hopeful analogy between New Zealand's strategic response to declining biodiversity—the concerted, daily work it requires from its people to repair and restore an endangered landscape—and the decolonial practices that would have us do the concerted, daily work it would take to truly reckon with our cultural history, knowing that to do that work is to honor the debt we have to our future:

> The Strategy is government-led, but cannot be achieved by government alone. All the myriad of resource management decisions made by land managers, resource users, iwi and hapu, and others, affect biodiversity. It will be changes in the day-to-day practices of all New Zealanders that will determine our record in biodiversity management. And the bottom line in management is that the loss of ecosystems and species is irreversible. Decisions that New Zealanders make today provide the biodiversity legacy or debt to their grandchildren.

BUT ALL DECOLONIAL WORK HAS ITS DETRACTORS. ON ANOTHER day, my partner and I hiked up Te Tapu-nui, or Queenstown Hill, another relatively steep uphill climb through a dark, mostly silent, shadowy fir forest, patches of which were actually dead, so that you occasionally felt as though you were moving through a dank natural grave. Many of the trees had silvered over time, so that it was as if you'd stepped into a world gone grayscale, alien and wrong, the way Antonioni once described the world lit by solar eclipse, or so I remember from a passage in an Anne Carson poem.

We walked through this funereal forest for a long time, mostly in inexplicably uneasy silence, until finally we saw, improbably, a light at the end of the tunnel: a patch of sunlight peeking through the tree canopy, where the fir line ended, and the path opened out into open, sun-baked native shrubland and grasses. This landscape looked so similar to the California landscape I grew up in that I immediately felt tender, at ease—and mostly just grateful to be back out in the sun, on open, variable ground of the kind I prefer to hike on: uphill, sandy, sunlit. At one of the summits—it was one of those hikes where you could go higher and higher, only to be rewarded with ever more shatteringly beautiful vistas—there was a descriptive placard next to a metal sculpture called the *Basket of Dreams*.

The placard read:

> You have just walked up the Queenstown Hill Walkway and are now looking across the resort's iconic mountain landscapes. Over these spectacular highlands grow beech forests, shrublands, and golden tussock grasslands that provide habitat for many native insects, lizards and birds including the karearea (New Zealand falcon).
>
> However, you may also notice many dead trees along your walk. This decay is a stark contrast to the usually healthy high country vegetation. What you are seeing is

the d[e][m][i][s][e] of [u][n]welcome "wildings," or weed trees.

The word *demise* and the *un* in unwelcome had been forcibly scratched out by someone, the plastic gouged out down to the metal backing. Scratched out by someone who didn't want people to know about the history of the trees they had just walked in, someone who didn't want to look that history in the face: a settler colonial history, a history not just of "neutral" or "universal" natural beauty, but of specific, historic, contextualized human destruction, and frankly, of death—the funereal atmosphere of the Douglas fir forest was accurate, as they grow so rapidly and become so large that they create a forest canopy that kills life beneath it, so that only poisonous, extremely Super Mario–looking mushrooms seemed to be thriving there.

I—this will come as no surprise to those who know me or indeed have read anything I have ever written—have approximately zero chill. Upon seeing this defaced placard, I proceeded to have a momentary rage blackout there on the summit; I don't remember exactly what came out of my mouth, only that I looked at my partner and said-barked something like: They erased it. I'm fixing it. Where's my pen.

Willful misreading is a violence. To warp the history of a place to serve one vision of the past—and therefore, preserve a specific vision of the present and future—is an obscenity, and yet we live in obscenities like this every day. The fact that

so few people know that the Philippine-American War produced a genocide in the archipelago is an obscenity. The fact
that so few Americans have any real grasp of their country as
founded upon a triumvirate of horrors, most principally as a
settler colonial society (which is to say, a society founded on
Native genocide), a slave economy (which is to say, a society
founded on the enslavement, exploitation, and degradation of
Black peoples), and a global empire (which is to say, a society
that took the lessons it learned as settler colonials and slavers,
and applied its lessons to other parts of the world, in particular the Philippines, whose ghostly presence in American history is nevertheless the secret key to understanding global
imperial American statecraft as we know it today)—is an obscenity.

This is changing, of course. I saw that defaced Queenstown placard in 2019; a year later, the removal of Confederate
statues—as well as other monuments to notorious imperialists
and colonialists—by antiracist activists in the wake of the historic Black Lives Matter protests sparked by the murder of
George Floyd has become one small part of a long-overdue
reckoning with America's bloodied history. Similarly vital acts
of damnatio memoriae have occurred in London, the city I
called my home for almost ten years, where some of the people
I love most in the world still live.

England's prime minister Boris Johnson (a small horror
film in five words) condemned the removal of slaveowner statues in London, where he once presided as mayor (a small hor-

ror film in six words), in a grotesquely disingenuous act of willful misreading:

> We cannot now try to edit or censor our past. We cannot pretend to have a different history. The statues in our cities and towns were put up by previous generations. They had different perspectives, different understandings of right and wrong. But those statues teach us about our past, with all its faults. To tear them down would be to lie about our history, and impoverish the education of generations to come.

The Guardian, reporting on Johnson's statement, added just one sentence as riposte, with that quintessentially bleak humor I loved so much when I lived there: "One of the statues of a slave-owner removed in London had only been placed in its present location in 1997."

Even if that statue hadn't, sickeningly, been put there in the twentieth century, the argument Johnson and zealous tradition-defenders like him often make—*we have to protect our history, our traditions, our legacy*—still doesn't hold up. Monumentalizing is already an act of editing (and censoring) the past; it *already* allows us to pretend to have a different history. Those statues don't just teach us about our past—they teach us how to *read* our past, and thereby how to live in our present. They deliberately teach us about slaveholders like Robert Milligan, whose statue was removed in 2020 from outside the Museum of London Docklands—a museum that opened in 2003, housed in an early eighteenth-century sugar warehouse, of the kind built to serve the West India trade routes, and the commodities gleaned via enslaved labor in the colonies. "Discover how the docks transformed London and made the city we know today," the museum boasts to visitors.

That people in the past had different perspectives, different understandings of right and wrong doesn't alter the fact that they *were* wrong—it cannot be controversial to ask us to agree that transatlantic slavery was a world-rending evil whose enrichment of the West has corruptively made the world we know today—and to memorialize those actors is to memorialize that wrong. In 2003, to choose to center the statue of a man like Robert Milligan is to make a deliberate choice—a choice about how to remember the docklands, how to remember that sugar warehouse and its uses, how to remember London and the history that made it. It's an act of reading, and it teaches all who view it a very specific way to read that history, too.

Where are the monuments to the enslaved people who built the wealth Britain benefits from today, or the indigenous peoples in the Caribbean who were massacred and dispossessed of their land to create sugar plantations for European enjoyment? Where are the monuments to the Windrush generation that— like the Turkish Gastarbeiter in Germany, or North African workers in France—helped rebuild postwar Britain, yet decades later were wrongly detained, denied legal rights and benefits (such as medical care and housing), and threatened with deportation (with at least eighty-three individuals wrongly deported) by Britain's Conservative government, in what became known as the Windrush scandal in 2018? Where is this seemingly ferocious commitment to not editing or censoring when it comes to those figures? Where is that much-romanticized—and much-instrumentalized—love of history when it comes to understanding just whom that history is actually built and peopled by?

In a statement on its website about the removal of Milligan's statue, the museum admitted, in a post by guest writer Kristy Warren:

> Requests to remove the Milligan statue are old. Activists, artists, communities, historians and a range of others have asked that something be done about it for a number of decades. . . .
>
> The inscription on the statue's plinth, while valorising Milligan's participation in commerce, said nothing about the enslaved people he claimed ownership of, nor those he bought in bulk from slave ships to sell to other enslavers. Before his death in 1809, Milligan claimed ownership of 526 enslaved people who were forced to work on his two plantations in Jamaica. When the London Sugar & Slavery Gallery was opened at the Museum of London Docklands in 2007 a black cloth was draped over the Milligan statue, but no permanent solution was resolved upon at that time.

Johnson doesn't have to worry about the removal of these statues being tantamount to lying about history, or impoverishing the education of generations to come—those statues have done the work for him. But the truth is, what he really means is that the removal of those statues will impoverish the education of generations committed to a specific historical reading—a specific way of interpreting the world, which has benefited people like Johnson, Milligan, and the descendants of Confederate slaveowners: built their estates, solidified their wealth, educated them at Eton, put them in power, carved their statues.

I'm reminded of a story I read in 2016, when I was still living in London, about Prince William and Kate Middleton, also known as the Duke and Duchess of Cambridge, having to hastily obscure the nameplate on a piece of art in their drawing room when then president Barack Obama came to England for a state visit. The painting was called *The Negro Page*. "The title is obviously the product of its age," *The Guardian* fretted at the time, "though given the thousands of other options some might have found said moniker faintly jarring for a receiving room." No attempt made to confront why, exactly, the future king and queen of England—future heads of the Commonwealth, made up largely of Black and Asian citizens, their faded monarchy's former imperial subjects—would choose, of all paintings, to display that "faintly jarring" one. Just a strategically placed fern, to help keep that persistent—and thus protected—history out of sight.

Most recently, in a similar act of censorship in England, conservative councillors in Essex censored Australian artist Gabriella Hirst's exhibition *An English Garden*, which "adopts the basic elements of a formal English garden, and is planted with Rosa floribunda 'Atom Bomb,' a rare rose plant," the artist's website details. "The rose bed is accompanied by a series of garden benches with brass plaques which allude to Britain's historical and ongoing relationship with nuclear armament, considering the British Imperial histories of 'gardening the world' . . . and Britain's nuclear weapons test program of the 1950s, which saw the devastating contamination of unceded Indigenous Lands in Australia."

English rose, indeed. And much like those people in Tāhuna who must have found an honest reckoning of the political history of the natural landscape before them so distasteful they had to deface a public placard, Tory councillors in Essex hastened to censor the work, removing Hirst's installation and claiming offensive content.

It's easy to simply drape a black cloth over or shove a big plant in front of a politically inconvenient object; it's easy to raze a rose garden when it asks us to do more than find it beautiful; it's easy to cynically calculate the momentary political expedience of minimizing one's tacit racism in "mixed" company (certainly it's telling that the black cloth only came to cover the Milligan statue when the museum's newest permanent exhibit, the London, Sugar & Slavery gallery, opened in 2007—not a good look right now, the museum must have concluded; not a good look right now, William and Kate must have also concluded, hiding *The Negro Page* while welcoming America's first Black president). It's much harder to actually confront the history that statues and paintings and artistic censorship not just represent but, quite literally, perpetuate: it being, after all, the job of statues to make things perpetual.

Firs, roses, statues—and the placards that adorn them—are like history books in public: they're civic sites of collective reading, where the statue tells us to read the ground we're standing on; to interpret it in a specific way. A statue of a slaveholder, on land stolen from Native peoples and developed and enriched by enslaved labor, is demanding a specific reading of that place; that building; that country. To challenge these monuments—to question the old story they've had so long to tell—is not only a vital act of civil disobedience. It's a revolutionary act of reading.

WHITE SUPREMACY AS BAD READERSHIP: A SCENE. AFTER ONE Auckland Writers Festival event about my book, an older white woman in the audience raised her hand during the Q&A. Her voice was North American, almost certainly American, but sometimes my ear for Canadian can go on the fritz, so I leave the possibility open.

She said something like: I teach at a school where there's over three hundred Filipina girls. I'm desperate for a list of Filipino and Filipino American writers I should read. *GO!*

She barked *GO* like shooting a starter pistol, letting me know when to begin running for my life. The audience audibly gasped, grew tense and uncomfortable, embarrassed. There were several options for responding that ran through my mind in that moment, not all of which would have allowed me to return home to the United States as a free person, so ultimately what I said to her was, dryly, *First of all, PayPal me the fee for that labor, because Google exists.*

This is obviously the kind of flippant reply that garners laughter and applause tinged with both shock and relief from some of the woker people in the audience. When that settled down, I was—in the manner of so many people of color endemically used to dealing with terrible white people, like having to take your Zyrtec during allergy season—gracious, of course. I laughed, too—deflated the moment for the comfort of the room, at the expense of my own—and said that, in the end, I was also a reader, and one of my favorite things to do was to give people, regardless of who they were, book recommendations, especially given that it was an opportunity to hype Filipinx writers I love, for the benefit of young Filipinx readers (kids whom I shudder to imagine in the care of a teacher like this). So I recommended a list of writers I love; said something about being honored to be living in and being the descendent of so much wonderful Filipinx and Filipinx American literature; and ultimately refocused the conversation on the Filipinx art I venerated.

I ended by repeating to her, *But yeah—PayPal.*

I don't have much to add to that anecdote; it was a shitty well-meaning moment engineered by a shitty well-meaning person. It was a moment of laziness and entitlement; an ethnographic moment. An encounter with someone who had always been an expected reader.

ON MY FIRST NIGHT IN AUCKLAND, I SAW A FILM CALLED *MErata: How Mum Decolonised the Cinema*, a documentary about Merata Mita, a hugely influential Māori director and presence in New Zealand cinema, who was an earlier supporter of an entire generation of indigenous filmmakers in New Zealand, among them Taika Waititi, the much-lauded director of *Boy*, *What We Do in the Shadows*, *Hunt for the Wilderpeople*, and of course, the film I spent at least a year semiseriously telling people was the Greatest Film of Our Time Just for That One Extremely Erotic Scene of Tessa Thompson Rakishly Saying "In a Minute" Before Leaping Off a Spacecraft to Fight Enemy Ships, *Thor: Ragnarok*.

I'd just arrived in Auckland from Queenstown, the day after Mother's Day, and I was so fucking exhausted I couldn't see straight. I was there for the writers festival, and I also had an eight-thousand-word deadline for a speech at the Roman Forum for Rome's International Literature Festival that I'd already missed by three days, so I knew I had to hunker down in the hotel room and not leave my self-imposed writing jail until I'd gotten some serious headway. I wrote for hours and hours—

some words of which appear in the pages of this book—and I think the motivation that kept me going was that I knew I was going to try to watch *Merata* at the Academy Cinema, not so far from my hotel.

The documentary had come out a couple of years prior, but was being rescreened all over New Zealand (with some screenings in the States, as well) for Mother's Day, and it had been seen and celebrated across the world; Ava DuVernay called Mita "an icon we should all know." When I finally got to the cinema, still dazed from my writing fugue and not having eaten anything all day but the pound of free chocolate kindly left in my hotel room by the festival organizers, I bought my ticket, and a bag of potato chips, and waited in the empty theater. Truth be told, there were not many people in the theater. I think in the end there may have been about five or six of us.

Merata: How Mum Decolonised the Cinema is a deeply tender, affecting, and ferociously radical portrait of the eponymous Merata Mita, shining light of New Zealand filmmaking, a legend and hero of Māori as well as global indigenous cinema. The film is made by her youngest son, Hepi Mita, and it is both tremendously intimate and radically intersectional in its attention: there are huge passages of the film that are devoted to showing Mita's struggles as a largely single mother of six children facing housing discrimination, sexual harassment, domestic abuse, the fight for reproductive rights (in particular for Māori women), all while she was producing art that confronted New Zealand's institutional racism and its legacy of colonial oppression and police brutality, as well as patriarchy, abuse, and sexism within her own Māori community.

There are scenes from Mita's thunderously powerful films—like *Bastion Point: Day 507*, for example, which follows the eviction of the indigenous Ngāti Whātua from their traditional land, and their peaceful yet absolutely heart-wrenching protest against the white settler colonial forces of New Zealand. The visual horror of seeing the all-white New Zealand police and army personnel come to remove the occupiers and demolish the temporary settlements they'd made is what the true power of documentary film is all about: it documents this horrifically momentous part of New Zealand's history, and the artistry of its shots, cuts, and framing brings us the spectacular form of politics at its most subversive and powerful—we cannot look away from the urgency of these images, and what they say about the country they are showing. In a similar vein, the film shows clips from Merata Mita's film *Patu!*, which documents the anti-apartheid protests in New Zealand during the notorious South African Springbok rugby tours (while many countries had closed their doors to the apartheid state, New Zealand had allowed the players to enter the country and tour there, likely related to an upcoming government reelection that required the votes of rural whites more likely to support the Springboks and, by virtue of that support, apartheid—a piece of political cynicism that felt very familiar to this American in the cinema). The scenes Mita captured of harrowing police violence enacted upon anti-apartheid protestors in New Zealand are indispensable viewing for anyone who thinks about police violence and state oppression, and how its strategies and practices mirror each other worldwide.

Mita became notorious in New Zealand for both the politics of her films as well as her relatively unconventional (at least by normative cis-hetero standards) domestic life, as the mother of seven children with three different partners (the film briefly but heartbreakingly details the loss of one of Mita's children, Lars, to cot death). Because of Mita's politics and films, she was routinely harassed by New Zealand police—a fact denied, of course, by the police themselves—and witnessed her own son brutally beaten at their front door. The searing trauma of these years very clearly had a profound effect on Mita's children—at least two of her children describe going down "antisocial" paths because of the police brutality they'd experienced; state violence had both psychologically and physically injured and hardened them to the world thereafter. One of Mita's children also describes the physical abuse Mita experienced at the hands of the younger Māori partner for whom she left her first husband (conventionally minded, white, uncomfortable with having a wife who worked). This younger Māori man, nine years Mita's junior, had once been her student. The tears that come to the son's eyes when he recalls the brutal beatings his father dealt his mother are wrenching; he describes episodes of bloodying assault that make a viewer's stomach go dead-cold with terror.

And yet in this scene, and all the scenes throughout the

film, we glimpse something that lies at the core of the film and is indeed its moral compass and force: how much Mita's children love her. Even after Mita's daughter admits that they went through immense hardship and poverty as a result of being, for many years, the children of a single starving artist, she declares passionately that she would do it all again: "for Mum." I don't think I can do justice to the life-claiming urgency with which Mita's daughter delivers this declaration, or the way the rest of her siblings agree.

Decolonial love pours out of every frame Merata Mita is in—there is an incandescent joy living at the heart of this film, which also doesn't shy away from depicting how pain, poverty, and trauma radiate out in a film and community for generations. There's also an unabashed vitality—an erotics, really—to the way Merata Mita moves through her life and politics; something exciting and liberating about how she obviously chased, and changed, her desires with an unapologetic freedom and conviction.

The more sober—yet no less vital—companion to this unabashed freedom is the way Mita confronts the fact that gendered liberation, and in particular sexual liberation, is incomplete without both reproductive rights and the dismantling of the patriarchal oppression that would withhold those rights. After having several children and living, at a certain point in her life, in what would be fair to call utter destitution, Mita describes finding herself pregnant. In the film she describes the decision she had to make, realizing that she was in no way financially or physically capable of raising another child, and yet the doctors she spoke to—cis men, of course—simply expected her to accept her lot, regardless of her economic circumstance. Mita says she was eventually able to find a clinic where she was able to have a successful abortion. From that point on, Mita says, she made it a point to talk about reproductive rights, contraception, and abortion, particularly so that Māori people in a similar position would have the resources necessary to make decisions about their own bodies, resources Mita felt she'd come of age entirely without. For a long time she'd never even heard of contraception, she admits at one point in the film.

This conviction Mita developed, in understanding that her particular experiences as a Māori woman, the particular crossroads she faced, were ones that would have universal value and impact if she simply told those stories—if she let them be heard by the people who needed them—is a conviction that resonates throughout the film. It reminds me that so much of the well-meaning yet intellectually flaccid liberal language around things like "diversity in film and literature" banks heavily on ideas like "giving voice to the voiceless," a sentiment I've always found repugnant and paternalistic. Mita's art, not to mention her politics—the *aliveness* of both—has no patience for that sort of white savior torpor, or for the notion that any of the people she puts onscreen have ever been voiceless. The decolonial point here is not to give voice to the voiceless, but to recognize the voices that have always been there—to recognize them, and to honor them. For what is it to *honor* something—

not to exploit it as a resource (either geographically, with a pipeline; or intellectually, with a novel one treats as prettied-up ethnographic data), not to deface it, not to hide its unsavory past, not to throw a black cloth over it or nudge a fern over it, not to raze it, not to let its hard-won promises molder under an injunction of secrecy—unratified, unrealized? What does the daily shape of that honor take in a world; in a life; in a life's work?

Much of this documentary, too, puts paid to that tiresome anxiety—the emotional support animal of mainly white, middle-class, liberal-minded practitioners of the arts—about whether or not making art has any viable, material, or sustainable purpose in times of crisis; that one should be out doing something more important, more actionable, more *more*. Does art matter in times of historical crisis, white middle-class artists always seem to be worrying, as if living in a time of crisis were new to them. And who knows—perhaps for these cramped gloomy minds, it is. Has it ever mattered? (Of course, if you ask those same artists if this anxiety therefore means they believe Black literature doesn't matter, or Native literature doesn't matter, or Asian literature doesn't matter, they're usually at pains to clarify that they didn't mean it *like that*; though in my experience, on the whole, Black, Native, or Asian art does not, generally—not to speak of materially or personally—matter to these artists, except in the sense that pretending it does matter is a protocol of good behavior, like always being nice to your maid.) The crux of that artistic anxiety is at once performatively self-annihilating and productively self-aggrandizing:

"contemporary art-making only produces mere laTe caPiTaLiSt coMmoDiTieS; *I* can't do anything about it but register *my* anxiety about it; having done so is sufficient discourse; place lampshade here and screw in." Slightly less anxiety, however, is devoted to the more immediate (and more immediately actionable) fact that white artists are better paid for their commodities than literally anyone else.

It reminds me that the concept "carbon footprint" was a PR tactic thought up by British Petroleum ("the company unveiled its 'carbon footprint calculator' in 2004," a *Mashable* article tells us) to steer people away from targeting rampant corporate greed or governmental collusion—like the British Petroleum oil spill in 2010 that wrought devastating environmental destruction on indigenous communities from the Amazon all the way to Louisiana's Gulf Coast. "Tracking one's carbon footprint" was instead an invitation to enter into an endless pantomime of individual piety, nihilism, and learned helplessness; eco-friendly, as opposed to eco-furious. Similarly, white middle-class anxiety about art's value is really only interested in its own carbon footprint: mapping it, framing it, putting it high on a mantel. It's an anxiety that pretends that being embarrassed about one's power is the same thing as divesting from that power. But *Merata: How Mum Decolonised the Cinema* is a documentary that knows, unsensationally and in the most practical sense, that *because* power matters, art matters (and for that matter, being protected against discrimination and paid an equitable living wage for one's artistic labor matters); *because* the impersonality of power matters, the personal and interpersonal matter. "The revolution isn't just running out with a gun," Mita says in the film. "If a film I make causes indigenous people to feel stronger about themselves, then I'm achieving something worthwhile for the revolution." And here we see Mita's honed understanding of the practical needs of resistance—she doesn't say *better*. She says *stronger*.

When I was researching Te Tiriti o Waitangi, I looked up the etymology of the word *treaty*. I like looking up the roots of words, knowing who their distant parents were, knowing what ground these words came out of, to eventually feed and name us. Take, for example, the Proto-Oceanic word that appears in te reo Māori, as well as in the Philippine languages of my parents, as in many languages with Austronesian roots. The word is *mana*. For te reo Māori speakers—obviously this will be a clumsy explanation, not being one myself—the word is one that denotes power, often of a supernatural kind; it describes someone's, or some place's, or some thing's, spiritual, sacred life force. Someone who has mana has an aura, a strong presence. For Tagalog speakers, *mana* means inheritance (though the Ilocano and Pangasinan of my parents have a different word for it, *tawid/tawir*). When someone inevitably tells my mother that I'm a pain in the ass, my mom will typically reply, "Mana sa nanay," which loosely translated means, "She gets it from her mom." Some researchers have suggested that the echo of the word *mana* and its cognates across all major divisions of Malayo-Polynesian supports theories of early prehistorical cultural contact between both Austronesian- and non-Austronesian-speaking peoples: forms of *mana* appear in the Meso-Melansian languages Roviana, Halia, Teop, Nehan, Tolai; in the Proto-Western Malayo-Polynesian of Tagalog, Bikol, Masbatenyo, Casiguran Dumagat; in Malay, in Aceh, in Buginese, Togian, Toraja Sa'dan; in the non-Austronesian languages of the New Guinea area, like Middle Wahgi, Warembori, Enga, Melpa, Nii. In a poetic interpretation, the echo also suggests that, for the Austronesian language family (which, before the sixteenth century's colonial era, was the most widespread language family in the world), another word for one's power, one's aura, one's sacred, impersonal life force, was: inheritance.

Treaty comes from the Latin *trahere*: to pull or drag, often violently. Eventually its meaning of "deal with, handle, especially in speech or writing" (example: the way I am "treating" empathy and art in this essay), which originated in the early fourteenth century, led to its use in medicine, which began in 1781, with *treat* used as a word to mean "heal, cure, or apply remedies."

The history of the word *treaty* begins with a violence, which then moves through something that deals with it—often writing. After which comes something like: healing. A remedy. All writing, then, and all art, is a kind of treaty—between the reader and the writing, between the art and the world, between the fire of the past that burnished us and the fire of the present that consumes us and the fire of the future we might forge. Honor the treaty.

THE LIMITS OF
WHITE FANTASY

Another day, another shit show involving J. K. Rowling; I'm starting to think there's a schedule. Now, I'm not particularly interested in rehashing the stale trans-exclusionary non-feminism that characterizes not just Rowling's work but her public persona, especially of late—particularly as it increasingly feels as though any sustained engagement with her scientifically and morally indefensible ideas around biology and gender only continue to give oxygen to those ideas, and reinforce the presumption that the existential reality of trans women's lives is a subject open for debate in the first place (not least of all, that it is open for debates led by and between cis women). For the purposes of this book, I want to focus on the effect her very public statements have had on the way people read her work, in an effort to rethink the way we've customarily read the mainstream white-authored fantasy narratives about identity, oppression, and justice that have become cultural touchstones for so many across the globe.

I'm not a Potterhead, so I have no skin in this game (if I had to sort myself in that universe, I wouldn't be in any of those houses, the class system of British boarding schools not being my particular kink—the closest thing I could imagine myself as would be a Squib, i.e., the nonmagical child of magical parents, which is another way of saying I'm the Virgo daughter of two Aquariuses), but I've seen enough friends and loved ones lament the loss, in their words, of nothing less than their entire childhoods—childhoods handheld by the characters in the Harry Potter universe, which (like so much of our most formative reading) taught them crucial things about difference, friendship, cooperation, loneliness, harm. I'm from the *X-Men* generation, myself—that classic American repository of allegories on oppression and difference, its entire narrative universe founded on the premise of marginalized people fighting for their right to exist without discrimination or exploitation; to be seen as equals, and to be loved in their wholeness.

Some part of me will always love that universe. But I also know that so much of what makes up our mainstream contemporary fantasy narratives, utopian or dystopian, has been written by white authors, from Rowling's Harry Potter to Chris Claremont's run of *X-Men* (still its most well-known incarnation) to Margaret Atwood's *The Handmaid's Tale* and its contemporary TV adaptation. They reach a global, cross-cultural audience even while their narrative universes overwhelmingly center white protagonists, both on the page and on the screen.

Yet all of those stories borrow freely from the histories of oppression and intergenerational trauma that have largely befallen communities of color: racial discrimination, enslavement, apartheid, mass incarceration, state disappearance of dissidents, forced pregnancy, sterilization, and state-sanctioned rape. For marginalized kids who have seen ourselves in these stories, it comes as no coincidence—those stories have literally been built off of the lives of people like us, our parents, our grandparents, our ancestors. We were constitutionally built to relate to those stories because those stories are, in every way, *about* us: in writing *The Handmaid's Tale* Atwood has described being inspired by, among other things, the murder of dissidents in the Philippines under the regime of dictator Ferdinand Marcos and the Argentinian junta's policy of child abduction; *X-Men*'s long-standing parallels to the civil rights movement have never been subtle, with fans commonly comparing Professor X to Martin Luther King Jr. and Magneto to Malcolm X. Marvel's Stan Lee never outright admitted that the characters were intentionally based on civil rights leaders like King—nor did he deny it. It proved beneficial, both culturally and financially, to simply allow the conclusion to be drawn by a wide swath of readers and consumers. (Here I'm also reminded of the fact that Chris Claremont's original art direction for the iconic X-Men character Rogue—the white Southern belle cursed to never be able to touch anyone without draining their life force—was that the character should look like Grace Jones; but artist Michael Golden didn't know what Jones looked like.) Certainly all the friends I grew up with saw themselves and their struggles in the X-Men, even as the stories themselves centered characters who rarely looked like us.

But that dynamic is endemic to white-authored fantasy: specific stories of oppression and marginalization that have been hollowed out of their historical context and replaced with white leading characters, in a kind of reverse *Get Out*. Apocalyptic narratives about people having to flee their homes because of climate disaster, or compete with each other over dwindling resources underneath a fascist state, or submit to a patriarchal regime that rules over their entire biopolitical reality—from *The Day After Tomorrow* to *The Hunger Games* to *The Handmaid's Tale*—overwhelmingly center characters whose racial specifics have been conveniently left unspoken, neutral. This means, of course, that when they are adapted to screen, these characters are nearly always played by white stars, Hollywood's way of saying the quiet part out loud: that neutral always means white.

This, despite the fact that, in our own apocalyptic present, it is patently not white people who will bear the brunt of our impending climate doom, and not white people toiling at the bottom levels of our capitalist fight club (not even poor white people; we know from a recent NPR report that, in fact, the median single-parent white family in the United States has more than twice the wealth of the median two-parent Black family—$35,000 and $16,000, respectively—suggesting that the advantage of whiteness these interlocutors are often so hasty to disavow, usually when they're trying to convince you how much harder poor whites have it than people of color, is much harder to cast off than they would like to admit). This combination of deliberate narrative withholding and the racialized assumptions it permits—which are then confirmed by Hollywood casting—tells us that stories about oppression and marginalization only become universally worthy, relevant, and relatable when the faces on the book covers and movie posters are white; when the bodies being systematically (and sympathetically) oppressed are white.

When Rowling's transphobia became more regularly discussed among the wider reading public (BIPOC readers have been pointing out the latent racism in the Potterverse since the books' publication), I often saw readers and fans lament their disappointment in Rowling's views, struggling to make those views line up with the allegories of difference and triumph that they had nevertheless found in those narrative worlds. I saw readers expend great intellectual and emotional effort to salvage what they had once treasured in her works, the characters and passages they'd been saved by—an effort I sympathize with, understand, and have gone through myself. I've personally never been particularly interested in separating the art from the artist, an impulse of exceedingly mild intellectual rigor, which has only ever really served the powerful and protected abusers (we never hear about separating the art from the artist when a writer of color wants her work to be read beyond the autobiographical, for example—people seem very keen to connect the art and the artist in that case—but god forbid someone tell the fuckboy who wants to read you another mediocre love poem that Pablo Neruda freely admitted to raping a Sri Lankan chambermaid during his posting as a diplomat there). What I would point out, however, is that this very dynamic—taking stories of oppression and marginalization, stripping them of most of their racial and historical specificity (leaving just enough to add a frisson of exotic/erotic flavor), and recasting them with white bodies—is at the heart of most white fantasy, and thus is also the source of the incongruence that minority readers later struggle with, when those authors turn out to care little at all about the oppression they once so beautifully illustrated.

How can a writer who wrote so convincingly about being a misfit be so indifferent to the plight of misfits in front of her? How could Marvel, home of *X-Men*, that supposed bastion of civil rights metaphors, be at the crux of such right-wing, misogynist, racist, homophobic fervor as Comicsgate, the reactionary harassment campaigns waged by fandoms against perceived "social justice warriors"—feminists, antiracists, queer artists and readers—out to ruin their precious comics? How could those fans miss the irony of attacking minorities while at the same time defending classic allegories of oppression, devoted to narratives of resistance and community-building?

The truth is, these worlds may have only ever nominally been interested in oppression and difference—that shallow, cosplay-like understanding of oppression makes itself clear when authors like Rowling are taken to task for their actual opinions on marginalized people. I can no longer muster up disappointment when white authors whose works supposedly deal in equality and justice show themselves (and the reactionary readers who love them) to not be remotely interested in either equality or justice—not when both the inception *and* the material effect of that work necessitate lifting from the historical struggle of racial, sexual, and economic minorities, and replacing those bodies with white, cis, straight characters. Were these works ever truly concerned by justice to begin with? Or were they simply enamored with and appropriative of its language—its culture, its aesthetic, its narrative style? Oppression chic, equalitycore.

Why wouldn't white antivaxxers adopt as a symbol of solidarity the three-fingered Hunger Games salute, first introduced by the fictional revolutionaries of Suzanne Collins's series and then more recently adapted by pro-democracy protestors in Hong Kong? Why wouldn't white seditionists, during the January 6 Capitol riots, chant—as they attempted to breach the civic building, in their systematic attempt at a coup—the Black Lives Matter rallying cry in memory of George Floyd, "I can't breathe"? Both of those facts lose any semblance of irony, even grotesqueness, when seen through the logic of white fantasy. For wasn't that the banal point, in the end?

As much as I will always love universes like those of the X-Men, I can't separate the metaphors that I've loved (and have often been saved by) from the realities of their circulation in the world; these were stories that deliberately hinted at solidarity, without ever doing the actual work, aesthetic or otherwise, of solidarity. And I can't ignore the fact that when Marvel began to take much-needed practical steps toward that solidarity, most explicitly in the company's hiring, pay structure, and storytelling, it was met with militant resistance by the mostly white, mostly male comics consumers who had always seen themselves, first and foremost, in the stories I loved. And why wouldn't they? All these years, those stories told them that it was fans like them who were the victims—the misfits, the minorities, the oppressed.

IN CONTRAST TO THE LIMITED IMAGINARY WORLDS LIKE *X-MEN* and the Potter universe, I can think of one contemporary example of narrative fantasy storytelling that goes beyond the gestures of oppression cosplay, and deals explicitly with the unbearably intimate relationship between heroism and historical trauma: HBO's *Watchmen*, specifically its first and sixth episodes.

White American showrunner Damon Lindelof called his series a "remix" of DC's *Watchmen* comics, created by white English author Alan Moore and artist Dave Gibbons. The show takes place over thirty years after the original comic series, in an alternate twentieth-century universe in which vigilantes— former superheroes—have been made outlaws. A fake alien attack on New York City in 1985, orchestrated by former vigilante Ozymandias, has wiped three million people from the planet, bringing previously battling nations together against their alien common enemy; postwar Vietnam has become the fifty-first state, and the birthplace of our protagonist, played by Regina King.

That's a lot to take in. But what I'm most interested in is how the show uses the structure of fantasy, specifically the superhero myth, to excavate the unnamed and often faceless histories hidden beneath those masks, under those capes. HBO's *Watchmen* relocates the action of the story to Tulsa, Oklahoma, in 2019 (mostly). A white supremacist group called the Seventh Kavalry has been waging a war against minorities and the police after a state policy has been put in place to administer reparations for racial injustice, stemming back to a specific— and historically accurate—event that *Watchmen*'s first episode orchestrates with titanic clarity and commitment: the Tulsa Race Massacre of 1921, in which mobs of white residents launched a mass attack on Black residents and Black-owned businesses in the Greenwood District of Tulsa, at the time the wealthiest Black community in America and sometimes called "Black Wall Street." I myself didn't learn about this massacre until I'd already graduated from college; certainly it was never taught in a single American history course I had growing up. And when I wrote this essay in the late winter, early spring of 2020, shortly after viewing *Watchmen*, Trump hadn't yet made the inflammatory political decision to host a rally in Tulsa on the anniversary of Juneteenth—only later changing the date.

HBO's *Watchmen* imagines that most alternate of alternate

universes: one where racial justice might be served—not permanently, not perfectly, but practically, and with intent. In this universe, descendants of those affected by the Tulsa massacre are entitled to reparations; a widely available DNA test determines the connection, and ancestry research is reimagined not just as a dubiously trackable data-collection opportunity for late capitalist self-actualizers, in the vein of 23andMe, but as an intimate, bodily inheritance that makes future justice possible. The show is entirely concerned with the living consequences of inheritance: inheritance and trauma, inheritance and justice. Here, a historical catastrophe like the Tulsa massacre is not just something we can know or unknow, something we can either be aware of or be simply, innocently ignorant of—history is a deposit in our bones, there in the blood and saliva.

Regina King plays Angela Abar, an orphaned police detective born to Black American soldiers in occupied Vietnam, now living in Tulsa, where her extended family is from. Ever since a pre-canon event described as the "White Night," in which the Seventh Kavalry attacked the homes of forty Tulsa police officers, laws protecting officers have enforced a policy of wearing masks while working. While ostensibly now making a living as a baker, Abar also moonlights as the vigilante Sister Night, tracking down Seventh Kavalry suspects when her daylight capacity as a cop falls short. When I first started watching the show and realized that the main characters were going to be police officers, my heart sank; so many American shows are obsessed with humanizing—and justifying—the presence of law enforcement and military command, from dramas like *Watchmen* to comedies like *Brooklyn 99* and tentpole movies like *The Avengers*. Try to get away from the police state in American narrative life: you won't get far. I didn't want to watch another show about a good cop, not in a country where you can't turn left or right without hearing about yet another instance of anti-Black police brutality. And until I watched *Watchmen*'s sixth episode, I was sure that it would be the kind of show I dreaded. I was, mostly, wrong.

Watchmen, it turns out, is entirely interested in humanizing a police officer, but not in sweeping under the rug the systemic racial discrimination of our inherently broken police state: it uses the loftier metaphors of heroism and vigilantism to ask questions about how we come to shape the figure that justice takes in our imagination—who we come to imagine as our heroes, and how we come to shape ourselves in their mold. The sixth episode of *Watchmen* imagines that Angela has taken an extreme dose of a drug belonging to her grandfather, Will Reeves, whom she's only just met—right after he's seemingly murdered her close friend, the white police chief of Tulsa, Judd Crawford. The drug is called Nostalgia, a pill manufactured to contain a person's memories, and which in the *Watchmen* universe has been outlawed due to its tendency to make its users psychotic. Angela takes her grandfather's Nostalgia in order to understand why he may have murdered her friend and colleague; what follows is a journey through American history unlike any I've seen on television.

Earlier in the episode, we'd opened on the conspicuously white—blue-green–eyed—face of the hero we've come to identify as Hooded Justice, a character that exists in the original *Watchmen* comics; the only vigilante in the original series whose true identity is never discovered. Hooded Justice is, as his moniker implies, hooded, with a cut-off noose around his neck. In the opening scene of the episode, we see Hooded Justice vigorously and bloodily applying his namesake to some homophobic policemen in an interrogation scene. Later, we realize it's all make-believe, a TV episode aimed at a rapt American viewing public. Here the show establishes a truth, which it will gradually begin to dismantle: this white man, the one with the blue-green eyes, is what Hooded Justice looks like—at least to most Americans.

When Angela travels deep down into her grandfather's memories, she discovers another face entirely. The show imagines that Angela quasi-becomes her grandfather, with some scenes glitching in between their faces and bodies, so the border between them dissolves; she is literally living his memories, in his clothes, in both her body and his. The scenes in the past take place in black-and-white, but certain images flicker starkly in color; like one scene where a supposedly innocent car drives away, but we see the full-color ghosts of Black people being dragged along by its fender: it's an image not only of that car's past, but its malevolent future. The show's choice to render this buried knowledge in color is a sharply visceral take on how we not only experience the past, but how the past informs our present terrors: how we literally experience the world, and how specific trauma can make specific ghosts remain vivid forever.

In Peter Handke's *Der Chinese des Schmerzes*, the notion of a crossed threshold is a convenient way to perpetually defer implication and responsibility, both as a character and as a storyteller; a way to be always-in-between. In HBO's *Watchmen*, the crossed threshold does the exact opposite: that in-betweenness brings Angela into an unbearably heightened intimacy with her grandfather, one in which she realizes how inescapably she is implicated in (and eventually, as she later learns, responsible for) events that make her life possible. In *Watchmen*, the violence of the vigilante isn't left mysterious, singular, and merely "existential," as a writer like Handke might have it; instead it is carefully given all the dignity and despair of its history, fully lived and deliberately realized. When Angela experiences firsthand the devastation of her grandfather's life, King telegraphs that grief and rage in a way that feels at once world-weary and newborn, like someone weeping from two different people's eyes. And isn't that, in the end, what intergenerational trauma feels like?

Slipping into these memories along with Angela, we meet a young boy, watching a silent movie in a Black-owned theater in Tulsa's Greenwood District, while his mother plays the accompaniment musical track on the piano. The movie is the child's favorite, containing one of the most formative scenes of his life: a scene in which white townspeople are saved from their corrupt white sheriff by a masked hero, a Wild West law-man who then removes his mask, to the excitement of the be-nevolent townspeople; the hero is a man named Bass Reeves, "the Black Marshal of Oklahoma," who tells them their own sheriff is the villain that has been stealing their cattle. Then he intones his fateful lesson: "Trust in the law!" Bass Reeves is another historically accurate addition to the *Watchmen* uni-verse, a reference to Bass Reeves, the first Black deputy US marshal west of the Mississippi, rumored to be the inspiration for the Lone Ranger (himself yet another example of an iconic American hero typically depicted as white).

The young child, Will, is smuggled by his parents out of Tulsa during the massacre, and he eventually meets the vul-nerable baby who will later become his wife (and Angela's grandmother), June. We watch this frightened, brave young boy grow up to be a frightened, brave young man—Will Reeves, taking his last name from his childhood hero. In Angelina Jade Bastién's luminously sharp and deeply moving critical cover-age of the show for *Vulture*, and this episode in particular, Bas-tién writes:

> [Will] believes that wearing a badge can not only do good for the world, but also help him find the justice he's been craving since he was a child. But alongside this de-sire for justice is a deep well of anger, which June recog-nizes. It's Angela whose face appears in the moment at the bar to say, "I am not angry," with a kind of calm that

belies just how angry both she and Will are. This is a part of her inheritance.

Preoccupied by the early lessons taught by his favorite hero, Bass Reeves, Will becomes a New York City police officer in an almost entirely white police force. The only other Black police officer, an older man named Sam Battle, is also the only one who agrees to pin Will's officer badge on him during his welcome ceremony. (Battle is yet another historically accurate character, a reference to Samuel Jesse Battle, the first Black NYPD officer.) Will says that he joined the police force because he looked up to Lieutenant Battle; Battle smiles a little wearily, then whispers to him, urgently: "Beware of the Cyclops."

We'll learn who and what the Cyclops is—or rather, Angela/ Will will learn, up close, and in the flesh. It comes as no surprise that Will's fellow police officers are actively and institutionally racist, undermining him at every turn and protecting white supremacists, like the one Will sees burning down a Jewish deli. Will's attempt to get justice—to do the job he signed up for—culminates in one of the most singularly horrifying sequences on American television, in which Will's police colleagues (the drivers of the car I described earlier) stalk, viciously beat, then proceed to lynch him. The show puts viewers behind Will's eyes as he wakes up behind the hood his attackers have put over him, the noose around his neck dragging him up, up, and up—until, at the very last minute, they spare him, laughing, with a warning.

It is the only example in American television I can think of that brings viewers into such profound, inescapable intimacy with one of America's foundational anti-Black terrors, the uniquely American practice of lynching. It shares space with the indispensable compilation *The Black Book*, edited by Toni Morrison, as one of the few cultural instances in which the American history of lynching is presented from a Black perspective (and not just through the eyes of white writers and their protagonists, as in Harper Lee's school staple, *To Kill a Mockingbird*). Will, in his dazed, broken survival, wanders the streets and randomly comes across a couple being beaten by thugs. Still wearing the noose, he puts on the hood his attackers had forced on him—reclaiming this dehumanizing anonymity for his own protection—and jumps upon the thugs, beating them back and ultimately saving the couple, who quickly thank their anonymous savior before fleeing.

We are witnessing the birth of Hooded Justice: not a white man with blue-green eyes at all, but a young Black man, an inheritor of the Tulsa massacre, who wears the noose and hood thrust on him by his would-be lynchers. It is a phenomenally radical imagining of an existing comic book character, one that takes the heroic vigilante trope so globally beloved and uses it to ask questions about the intimate, gut-deep agonies of trauma, oppression, and justice. Will, like any number of scared, traumatized kids, watches a man who looks like him become a hero through a fantasy of law enforcement—"trust in the law"—so he, too, becomes a police officer. But his life shows him that the violence that led him to believe in that heroic fantasy is the same violence that will wake him from it. Here there are no grateful white townspeople; when you reveal the corrupt white sheriff, you get beaten and lynched. Will turns from his Bass Reeves fantasy to a grimmer identity; takes the horror that has been dealt to him, and turns it into a weapon.

And this is where the episode—which has already been extraordinary—finally fulfills the promise that its pilot made by centering the show in Tulsa to begin with. The episode isn't interested just in how Will becomes disillusioned with the police state and thus steps into his true, fulfilling self as the vigilante Hooded Justice—another narrative path I was dreading. No, the show is invested in something much deeper, much harder to parse: the persistence of intergenerational trauma and its effect on a person's physical and emotional growth; the unforgiving war of attrition that the pursuit of justice can often feel like, especially for those restlessly seeking it alone, against an indifferent world. The show is interested in how the longing for justice, unfulfilled, can literally break us down: break our families apart, break our bodies apart. It asks impossible questions, like why do people—people of color in particular—sometimes paradoxically long for the heroic validation and redemptive power promised by law enforcement, when their own histories so clearly show that law enforcement has rarely been their friend? It's something I wonder about my own Filipinx community, one that bears the traces of having once been the fought-over Pacific property in America's colonial real estate grab, a conflict that culminated in a policy of genocide that claimed, some say (the official American documents of the period are, of course, to be mistrusted), over a million native lives. And yet my extended family is punctuated with proud US Army and Navy soldiers stationed everywhere in the world; trusting in the law.

We discover later that Hooded Justice is a closeted gay man; he has to meet his white lover, fellow vigilante Captain Metropolis, in secret. It's not just a double life, but a triple life, a quadruple life. Captain Metropolis urges Hooded Justice to keep his identity hidden from their fellow vigilantes, who aren't as "tolerant" (that buzzword of the white liberal racist) as he is; Hooded Justice regularly wears white makeup around the parts of his eyes visible through the hood's gaps. Tangled knot after tangled knot weaves in Hooded Justice's psyche, there where the self meets mask, where the hunger for power and justice settles for the exhausting cycle of violence and vengeance, where the desire for true connection and sexual fulfillment settles for condescending companionship and racialized fetishizing. When Will finally stumbles upon the grand plan of the Cyclops (the obvious KKK stand-in, who are plotting to gain societal power through mind control, and whose presence in *Watchmen* is drawn from our own very present realities: a 2006 FBI intelligence assessment detailed organized white supremacist infiltration in state police forces, such as neo-Nazi gang the Lynwood Vikings, which thrived in the Los Angeles

County Sheriff's Department), Will asks for help from his lover and supposedly fellow masked heroes. But he soon realizes they're not in this fight together; they're not even in the same fight. Again, he is alone, against a group of white people not there to help him, in a hood, with a noose around his neck.

Mainstream heroic wisdom, especially in the settler colonial American psyche, still so enthralled with its hardy independence and its pioneering spirit, asks us to worship the figure of the vigilante hero as a singular aberration and miracle—a superhero, unique unto himself. The mainstream vigilante's spectacular acts of violence or heroism are coded as nonpolitical eruptions in the nonpolitical everyday: vigilante heroes vote libertarian (if indeed they vote at all). This vision of the vigilante is, above all, *special*. But in *Watchmen*, the vigilante's origin story has at its foundation our inescapably political and inextricably shared everyday: the pain, violence, and grief in Will's story isn't an aberration at all, but the pangs of a much greater—and much more joint—malady.

The show points to the lone vigilante in American culture and reveals that he has always been a lie: the work of justice was never meant to be solitary. We inherit that work from each other; we inherit it from people we don't even know. Our history is *in* each other, like deposits in the bones, there in the blood and saliva. In this we are not special. Most poignant of all is the realization that Hooded Justice is—horrifically, historically—ordinary. He's not just a vigilante, not just a superhero. He's an American.

IT'S UNFORTUNATE, THEN, THAT THE SAME SPECIFICITY AND attention wasn't as attuned when developing *Watchmen*'s Vietnam story line. The show takes place in a universe in which a postwar Vietnam has become the fifty-first American state; Angela is born there to military parents, a child of the occupier. When her parents are killed in an antioccupation attack by a Vietnamese insurgent who plants a bomb, the young Angela personally requests to listen to the shooting of her parents' killer; the young female Vietnamese police officer gives her a badge and a wink. Thus is born this generation's Bass Reeves, marshal of Saigon. (And like her grandfather, Angela also grew up on a favorite cinematic heroine, the blaxploitation protagonist Sister Night, from whom Angela later takes her vigilante name; what's past really is prologue, the show tells us.)

Yet the show never really delves too deeply into the complicated legacy of Angela's parents in Vietnam as military occupiers; it never truly lingers on the messy mix of anti-imperial *and* anti-Black resentment made apparent to Angela through the unkind Vietnamese woman who runs the Saigon orphanage where she is placed. There is no long deep-dive episode into the psyche of any of the Vietnamese characters to understand how the show's imagined imperial annexing of Vietnam contributed to the kind of intergenerational trauma that brought that young man to plant a bomb. We do get the delightfully complex performance of Hong Chau—shifting lightning-fast between droll amusement and razor-sharp calculation—as Lady Trieu, the trillionaire Vietnamese founder and CEO of Trieu Industries, the multinational conglomerate that successfully produced the Nostalgia pills that Angela takes from her grandfather. (One of the show's motifs is around naming and inheritance and the name "Lady Trieu" also refers to a historical figure: a female warrior who resisted the Chinese occupation in third-century Vietnam.) But the way the show eventually resolves Lady Trieu's story line disappoints the promise of its earlier episodes. We discover that Lady Trieu's mother, Bian, artificially inseminated herself with the semen of white vigilante megalomaniac and genius Ozymandias, played by Jeremy Irons. As she's inseminating herself, she says: "I want to ride the strong winds, crush the angry waves, slay the killer whales in the eastern sea, chase away the Wu army, reclaim the land, remove the yoke of slavery. I will not bend my back to be a slave. Fuck you, Ozymandias."

Her lines are an echo of a documented quote from the historical Lady Trieu: *I'd like to ride storms, kill sharks in the open sea, drive out the aggressors, reconquer the country, undo the ties of serfdom, and never bend my back to be the concubine of whatever man.*

The reference is elegant enough, but rings hollow as the narrative arc becomes evident: Bian, a Vietnamese woman living under the occupation of a white supremacist country, makes herself pregnant by a white man, in an act that's meant to be read as defiance. But besides the fact that the show writes this scene with no apparent willingness to engage with the sexual history of empire, as ugly and common in Vietnam as it is in the Philippines and the rest of America's colonial project (think of that Ocean Vuong line, "An American soldier fucked a Vietnamese farmgirl. Thus my mother exists. / Thus I exist. Thus no bombs = no family = no me"), by making Bian say "Fuck you, Ozymandias" instead of—oh, I don't know—"Fuck you, America," it reduces the motive of her defiance to one of individual self-actualization (personal rebellion, not communal revolution).

Worse even than Bian's weirdly underwhelming act of personal-growth-via-sperm-donor is the later admission by Lady Trieu that her "genius" comes from her father—that is, her distinctly *Jeremy Irons–looking* father, and not her Vietnamese mother, who, besides tantalizingly quoting third-century female warriors, nevertheless remains woefully underwritten, so that the show's deliberate historical Lady Trieu callback ends up functioning as little more than a writerly placeholder: quoting a third-century female warrior, to avoid having to actually write a twentieth-century Vietnamese woman. The admission is not only tantamount to saying that a biracial kid's intelligence comes from her white parent (yikes), but also fails to make the effort to do what a verse like Vuong's attempts: trying to solve the impossible calculus of one's family lineage, in its relation to sex, power, and imperial violence, and asking the answerless questions about how that lineage makes a life.

The show's heartbreaking failure in these later episodes—its failure to go beyond the empty promises of empathy into the richer labor of intimacy, the way its previous episodes dare—is furthermore upsetting because there were some moments in those episodes that I found genuinely exciting and novel, not least of them the tense, opaque, sometimes deliciously combative scenes between Angela and Lady Trieu. It felt like the woman of color version of the Bechdel test; I so rarely get to see women of color, especially women of color from different backgrounds, encountering each other onscreen in this way, each bringing a dense history behind her—let alone in a superhero tale. Asian anti-Blackness, American colonialism, the history of Black soldiers conflicted about their role in twentieth-century American imperialism in the East, women grieving traumatic parental loss: the air between them during these encounters felt electric with possibility, thanks in no small part to both King's and Chau's shrewd, magnetic performances. There were so many questions to ask: What was Lady Trieu's relationship to Angela's grandfather, with whom she seemed, at least temporarily, to be in complicity? What new stories might come out of the friction produced when these characters rubbed up against each other?

In the end, when Lady Trieu is revealed to be the boring megalomaniacal villain the show spent so many episodes hinting that she wasn't, she's more or less snuffed out. And when Will Reeves discovers the news of her death from Angela, he more or less shrugs it off—this, despite the fact that he and Lady Trieu had worked together to bring Angela into the revelations that brought granddaughter and grandfather together in the first place. It's oddly anticlimactic. It wouldn't be impossible to make me believe that Will Reeves would have genuinely wished for the demise of the lady trillionaire whose services he needed for a moment—to write the tale of how we enter into uneasy alliances with morally murky people because we think the ends will justify the means—but the show makes no substantial gesture at that deeper story.

In the end, what these failures tell us is that there *are* things to be vigilant about, and storytelling is one of them. That *Watchmen* could create such meticulously extraordinary American art in one breath, then so easily vacate the capaciousness of its own imagination in the next, only means that we can't take the stories we tell, and how we tell them, for granted. It's that easy to forget our inheritances. It's that easy to suddenly see ourselves again as the lone hero—shining in the sun, trusting in the law.

MAIN
CHARACTER
SYNDROME

I think I left America because I died so often.

ANNA MAY WONG, A CALIFORNIAN

At this point, it's almost boring to say you hate Joan Didi-on's work, but in this instance (and here I'm also speaking in my capacity as part of that globally oppressed class, Earth signs) I'm perfectly comfortable being boring.

Look—I never really liked her work. Even as a younger reader. But as I get older that instinctive, largely-left-unexcavated dislike and suspicion have bloomed into full-blown antipathy and impatience. Not least of all because, along with John Stein-beck, she has long been crowned as the preeminent chronicler of Californian life: Didion, a famously aloof journalist whose imperious detachment (often rendered as "cool") and distinc-tively epigrammatic style have been fetishized and imitated by would-be Californian malcontents the world over. In Stein-beck's case, it bears remembering that he stole the research for that seminal staple of high school syllabi all across the nation, *The Grapes of Wrath*, from Sanora Babb, a white woman born on Otoe territory in Oklahoma, whose marriage to the Chinese

American cinematographer James Wong Howe was not recognized in California due to the state's miscegenation laws. After Steinbeck's novel was published, the novel Babb was doing her research for was shelved until 2004. (What a novel *that* history would make.)

In Didion's case, books like *Slouching Towards Bethlehem* have of course become talismanic Californian commodities—but none greater than the image of Didion herself, appearing on literary tote bags and in Céline ads alike, as shorthand for a certain strain of bourgeois intellectual white feminism so beloved by luxury capitalism for the veneer of authenticity and depth it provides: the cool white girl as elder stateswoman, remote in her thousand-dollar sunglasses.

It's a seductive pose; the sunglasses look great. But as critic Sarah Nicole Prickett writes, after revisiting Didion in a 2017 review for *Bookforum*:

> No elite is more coastal than she. Reading *The White Album* in full for the first time in years, I saw that what once seemed a coolness that precluded the need for opinions is perhaps what Mary McCarthy called, in her review of *Democracy*, a "stunned aversion from thought." Didion is useless in a maelstrom, out of her intellectual range in a women's movement led by Shulamith Firestone, unable to witness a press conference with Huey P. Newton and hear a question as simple as "Isn't it true that racism got its start for *economic* reasons?" without find-

ing it all a "weird interlocution" and complaining that the fluorescent light in the room hurts her eyes. Yet when she loiters or toils in a Los Angeles she calls "the invisible city," talking to gambling addicts in Gardena, befriending a Mexican orchid-grower before his greenhouse burns down, observing "casual death" in biker films at drive-ins, eavesdropping on desperate affairs in Encino piano bars, there arises a conviction that no one else *does* see what Didion sees, or that if she didn't see it, neither would we. Her performative empiricism (only what is describable is true) is hard to distinguish, in effect as in theory, from a pure and almost purifying solipsism (the limits of one's language are the limits of the world). Work keeps the mind clean, as I learned at age fifteen from *Heart of Darkness*.

Didion's characters *look* at things a great deal; her narrators often put themselves forward as consummate observers. But what are they really looking at—and what do they so consistently fail to see? One of Didion's greatest failures of seeing is exemplified by her novel *Democracy*.

The novel's main character is Inez Christian Victor, the wife of a United States senator who is running a campaign for president—it was very weird to reread this novel in early 2020—and whose dissolute journey through the discontents of neglectful motherhood, colonial wealth, and racial privilege are the backdrop to her indistinctly sketched twenty-year romance with Jack Lovett, a character who is, quite literally, an *international man of mystery*: a shady figure who hovers somewhere in between James Bond and regime-destabilizing CIA agent—if there is a between, there. The library copy I borrowed was, amusingly and fittingly, millennial pink, long before millennial pink was a thing.

But the true backdrop—to the inhibited motherhood, the colonial wealth, the Racial Privilege (that old canard), and the twenty-year romance with the man of mystery—is the Orient. All of the book's main characters are white, of course, but much of the novel itself takes place in either Asia or Hawai'i; I specify the Orient because that is the precise term for what places like Asia or Hawai'i mean to these particular twentieth-century characters. The characters are always just jetting off, in the great motion picture drama of their lives: on the night flight from Honolulu to watch the dawn break over Hong Kong and then on to Saigon; taking refuge in Kuala Lumpur from the boredom and misery of their upper-class political marriages (though *misery* is perhaps too strong a word for such anodyned persons); in their teenage years, they're in the car with their boyfriends, the young white dauphins of Hawai'i's ruling class. When people fly in from Subic Bay, they say they just came in from "Clark," as in Air Base: the notorious US colonial military outpost in the Philippines, just another old gentleman's club. "Couldn't walk. No place to walk," Jack Lovett says to Inez Victor of Manila. "Couldn't write anything down, the point of the pen would go right through the paper, one thing you got to understand down there was why not much got written down on those islands." Such cool, colonial intellects require as their foils the hot, colonized tropics; warm and permissive, mute and blank: a place with supposedly scant surviving literature, not because of centuries of colonial erasure and genocide, but because of the—weather. (By some miracle I have on several hot-weather occasions managed to use a pen in Manila without ripping the paper—but I accept I may be inordinately gifted.)

When things go badly for these characters, they don't just go to Skid Row; they take a Lockheed C5-A military transport to Vietnam. Inez's daughter Jessie, recovering from an emotionally and politically inconvenient heroin addiction, is recommended by her fourth therapist a schedule of methadone and a part-time job "as a waitress in a place on Puget Sound called King Crab's Castle." Later in the book, Jessie somehow escapes from her handlers, all with the blithe entitlement familiar to many young scions of her genre: "walked out of the clinic that specialized in the treatment of adolescent chemical dependency and talked her way onto a C-5A transport that landed seventeen-and-one-half hours later (refueling twice in flight) at Ton Son Nhut, Saigon." Janet, Inez's sister and foil, says things like "when Lowell and Daddy went to Fiji together," "the time Daddy wanted to buy the hotel," and "A hill station. . . . Divine." The book finds its ostensible center (it would perhaps go too blushingly far to say "heart") when Janet is found murdered, along with Wendell Omura, an older second-generation Japanese American Democratic congressman, on the lanai of Inez and Janet's family estate in Hawai'i—the murderer likely Inez and Janet's oligarch father, for reasons of political or patriarchal shame (and aren't the two, in the end, family?).

Sordid affairs, racial tensions, wealth and power, addiction and grief, womanhood and motherhood, sex and scandal: *Democracy* is built on the stuff of melodrama, at the narrative level of a *Madame Butterfly* (originally published in 1898 by American author John Luther Long, "based" on his sister's Methodist missionary work in Japan and heavily influenced by French colonialist Pierre Loti's novel 1887 *Madame Chrysanthème*). Yet *Democracy* reads, often, like an embarrassed book, self-conscious and reflexive (as opposed to self-consciously reflexive). The narrator—also named Joan Didion—is constantly zooming in and out of the shot, like a brooding film student's senior thesis, reframing and relitigating the scenes unfolding in front of us. But the distinct timbre of performative philosophical distance Didion-the-narrator insists on means that all of this litigating and reframing serves not to deepen the characters or the narrative—not to invite us to see its claustrophobic political jet-setters' world from multiple angles, slant or straight—but, instead, to provide what amount to literary disclaimers: like someone saying all narrative is generally unreliable, in order to distract from the fact that one's own narrative may be in bad faith. *Democracy* is a book that pretends to be suspicious of melodrama and authority, to mask its compulsively melodramatic and authoritarian nature. The book is always at pains to let you know how much it knows how very problematic (that nothing-burger of a word), how very boring, deep down, how very hollow, really, it is to be white and rich in the colonies. Archly, it holds itself above everyone and everything, including its own whiteness and wealth—which it despises, and cannot survive without.

Herein lies its tragedy, for the book is undeniably tragic (in both the literal and the colloquial sense, i.e., girl, it was tragic): it's a book that not only believes in its own coping mechanism, but has enshrined that mechanism as a moral and narrative framework. Which would be fine—even perhaps momentarily interesting, like if Jordan from *The Great Gatsby* wrote a novel—if the plot, and its delicate corset of emotionally shut-down upper-crust glamour didn't rely entirely on the warm, silent, ever-laboring welcome of the tropical Orient to make all that coolness possible. Every self-respecting gal in the colonies needs a houseboy with a fan, it turns out. *Democracy* sometimes reads like a funhouse mirror *Eat Pray Love*—they are cut from the same still-somewhat-lucrative cloth, wherein white people, very preoccupied with their own melancholy, are adrift in Asia or Africa or Latin America, the exotic background providing just enough texture and detail to make the old operatic agonies novel again. The inevitable redemption arcs are always scaffolded by the one or two noble-hearted natives in the piece, who usually end up dying in the finale, stage left. "Inez also remembered that the only person killed when the grenade exploded in the embassy commissary was an Indonesian driver from the motor pool."

—————

HAVING ZOOMED OUT OF THE SHOT, LET'S ZOOM BACK IN—
to look upon its characters. At a reception for her husband,
Harry, which takes place in Jakarta the night before the grenade explodes in an American embassy (killing "only" "an"
Indonesian driver from the motor pool),

> Inez remembered Harry saying over and over again that
> Americans were learning major lessons in Southeast
> Asia. She remembered Jack Lovett saying finally that he
> could think of only one lesson Americans were learning
> in Southeast Asia. What was that, someone said. Harry
> did not say it. Harry was too careful to have said it. Fran-
> ces Landau or Janet must have said it. What was that,
> Frances Landau or Janet said, and Jack Lovett clipped a
> cigar before he answered.
>
> "A tripped Claymore mine explodes straight up," Jack
> Lovett said.

It's a typical, classically Didion line: clipping a cigar like a
member of the Rat Pack and delivering a well-crafted and precisely placed zinger, meant to say everything in the hopes that
no one will notice it doesn't really say anything—meant to sum
up the political difference between her conservative (in the generic, not merely partisan, sense; though "major lessons" does
sound like it comes directly from a Trump memo) husband and

her hard-boiled CIA lover, meant to cover the vast history of American imperialism in Southeast Asia with the powers of its perfect observation. It's also typical, in that nothing more really materializes of this crystalline observation once deployed: having done his narrative heavy lifting, Jack wants to manfully taper the discussion off, let the characters wander unsteadily back to their pomegranate drinks. "I believe some human rights are being violated on the verandah," he says, pithily (also as in: helmet, pith). Still, Didion doubles down on the importance of *seeing*—like someone telling you that if you aren't satisfied with their shoddy explanation, you're the idiot—with Jack insisting to Harry: "You don't actually see what's happening in front of you. You don't see it unless you read it. You have to read it in the New York *Times,* then you start talking about it."

This is such a weird, clumsy accusation-as-deflection by a character who, after his wife left him ("packed her huaraches and her shorty night-gowns and her Glenn Miller records and picked up a flight to Travis"), started fucking a teenager (Inez is seventeen when she and Jack begin their affair: "she smelled of beer and popcorn and Nivea cream") and began to indulge in a little neocolonial war profiteering ("By September of 1952, when Inez Christian left Honolulu for the first of the four years she had agreed to spend studying art history at Sarah Lawrence, Jack Lovett was in Thailand, setting up what later became the Air Asia Operation"). Of course, like most such apologist literary narratives about the romance of divorced adult men wanting to fuck teenagers, the girl in question is preternaturally cool, mature, and self-possessing.

Jack Lovett is the king of crackpot realists, that term coined by Texan sociologist C. Wright Mills to describe the all-knowing political cynicism and nihilism masquerading as (and used to justify) martial realism, and therefore military action: "America—a conservative country without any conservative ideology—appears now before the world a naked and arbitrary power, as in the name of realism, its men of decision enforce their often crackpot definitions upon world reality. The second-rate mind is in command of the ponderously spoken platitude. In the liberal rhetoric, vagueness, and in the conservative mood, irrationality, are raised to principle." A crackpot realist like Jack Lovett (or, indeed, Joan Didion) abhors both the effete machinations of a political stooge like Harry Victor and the pie-eyed idealism of revolutionaries in the street; unlike all those chumps, these practical men of action know how things really are in Vietnam, in the Middle East, at the eternal frontier. We the sheeple can't see—not as well as these cynical visionaries, omnipotently peering down at us from the perch of a UH-1 Iroquois "Huey" helicopter.

"In the name of realism they have constructed a paranoid reality all their own," writes Mills. "They have replaced . . . intellectual ability with agility of the sound, mediocre judgment; [they have replaced] the capacity to elaborate alternatives and gauge their consequences with the executive stance." Like Didion (contriving a reality to be paranoid about; agile without being intellectual; executive without being consequential), Jack Lovett's cryptic yet vaguely prophetic terseness and his man-among-boys practicality are meant to convey immeasurable depths of lived, firsthand knowledge about the boots-on-the-ground truth of American interference abroad. This world-weary teen-fucking Rick Blaine knows about claymore mines; ergo, he knows more about Southeast Asia than everyone at this party, including you. Which, again, would be tremendously funny, if *Democracy* actually functioned as the political satire it's often charitably mistaken for.

Here's a sexy zinger to do some narrative heavy lifting about Southeast Asia, for men like Jack Lovett and their ancestors: the M1911 .45-caliber pistol was invented because US line officers during the Philippine-American War begged for a stronger firearm when they discovered that their standard-issue .38-caliber service revolvers didn't pack enough stopping power against the sword-bearing Moro resistance in the Philippines. With a .38, you had to shoot a man up to a dozen times before he'd go down, and even then his last lethal move would be to throw his barong sword at you. A tripped claymore mine explodes straight up; a bolo thrown by a dying juramentado at ten paces can still decapitate a man.

THE TRUTH IS, NO ONE IN THE NOVEL IS PARTICULARLY GOOD at seeing or knowing what's happening in front of them; they are, however, fully committed to a performative kind of seeing, a performative kind of knowing, like the guest at the party who knows just what specific-enough details to drop so he sounds like he knows what he's talking about in every conversation. Facts and details are scattered in the book like tchotchkes, and they ultimately serve as narrative placeholders that might as well read, to paraphrase fellow noted settler colonial Elizabeth Warren, *Insert Story Here*.

"Letter from Paradise, 21° 19' N., 157° 52' W." Didion's anxious love song to Hawai'i, which appears in perhaps her most famous essay collection, *Slouching Towards Bethlehem*, is helpful to read alongside *Democracy*, not only because Didion-as-narrator claims that *Democracy* is the novel she wrote instead of writing a book about Inez's dynastic Honolulu family, but crucially because it's in the former that Didion maps out the way she thinks about places like Hawai'i, and the position from which she writes. With the haughty vim of a good colonial soldier, Didion writes: "I do not believe that the stories told by lovely hula hands merit extensive study. I have never heard a Hawaiian word, including and perhaps most particularly *aloha*, which accurately expressed anything I had to say."

Anyone familiar with the travel genre of dissolute white women finding themselves in the tropics will recognize the tone of the following lines: "I am going to find it difficult to tell you precisely how and why Hawaii moves me, touches me, saddens and troubles and engages my imagination, what it is in the air that will linger long after I have forgotten the smell of pikake and pineapple and the way the palms sound in the trade winds." The entirety of "Letter from Paradise" (letter to whom? paradise for whom?) is centered on the experience of wealthy white families in Hawai'i—the white Hawaiian oligarchy, Didion herself calls them. In her consummate pilgrim's style, the earliest historical date she mentions in the essay is 1842: "a great-great-grandfather . . . taught there as a young missionary in 1842, and I was given to understand that life in the Islands, as we called Hawaii on the West Coast, had been declining steadily since."

Of course, the motivational thrust of the critique more commonly known as the "why doesn't this white author ever write about people of color" argument has been feeble since the aftermath of *Girls*, if not Austen; no one wants your Shein haul of Diverse Characters. So it is with an entirely mathematical spirit that I note for you here that, obviously, not once in the essay does Didion concern herself with the history of Hawai'i as it might be seen by anyone other than this rarified class of pickled whites—least of all native Hawaiians. When she does finally bring herself to remark upon the presence of nonwhite people and the realities of race relations on "the Islands," it's with a characteristic kind of glazed-over passivity, which for so long has been allowed to pass as the occupational detachment of Real Journalism: "'I wouldn't exactly say we had discrimination here,' one Honolulu woman explained tactfully. . . . Another simply shrugged. 'It's just something that's never pressed. The Orientals are—well, discreet's not really the word, but they aren't like the Negroes and the Jews, they don't push in where they're not wanted.'" Didion continues (it would be too generous to say she *explains*):

> Even among those who are considered Island liberals, the question of race has about it, to anyone who has lived through these hypersensitive past years on the mainland, a curious and rather engaging ingenuousness. "There are very definitely people here who know the Chinese socially," one woman told me. "They have them to their houses. The uncle of a friend of mine, for example, has Chinn Ho to his house all the time." Although this seemed a statement along the lines of "Some of my best friends are Rothschilds," I accepted it in the spirit in which it was offered—just as I did the primitive progressiveness of an Island teacher who was explaining, as we walked down a corridor of her school, about the miracles of educational integration the war had wrought. "Look," she said suddenly, grabbing a pretty Chinese girl by the arm and wheeling her around to face me. "You wouldn't have seen this here before the war. Look at those eyes."

"These hypersensitive past years" is a description that would be at home with the sweatily pious conservative commentators who call progressive activists "snowflakes"; a way of pathologizing and thereby intellectually minimizing the effect of the political movements of the 1960s, when Didion's essays were published. It's a way of making the struggles for racial and

economic justice seem like an epidemic of "hypersensitivity"—
which, as we know, is precisely how many people in our country still view these ongoing struggles. The accommodatingly
neutral way Didion makes space for the teacher's neocolonial
racism—"I accepted it in the spirit it was offered," as the woman
literally grabs a Chinese girl's arm and shows her off like a vase—
passes just under the wire for what might constitute journalistic neutrality, but is also akin to those taxing moments when
white people, always in a demonstration of their vaunted ratio-
nality and open-mindedness, try to tell you, very objectively,
all about someone else's racism, the better to deflect from any
scrutiny of their own.

Much of the essay obsesses over "war" as the defining
cataclysm of the Hawaiian experience, but one realizes very
quickly that the only war Didion is referring to is World War II:

> War is in the very fabric of Hawaii's life, ineradicably
> fixed in both its emotions and its economy, dominating
> not only its memory but its vision of the future. There is
> a point at which every Honolulu conversation refers back
> to war. People sit in their gardens up on Makiki Heights
> among their copa de oro and their star jasmine and they
> look down toward Pearl Harbor and get another drink
> and tell you about the morning it happened.

Didion is being very clear about just what she means when
she says "war," and just who she means when she says "people":

wealthy, mostly white, mostly drunk people "up on Makiki Heights"—the people who "look down toward Pearl Harbor." For this precious minority, the bombing of Pearl Harbor is the foundational terror of their Hawaiian experience. In one long section, she describes the wealthy families of prewar Hawaiʻi ("the pleasant but formidable colonial world in which a handful of families controlled everything Hawaii did") and their business empires, from sugar to shipping to insurance, throwing out names like Brewer, Davies, Castle & Cooke, Alexander & Baldwin, Sears, Roebuck, Liberty House, Mason Navigation.

"That was Hawaii," Didion pronounces, like God naming Adam. "And then World War II came."

To hear Didion tell the story, you would never know (in the mathematical sense, of course) that anyone lived in Hawaiʻi at all before that great-great-grandfather of hers came as a missionary (to whom?) in 1842. The only time she mentions Queen Liliʻuokalani, it's to describe the possessions Didion's white family members took from Hawaiʻi upon immigrating to California: "their token mementos, the calabashes and the carved palace chairs and the flat silver for forty-eight and the diamond that had been Queen Liliuokalani's and the heavy linens embroidered on all the long golden afternoons that were no more." The Hawaiian Sugar Planters' Association, founded in 1895, actively recruited migrant labor to work its plantations— they opened Philippine offices in Manila and the city where my father is from, Vigan, the capital of Ilocos Sur. By 1906, Filipino laborers (alongside Japanese migrant laborers, with whom the solidarity was complicated and tenuous) were working on Hawai'i's sugar plantations, only four years after the end of the Philippine-American War. The grueling labor conditions and relentless racial discrimination they faced meant that in the first half of the twentieth century, Filipinos—long stereotyped as violent actors, prone to fits of emotion and criminality— were the number one race in Hawai'i to be sentenced with the death penalty. During the 1924 Hanapepe Massacre, sixteen Filipinos were murdered during an organized labor strike, with over a hundred arrested and tried, and around fifty imprisoned and later deported. The massacre effectively marked, in many ways, the end of the labor movement in Hawai'i during that period. Some of the names Didion mentions (Castle and Cooke, Alexander and Baldwin, C. Brewer & Co., Theo H. Davies & Co.) were part of the Big Five, the oligarchic group of settler-colonial-owned sugarcane corporations in Hawai'i, which amassed significant political power during the early twentieth century, largely throwing their weight behind the Hawaiian Republican Party.

At one point, Didion even uses the word "ante-bellum Hawaii," making the parallels unmistakable, casting herself as a Scarlett O'Hara of the Islands: bemoaning a bygone paradise (for whom?), mourning *the loss of our way of life.* None of the other degenerate colonials remember the islands the way she does—the entire essay is essentially a "not like the other girls" argument about which type of rich white settler loves Hawai'i best (her, of course).

In fact, there is perhaps no description that captures Didion's work better than to say that it is consummate pick-me writing. Her pitiless, colonially inflected reportage, and the wider misapprehension of Didion's style as unsentimental (usually dog whistle phrasing for "unfeminine, thank God") is at the very core of Didion's cultural popularity and critical approval. When Didion is praised, it's often in a specific kind of chiaroscuro: she's not like other women writers. (If I must contribute to the competition: in the drunk-white-colonial-dame-having-hot-sex-in-Asia genre of literature, I prefer Marguerite Duras; in the white-American-woman-excoriating-her-oppressive-aristocratic-background genre of literature, I prefer Edith Wharton.)

Didion makes little to no mention of the colonial war of 1893, during which the Kingdom of Hawai'i was overthrown in a coup d'état, and Queen Lili'uokalani removed from power by a US-backed, majority-foreign (back when white people at least knew they were foreign to Hawai'i) insurgency, her wealth appropriated by people like Didion's family. Didion never once considers that it's this war that is Hawai'i's true, originary disaster—that for some, every day since 1893 has been another Pearl Harbor.

In 1898, the islands were annexed to the United States. All so that years and years later, families just like Didion's could look down at the island from their great houses in the hills, and sing to you the long and lovely song about the pikake and the pineapple and the trade winds; the long and lovely song about how much Hawai'i means to them.

"AERIALISTS KNOW THAT TO LOOK DOWN IS TO FALL," WRITES Didion in *Democracy* (or rather, the fictional character "Joan Didion" in *Democracy*):

> *Writers know it too.*
>
> *Look down and that prolonged spell of suspended judgment in which a novel is written snaps, and recovery requires that we practice magic.*

The line is another classic Didion gem, imperious as the Wizard of Oz, right before he reveals to Dorothy that he's just a con man, an old settler from Omaha.

Is this what writers know? Is this what writers do? Force themselves to never look down into the depths beneath the tightrope they're walking, just in order to write? There's a deliberately mystifying and self-aggrandizing tenor to this way of thinking about the holy work of the writer that I've never found truthful, let alone helpful. This is writing as sleight of hand, as balancing act, writing as parlor trick to be pulled off—not writing as a practice of being in the world, being *of* the world. It seems to me that if we're to take Didion's metaphor seriously at all, then the real job of the writer-as-tightrope-walker is *precisely* to look down. But a fixed-forward-gaze theory of fiction makes sense when you read a book like *Democracy*, so committed to its singularly unblinking, unseeing stare, protected behind huge sunglasses. This way of writing is like a paramilitary goon flying briskly away from the careless graveyard he's made of a foreign country. And like so many great American wizards, the effect of much of Didion's writing, from *Slouching Towards Bethlehem* to the equally fetishized *White Album*, has the spell-like effect of a particularly impassive astrologer, an evasive Sactown psychic phoning it in. Didion's writing divines more than it diagnoses. Her auguries retain just enough blurriness at the edges for anyone—well, almost anyone—to see themselves in the fortune told.

The novel closes with Jack Lovett's death, "at approximately eleven o'clock in the evening in the shallow end of the fifty-meter swimming pool at the Hotel Borobudur in Jakarta. After swimming his usual thirty laps." Inez embarks on a long journey to retrieve her longtime lover's body, and bury him in the Schofield Barracks cemetery in Honolulu. The journey from Indonesia to Honolulu requires, of course, help all along the way:

The colonel who had been her contact at Schofield had been extremely helpful.

Extremely cooperative.

Extremely kind really.

As had her original contact.

Mr. Soebadio. In Jakarta. Mr. Soebadio was the representative for Java of the bank in Vila and it turned out to be his telephone number that Jack Lovett had given her to call if any problem arose during the four or five days they were to be in Jakarta.

Jack Lovett had not given her Mr. Soebadio's name.

Only this telephone number.

It's difficult, in this post-Trump era, to read a character vaguely complimenting someone as "extremely helpful, extremely cooperative, extremely kind really" and not think their grasp on the subtleties of the world has something in common with our forty-fifth president's equally empty superlatives in press conferences and State of the Union addresses alike; the novel's called *Democracy*, after all. But beyond Inez's grief-numbed reactions to her lover's death, what's most striking about the novel's denouement is how entirely it rests upon the work of Asian side characters like Mr. Soebadio, or the Tamil doctor (no name given) who attends to Jack Lovett's drowned body at the pool:

It was Mr. Soebadio who had brought the Tamil doctor to the pool.

It was Mr. Soebadio who worked Jack Lovett's arms into his seersucker jacket and carried him to the service area where his car was parked.

It was Mr. Soebadio who advised Inez to tell anyone who approached the car that Mr. Lovett was drunk and it was Mr. Soebadio who went back upstairs for her passport and it was Mr. Soebadio who suggested that certain possible difficulties in getting Mr. Lovett out of Indonesia could be circumvented by obtaining a small aircraft, what he called a good aircraft for clearance, which he happened to know how to do. He happened to know that there was a good aircraft for clearance on its way from Denpasar to Halim. He happened to know that the pilot, a good friend, would be willing to take Mrs. Victor and Mr. Lovett wherever Mrs. Victor wanted to go.

It's an extraordinary passage, a narrative master class: how to write about a side character without writing about him at all; how to write about a side character, stripping him of any quality he has that does not directly service the story's main characters. Mr. Soebadio is an Indonesian deus ex machina for the book's white people in crisis: putting the clothes back onto a corpse, fetching Inez's passport, arranging the plane that will allow her to bury Jack's body in Hawai'i. "He happened to know that the pilot, a good friend, would be willing to take Mrs. Victor and Mr. Lovett wherever Mrs. Victor wanted to go." Well, of course he did; it's his narrative job, to happen to know these things. He exists to be the soothing voice on the end of a phone number, the capable arms hauling the dead body to the car; like many characters of color in such works, he operates primarily as a satellite to the central white narrative, the way queer characters will often function as reflective handmaidens in central hetero narratives, with those narratives expecting readers and viewers to be grateful for the existence of those characters at all. Representation matters, etc.

Still, it's in this last act that the perfection of *Democracy*'s title actually becomes clear. Didion's sardonic yet succinctly self-serving vision of democracy encompasses the primal sense of the word—flush with all its history, from ancient Greece to early America: the early iteration of democracy as the noble dream of slaveholders and land thieves. Here, democracy is still just a parlor trick of equality, a half-written story—with a crew of side characters down in the depths, doing the dirty work.

FEW OTHER WRITERS, OTHER THAN STEINBECK, ARE ASSOCIATED with California more than Didion. She is the reference of references when people want to harp on about what's often palely described as "the West," and nearly every article about Didion I've ever read appears contractually obligated to make the same breathlessly, quasi-fetishistic observation: that she is a "fifth-generation Californian." *Fifth-generation Californian* is a way of reminding first-generation Californians like myself that our stories mean less, matter less, weigh less: four generations less, to be exact. *Fifth-generation Californian*, rather than read as a distinctly banal American settler colonial horror story, is recited like a land deed, ready to evict those of us with frailer claims to California; frailer claims to the right of telling its story. Didion is baptized in what passes for Californian authenticity, circa the mid-nineteenth century: "Didion grew up in Sacramento," Robert Lacy writes in "Joan Didion, Daughter of Old California." "Her family were members of the landed gentry, a benefit of having got there early."

By "people who want to talk about what's largely called the West," I generally mean non-Californians, for it's non-Californians who are the true audience of Didion's California observations. It's non-Californians who tend to worship at the feet of Didion's "Western" writing, for it's non-Californians who have always most faithfully, most desperately, nurtured this dream of California: its vastness, its emptiness, its grim ugly cool, its sun-bleached corridors there at the tantalizing edge of civilization, the utopian place par excellence for weary American settlers—or middle-class intellectual refugees fleeing colder coasts—to rest their bones. Indeed, with all of Didion's writing, her primary audience is always everyone *but* the people who live in the places she's writing about, from California to Colombia. Didion and colonial bureaucrats alike share the romanticized postwar posture of "Our Man in [Blank]," where the [Blank] might be Havana, Jakarta, Manila, Bogotá, or Los Angeles. Where there be blanks, there be monsters: anyone who knows Western history knows that.

Perhaps Didion's most telling understanding of the West appears in her *New York Times* review of Norman Mailer's *The Executioner's Song*:

The authentic Western voice, the voice heard in "The Executioner's Song," is one heard often in life but only rarely in literature, the reason being that to truly know the West is to lack all will to write it down. The very subject of "The Executioner's Song" is that vast emptiness at the center of the Western experience, a nihilism antithetical not only to literature but to most other forms of human endeavor, a dread so close to zero that human voices fadeout, trail off, like skywriting. Beneath what Mailer calls "the immense blue of the strong sky of the American West," under that immense blue which dominates "The Executioner's Song," not too much makes a difference. The places at which both Gary Gilmore and his Mormon great-grandfather came to rest was a town where the desert lay at the end of every street, except to the east. "There," to the east, "was the interstate, and after that, the mountains. That was about it."

One would be hard-pressed to find a modern description of the West more devotedly settler colonial in its tenor than this; one would have to go back to literal settler colonial documents to find a description so rich with all the clichés of what places like Utah or California represented to its newest occupiers: its vastness, its emptiness, its nihilism and dread. Toni Morrison has written extensively about the tendency in early American literature—what's often taught to us in school as the Romance era of Poe and Hawthorne—to display the profound anxiety and terror of white European settlers, faced with what they viewed as their savage, uncivilized new country, a terror foregrounded by the colonizer's particular blend of hope and curiosity—escaping rigid, oppressive European society for the freedom of the West, the dream of Santorum and his forebears: "One could be released from a useless, binding, repulsive past into a kind of history-lessness, a blank page waiting to be inscribed." That it was paramount for white settler colonials to believe the lie that the land they were occupying was "a blank page waiting to be inscribed," that it was this lie that allowed America to tell the story of itself (and fifth-generation white Californians like Didion to tell the story of California)—is the lens through which all writing about the West must be scrutinized. Who is this writing for? What vision of California and the West is it upholding, and why?

When Lacy describes, as many of Didion's critics also often remark upon, "the gloominess that has always characterized Didion's writing," I think of how Morrison characterized our early American literature: "The body of literature produced by the young nation is one way it inscribed its transactions with these fears, forces, and hopes," Morrison writes.

> And it is difficult to read the literature of young America without being struck by how antithetical it is to our modern rendition of the American Dream. How pronounced in it is the absence of that term's elusive mixture of hope, realism, materialism and promise. For a people

who made much of their "newness"—their potential, freedom, and innocence—it is striking how dour, how troubled, how frightened and haunted our early and founding literature truly is. . . .

Romance, an exploration of anxiety imported from the shadows of European culture, made possible the sometimes safe and other times risky embrace of quite specific, understandably human, fears: Americans' fear of being outcast, of failing, of powerlessness; their fear of boundarylessness, of Nature unbridled and crouched for attack; their fear of their absence of so-called civilization; their fear of loneliness, of aggression both external and internal. In short, the terror of human freedom—the thing they coveted most of all.

All of these early American anxieties are at the heart of Didion's work: its conflict between privilege and risk, between safety and danger; its distinctly white upper-class obsession with social and psychic disintegration and the loss of boundaries; most of all the way it stares, administratively, into what it considers the subaltern, then turns back over its shoulder to report back to its colleagues. Always flitting about her pages is the hypochondriac terror of Kurtz's ghost, going native. "Funny that every place Joan Didion visits is falling apart," Prickett remarks.

The beginning of "Some Dreamers of the Golden Dream," the essay that opens *Slouching Towards Bethlehem*, contains some of Didion's most totemic writing about California—and like all totems "owned" and then proffered by white people, one must be skeptical not only of their warped meaning but their provenance:

This is a story about love and death in the golden land, and begins with the country. The San Bernardino Valley lies only an hour east of Los Angeles by the San Bernardino Freeway but is in certain ways an alien place: not the coastal California of the subtropical twilights and the soft westerlies off the Pacific but a harsher California, haunted by the Mojave just beyond the mountains, devastated by the hot dry Santa Ana wind that comes through the passes at 100 miles an hour and whines through the eucalyptus windbreaks and works on the nerves. October is the bad month for the wind, the month when breathing is difficult and the hills blaze up spontaneously. There has been no rain since April. Every voice seems a scream. It is the season of suicide and divorce and prickly dread, wherever the wind grows.

The Mormons settled this ominous country, and then they abandoned it, but by the time they left the first orange tree had been planted and for the next hundred years the San Bernardino Valley would draw a kind of people who imagined they might live among the talismanic fruit and prosper in the dry air, people who brought with them Midwestern ways of building and cooking

and praying and who tried to graft those ways upon the
land.

It's paragraphs like these that bring critics to speak of Didion's razor-like unsentimentality, her sharp attention to lin-
guistic rhythms, her singular instinct for beats, her unsparing
and seemingly novel (at least, to non-Californians) approach
to writing about the West. The language Didion uses here is an
archive of settler colonial terror and anxiety: "an alien place,"
"harsher," "haunted," "devastated," "whines," "works on the
nerves," "bad month," "breathing is difficult," "every voice
seems a scream," "suicide," "divorce," "prickly dread," "ominous." As the queer Chicana writer Myriam Gurba deftly notes
in her essay "It's Time to Take California Back from Joan Didion,"
describing the way Didion's settler colonial language inflects
her writing about both Californian and Mexican landscapes:
"México is something for gringos to do in their piyamas, o quizás
en cálzon, on rainy days. . . . The further south [Didion and her
family] drive, the more her prose approaches the infernal."

What's most distinctive about the opening to "Some Dreamers of the Golden Dream," and the way it situates its narrator
and its readers in a particular positioning within California,
is precisely *what* sparks this flood of anxiety and terror. An
alien place, haunted—by the Mojave. Devastated—by the hot
dry Santa Ana wind. The passive voice Didion deliberately
chooses puts us into the aggrieved, nervy body of a white
settler, who sees the Mojave and the Santa Ana as enemies,

with the same cocktail of attraction and repulsion to the natural landscape and its visceral effect on white European immigrants that Toni Morrison so aptly identified in our early American literature. It's this genre of California writing that appeals to non-Californians, because, as Gurba astutely points out in Didion's relationship to Mexico ("the spiritual tradition of extranjeros palidos using México as a portal"), it reinforces the idea of California and the West as a fantasy space *for non-Californians*; a place that remains—intrinsically, anxiously, seductively—at once alien and alluring, fecund and hostile forever. And while Didion is regularly considered the high priestess of New Journalism, the altar at which her writing really worships, as passages like these show, is Western Romance, in the Morrison understanding of the genre:

> For young America it had everything: nature as subject matter, a system of symbolism, a thematics of the search for self-valorization and validation—above all, the opportunity to conquer fear imaginatively and to quiet deep insecurities. It offered platforms for moralizing and fabulation, and for the imaginative entertainment of violence, sublime incredibility, and terror—and terror's most significant, overweening ingredient: darkness, with all the connotative value it awakened.

In her review of Mailer's book, Didion describes the "Western" sections of the novel as "a fatalistic drift, a tension, an overwhelming and passive rush toward the inevitable. . . . The women in the 'Western' book are surprised by very little. They do not on the whole believe that events can be influenced. A kind of desolate wind seems to blow through the lives of these women. . . . The wind seems to blow away memory, balance."

This passive, barren portrait of white women's interiority in the West is not just textbook Didion but textbook Americana: it's a deliberate characterization of white colonial femininity as grimly but unoperatically tragic; helpless and blameless. (Sometimes, the defense of Didion's writing from critique takes a page from this proto-girlboss handbook, i.e., that to criticize her is misogynist; defending white heroines is, after all, a totemic American pastime.) The women are fragile but hard; too scattered and distracted to ever be anything as overt as a heroine or a villain; always imperiled but somehow never quite vanquished—most of all, they are ethically neutral objects through which history happens, not decisive actors of history themselves. Their presence in the West is not an active project of occupation, but an inevitability; nobody's fault.

It cannot furthermore escape anyone's notice that many of the articles praising Didion's work take pains to mention, quasi-fetishistically, the author's physical build—often emphasizing the combination (not quite contrast) of her appealingly laconic, "masculine" prose with her sylphlike thinness: again and again we are encouraged to appraise her apparent fragility as well as be impressed by her severe, distilled purity; the pale pared-down sliver of her. That casual fatphobia should also have its comfortable nook in literary criticism, as in all reaches of society, comes as no surprise; writers like Sabina Strings, in her book *Fearing the Black Body: The Racial Origins of Fat Phobia*, help coax out the psychosocial regimes of control, refinement, and respectability that govern the glorification of thin wealthy white femininity, in contrast to the supposedly overflowing appetites—and ungovernable bodies—of poor women, immigrant women, women of color (not even always women; think of the racist and fatphobic experiences recounted by the late great aesthete and indisputable fashion polymath André Leon Talley). Strings writes that at the end of the nineteenth century, "it was incumbent upon Anglo-Saxon women, then, to serve as the flag bearers of a new standard of beauty, one rooted, 'thanks to our benign religion and better civilization,' in morality, health and racial pride. . . . The new standard of beauty . . . that of the tall, slender, Anglo-Saxon Protestant woman, did arrive. It would come to be known in many New England circles as the 'American Beauty.' "

The appraisal of Didion's slimness always goes hand in hand with the celebration of her style. On this point, it bears remembering the modern fashion witticism "Is this outfit good, or is she just skinny and white."

(Incidentally, whenever I hear the line "Nothing tastes as good as skinny feels," a line attributed to Kate Moss—another bona fide Skinny Legend; often venerated by those who venerate Didion—a line the model later wisely distanced herself from, I am reminded, as someone who lived and thus was obligated to eat in England for many years, that the indigenous cuisine of the white English populace is not, shall we say, universally esteemed as one of the globe's great culinary treasures. Obviously nothing tastes as good as skinny feels if all you're eating is stale underfried chips and cucumber sandwiches, but—to paraphrase June Jordan—some of us did invent seasoning.)

As an erstwhile classicist and not quite as erstwhile spender-of-money on discounted HAY side tables at Design Within Reach, I've also sometimes sensed, in the exaltation of Didion's aesthetics, a soupçon of Laconophilia—not just the love of the laconic, a quality that is of course synonymous with Didion's writing, but the love, literally, of Laconia: the area in Greece famously home to the Spartans, and their notorious culture of martial austerity, bodily control, and rigid aristocracy, all things that Didion's writing, even when ostensibly critical of the military-industrial complex or indeed her own aristocracy, nevertheless holds close, like tarnished heirlooms. What *Democracy* finds most appealing about Jack Lovett is his martial stoicism and competence, his crackpot's willingness to get shit done (and of course one must admire the delicious irony of a book called *Democracy*, written by arguably one of the least democratic writers in the American canon). Famous Laconophiles included founding father Samuel Adams, Jean-Jacques Rousseau, and Karl Otfried Müller, whose writings on Spartan culture heavily influenced the concept of Nordicism, which in turn saw its theories on race and society adopted by

such Third Reich luminaries as Hans F. K. Günther (a eugeni-
cist whose nickname was Rassenpapst, the Pope of Race) and
theorist Alfred Rosenberg (an early student of art and ar-
chitecture, later head of the NSDAP—Nationalsozialistische
Deutsche Arbeiterpartei—Office of Foreign Affairs from 1933
to 1945, before his conviction for war crimes in Nuremberg in
1946). It's a strain of thought that reverberates through contemporary aesthetic theory; Kyle Chayka's *The Longing for Less:
Living with Minimalism* identifies the submerged elitism (and
in the case of famed architect Philip Johnson's Glass House,
latent fascist sympathies) in minimalism's allure, the cost of its
seductively utopian promise of reduction, distillation, and pu-
rification.

Like the mannered ascetism of the 1 percent, Didion
fandom—its hygiene, its class signifiers; the codes of its
brand, to use the language of luxury fashion, which it most
resembles—has a distinctly aspirational bent. Take, for example, the famously Spartan capsule wardrobe to end all capsule
wardrobes, the list that launched a thousand mood-boards,
Didion-as-reporter's packing inventory, itemized in "The White
Album": "2 skirts / 2 jerseys or leotards / 1 pullover sweater / 2 pair
shoes / stockings / bra / nightgown, robe, slippers / cigarettes /
bourbon."

"Note the deliberate anonymity of the costume . . . I could
pass on either side of the culture." Didion writes, of a list "made
by someone who prized control, yearned after momentum,
someone determined to play her role as if she had the script,

heard the cues, knew the narrative." In a marvelously Carrie Bradshaw–like self-own passing as a flex, Didion later notes the one thing she always forgot was a watch. "In other words I had skirts, jerseys, leotards, pullover sweater, shoes, stockings, bra, nightgown, robe, slippers, cigarettes, bourbon . . . but I didn't know what time it was. This may be a parable, either of my life as a reporter during this period or of the period itself."

"The wind seems to blow away memory," Didion writes in her Mailer review. In *Democracy*, the character "Joan Didion" writes of her protagonist: "During the 1972 campaign and even later I thought of Inez Victor's capacity for passive detachment as an affectation born of boredom, the frivolous habit of an essentially idle mind. After the events which occurred in the spring and summer of 1975 I thought of it differently. I thought of it as the essential mechanism for living a life in which the major cost was memory. Drop fuel. Jettison cargo. Eject crew."

It's an unwittingly hopeful, luxurious, American approach to history. White settlers would certainly love to think that "the wind seems to blow away memory," wouldn't they? Drop fuel; jettison cargo; eject crew. In the end, the most honest— and most self-exonerating—word in "Some Dreamers of the Golden Dream" is: *some*.

IF *DEMOCRACY*'S INEZ CHRISTIAN VICTOR (HOW AMUSINGLY literal) is the heiress not merely to one white colonial dynasty in Honolulu, but of the entire settler enterprise of Christian victors in the West, then her lover Jack Lovett's obvious model is not actually James Bond (too English), not Rick Blaine (too short), but, of course, the American hero par excellence: John Wayne. In her encomium "John Wayne: A Love Song," the essay that directly follows "Some Dreamers of the Golden Dream," Didion lays out, in full gleaming Technicolor, the erotics of the colonial imagination that built her childhood: "Saw the walk, heard the voice. Heard him tell the girl in a picture called *War of the Wildcats* that he would build her a house, 'at the bend in the river where the cottonwoods grow.'"

The War of the Wildcats (its original title was *In Old Oklahoma*) is a 1943 movie about Catherine Allen, a liberal white woman and schoolteacher seeking refuge in the West from her stuffy bourgeois milieu back East, who have excommunicated her for writing a romance novel. The protagonist is quite literally a spiky, independently minded, but otherwise entitled and naïve white woman writer; she's not like the other WASPs, you see. Our brave heroine is on a quest for—you'll never guess—"life, love and freedom" in the West. Like a plot from one of her pulps, Catherine meets two eligible bachelors, Jim Gardner and Dan Somers, who compete, not only for her love, but for oil lease rights on Native land in Oklahoma, with the obligatory uncredited white actors in redface.

We know immediately that young John Wayne's Dan Somers is the hero, not only because he's serving us his best himbo-twunk-with-a-heart-of-gold (in the vein of good-outfit-or-just-skinny discourse, Wayne is a perfect incarnation of "is he hot or just tall" discourse), but because he valiantly defends the Indians from being excessively scammed out of their lands by Jim Gardner's leering tycoon. Dan's a fair-minded settler, he is. Anointed as the chosen son by the good reliable working-class stock of the local farmers, as well as by the Natives (air quotes here would not go amiss) who approve of his inherent decency, Dan goes straight to President Roosevelt (okay) to claim the oil rights for himself; you know, for the greater good. Roosevelt immediately recognizes Dan as a war hero: "Where did you disappear to after Cuba?" "I wound up in the Philippines." And since the film's version of Roosevelt is apparently very pro-indigenous rights (the same Teddy Roosevelt who said in 1886: "I don't go so far as to think that the only good Indian is the dead Indian, but I believe nine out of every ten are, and I shouldn't like to inquire too closely into the case of the tenth. The most vicious cowboy has more moral principle than the average Indian"), he favors Dan's proposal to give the Natives not a paltry 12, but a magnanimous 50 percent of the royalties. For oil extracted from their own land.

"Gentlemen, our country owes all of its progress to a small detachment of pioneers," movie Roosevelt says, sounding a little more familiar. "Men who asked only for the chance to take a test. That spirit is the essence of America!" Later, Catherine delights in picking up the sledgehammer to be the first to break ground on the lands of the reservation; now Dan's oil fields. The essence of America.

In the psychosexually formative scene Didion describes in

her essay, what Wayne's character, Dan, actually says in the film is:

> You know the bend in the river where the cottonwoods grow? I'd build me a house right there. . . . Oh, I've been thinking about it ever since I was a little tyke. I even thought about it over in the Philippines. I could see it just as plain: smoke coming out of the chimney, nice horse in the corral. I could even see a girl with sorrel hair, standing in the doorway.

A soft-focus fantasy of colonial domesticity at home; a place to put up one's feet, after colonial genocide abroad. Didion continues, ruefully: "As it happened I did not grow up to be the kind of woman who is the heroine in a Western." Again, the protagonist of *War of the Wildcats* is literally a white woman writer and settler who scorns her upper-class community. And exactly as in *Democracy*, Catherine's scandalous romance novel is about a woman choosing between a man who promises dull security and a man who promises thrilling adventure. "And although the men I have known have had many virtues," Didion writes, "they have never been John Wayne, and they have never taken me to that bend in the river where the cottonwoods grow. Deep in that part of my heart where the artificial rain forever falls, that is still the line I wait to hear."

Democracy's Jack Lovett is a John Wayne character with a CIA clearance; the definition of the cowboy who takes you to the bend in the river where the cottonwoods grow. "[Wayne] had a sexual authority so strong that even a child could perceive it," Didion writes, proving that BDE is a commonly misdiagnosed condition. We all of course reserve the right to our problematic faves (though as friends at my dinner table know all too well, we do not reserve the right to never be roasted about them), but sometimes a particularly fulsome hagiography fancies itself a greater revelation of cultural wisdom, purporting to discover the last terra incognita about masculinity, or freedom, or the American way, or whatever. "And in a world we understood early to be characterized by venality and doubt and paralyzing ambiguities," Didion waxes on, with the alas-those-simpler-bygone-times nostalgia favored by the chicest of far-right nationalists, "[Wayne] suggested another world, one which may or may not have existed ever but in any case existed no more: a place where a man could move free, could make his own code and live by it; a world in which, if a man did what he had to do, he could one day take the girl and go riding through the draw and find himself free."

"John Wayne: A Love Song" ends with Didion and her husband at dinner in Mexico, in "an expensive restaurant in Chapultepec Park," with Wayne and his Peruvian wife, Pilar (whose name, along with the name of Wayne's previous wife, Mexican actress Esperanza Baur, perhaps hints at another reason why Mrs. Christian Victor in *Democracy* is named Inez in the first place; no shame about a little self-insert fanfic, after all), drinking Pouilly-Fuissé "and some red Bordeaux for the

Duke." Suddenly three men appear "out of nowhere," carrying guitars.

A haze falls over this last paragraph of the essay, like someone reapplying Vaseline to the lens. The musicians begin to play "The Red River Valley" and the theme from "The High and the Mighty," in a scene of either profound Western Romance or High American Camp or Classic Mexican Horror, wherever you happen to fall. "They did not quite get the beat right," Didion tries, and once again fails, to keep from rhapsodizing, "but even now I can hear them, in another country and a long time later, even as I tell you this."

THE STORY I REMEMBER ABOUT JOHN "I BELIEVE IN WHITE SU-premacy until the Blacks are educated to the point of responsibility" Wayne is the one that Sacheen Littlefeather told after she attended the 1973 Academy Awards, declining Marlon Brando's statuette on the actor's behalf. Littlefeather gave a speech (to a shell-shocked mix of boos and applause) that drew attention to the portrayal of Native Americans in film and television; a speech that, watching it again now, rings as exceedingly mild and accommodating, for all the furor it swiftly attracted.

"During my presentation," Littlefeather said of the great hero, the one cast as the kind of man who dreams of building the white woman a house, there at the bend in the river where the cottonwoods grow, "[Wayne] was coming towards me to forcibly take me off the stage, and he had to be restrained by six security men to prevent him from doing so."

Presenting best pictures soon after (also for *The Godfather*), Clint Eastwood quipped: "I don't know if I should present this award on behalf of all the cowboys shot in all the John Ford westerns over the years." When Littlefeather got backstage, she says, there were people making stereotypical Native American war cries at her and miming chopping with a tomahawk.

IN LINES THAT FULFILL MORRISON'S AMERICAN DIAGNOSIS, Didion writes of the women in Mailer's *The Executioner's Song* (though she could just as easily be writing about the women in her own novels): "These women move in and out of paying attention to events, of noticing their own fate. They seem distracted by bad dreams, by some dim apprehension of this well of dread, this 'unhappiness at the bottom of things.' . . . She has no idea 'how much was her fault, and how much was the fault of the ongoing world that ground along like iron-banded wagon wheels up the prairie grass.'"

"When I read this," Didion confides to us, "I remembered that the tracks made by the wagon wheels are still visible from the air over Utah, like the footprints made on the moon. This is an absolutely astonishing book." Thus endeth the review.

I can think of few lines that more succinctly sum up the American settler colonial project in the West—its fatuous insistence on exceptionalism, its jejune self-astonishment (for that is the word Didion deploys): "the tracks made by the wagon wheels are still visible from the air over Utah, like the footprints made on the moon." Didion deploys the line without affect besides astonishment (the better to "pass on either side of the culture," my dear). And indeed, what radiates here—beneath the coolness, beneath the detachment, beneath the redactions, beneath the sunglasses, astonished and astonishing, as wide-eyed and innocent as America's dream of itself, like the chilly glare of the sun off a glass house—is wonder. It is the hushed, forgetful wonder of the settler colonial: that their foundational crime may not only persist, but go on to become a country. Its imprint visible from space. Its legacy traveling all the way to the moon.

THE VISION OF CALIFORNIA THAT I HAVE RETURNED TO, AGAIN and again since reading it for the first time only a few years ago, is to be found in Tommy Pico's epic work of poetry, *Nature Poem*. It contains, for me, the greatest contemporary writing about California by one of our most important living writers about California, and I am purposely using the kind of magisterial language that regularly buffers all discussion of Didion, because this is the kind of language that *should* attend the work of writers like Pico: a queer indigenous writer from the Viejas Indian reservation of the Kumeyaay Nation in Southern California, now based in Brooklyn, whose work swerves masterlessly between the sublime and the quotidian, in ways that remind us that the two are one and the same. I thought of call-ing Pico's work peerless, but that would be to subscribe to a genre of literary critique that asks us to elevate singular voices from a minority, the better to close the door on everyone else. On the contrary, Pico's writing is peer*ful*: it is joyfully, pain-fully, brattily, determinedly (in the particular shade of deter-mination that all inheritors to histories of genocide know well, there where survival must be a kind of *de*termination, as an antidote to *ex*termination) full of peers—from friends with benefits to one-night stands, from parents to roommates, from the defiantly living to the numberful dead. *Nature Poem* is the kind of writing that quite literally restores—it has at its long-form heart the thorny, difficult, long-form work of repair, even as the narrator runs from that work, avoids it, curves it, doesn't answer its call.

The premise of *Nature Poem* is of a queer Native writer who absolutely does *not* want to write the cliché Native nature poem: "I can't write a nature poem / bc it's fodder for the noble savage / narrative. I wd slap a tree across the face, / I say to my audience," Pico writes toward the beginning of the collection. Few writers use bathos more trenchantly than Pico, or wield it to build such surprising and devastating effects. And where Didion's Californian writing sees the dread of empty, hostile land waiting to be ripened then ruined by settler industry, Pico's Californian writing sees an entire already teeming world: with humor, with tenderness, with a son's embarrassment of his parents, with a city immigrant's embarrassment of the country back home, with a Native narrator's awareness and anxiety of what contemporary indigenous reservation life looks like to largely non-Native urban audiences. Not the anxiety of the white settler colonial in the face of the dreadful and peopleless prairie—but the anxiety of someone who had to grow up in the shadow of that too long, too loud story. Both are true stories about California, of course—but it's the former that gets the Céline ad.

Humor runs through *Nature Poem* like a major artery, and plays just as vital a role in the body of its poetry: nick it, you die. Its vise grip on the comic reminds us that people familiar with genocide are usually pretty funny—there has to be at least a little laughter on the other end of survival, to make it worth anything. But Pico's narrator is equally aware that the humor of people who've known intergenerational trauma is also nearly always a defense mechanism, a way to deflect, a practiced jujitsu that survivors use to make their way through the world, always blocking and redirecting the unexpected blows: "invent myself some laughs in an / attempt to maneuver from a sticky kind of ancestral sadness, being a / NDN person in occupied America." It's Pico's sharp attention to both the places he looks at *and* the places he avoids that makes *Nature Poem* so remarkable; the way the narrator lets us into the world-building that goes into writing a poem, while questioning the very nature of poetic world-building, especially when it comes to the tradition of nature poems in American, and specifically Californian, literature.

It would be easy to describe Pico's *Nature Poem* as the act of a queer Native poet reclaiming the pastoral genre from its white colonial history, but what Pico is doing is so much more complicated than reclaiming ("Reclamation suggests social / capital," he writes), and resists the simplified heroics of these kinds of literary reparations: the idea that it must be necessarily positive for minoritized writers to "reclaim" spaces in which they have been erased, that the Western genre can be redeemed if we just populate it with the Native, Black, Latinx, and Asian people who actually made Western history possible in the first place (a favorite posture taken up by the tired, corporate-friendly "representation matters" crowd). It's a seductive thought (and it certainly is a popular way to get people of color on the page and onscreen nowadays—which, hey, I use my Netflix subscription, too), but poetry like Pico's knows to be wary of the claiming impulse in the first place. "Who is the 'I' but its inheritances," he writes.

In an oft-quoted passage from her 1976 essay "Why I Write," Didion writes:

> In many ways, writing is the act of saying I, of imposing oneself upon other people, of saying *listen to me, see it my way, change your mind*. It's an aggressive, even a hostile act. You can disguise its aggressiveness all you want with veils of subordinate clauses and qualifiers and tentative subjunctives, with ellipses and evasions—with the whole manner of intimating rather than claiming, of alluding

rather than stating—but there's no getting around the fact that setting words on paper is the tactic of a secret bully, an invasion, an imposition of the writer's sensibility on the reader's most private space.

I'm reminded, when I read this, of a proverb dear to people of color: white people tell on themselves. The fact that writers like Didion see writing as necessarily the tactic of a secret bully *is* telling: it's telling about how writers like this think about writing, and the silent but inevitable combat they arm themselves for when they write, like a homesteader keeping a shotgun by the door. Writing as invasion, writing as imposition, writing as occupation.

It is also a peculiar kind of artistic self-absolution: *all writers are bullies, therefore by being a bully myself, I'm just doing what writers do.* There is no space here for writing as invitation, or as a place for mutual intimacy or vulnerability. There is no space for the complicated, peerful way Pico imagines the "I," diametrically opposed to Didion's imagined "I," a bully brimming with impositions and aggressions. Pico instead asks: "Who is the 'I' but its inheritances"? Here we have a self not as secret bully, not as imposing "I," not just Andrew Jackson and all his cursed children—but a small dot, unalone, part of a long and living flock. There's a defiant humility to the way Pico's narrator places himself and the people in his life, not just in the California landscape, but California history: "The sky was yellow at dusk," Pico writes, "and we were like cameos, flushed against the mountains."

For all the talk of being a fifth-generation Californian, writing like Didion's doesn't actually ever want to think of the "I" as made up of its inheritances, because then it would have to think of the "I" as also made up of its indebtedness. And if the settler colonial "I" was ever tasked to focus on its debts rather than its dread, the whole tawdry American story would collapse in on itself, like a black hole finally swallowing up the place where a star used to glint.

Didion writes:

> In a world where every road runs into the desert or the Interstate of the Rocky Mountains, people develop a pretty precarious sense of their place in the larger scheme. People get sick for love, think they want to die for love, shoot up the town for love, and then they move away, move on, forget the face. People commit their daughters, and move to Midway Island.

No. Not just: "people." It's specifically white settlers and their descendants Didion is describing in the passage above—whether it's a white cowboy dual-wielding Schofield revolvers in the saloon or a young white man aiming an assault rifle at schoolchildren and protestors—once again assuming that we'll take their experience of the world as universal. It's largely the white monied class who commit their daughters to institutions—they're used to it, having spent so many generations committing indigenous people to boarding schools and reservations. It's white settlers who built every road that ran into the desert, because it's white settlers who didn't know the land to begin with; it's white settlers who saw only desert in the first place ("to truly know the West is to lack all will to write it down"—again mistaking her own myopia and impotence as everyone else's), there where others might also see chaparral; not just desolation, but: acorns, scrub oak, manzanita, buckeye, cypress, yucca, foothill pines, mountain mahogany, jewelflowers, and of course, the live-forever, that extremely rare plant found in the San Gabriel Mountains sandwiched between the Los Angeles Basin and the Mojave Desert that Didion found so—haunting.

And it's largely white settlers and their children who can then: move away, move on, forget the face. "The Mormons settled this ominous country, and then they abandoned it." "People sit in their gardens up on Makiki Heights." Soon enough a reader learns that whenever Didion says people, she doesn't actually mean *people*—she means the only people that writers of her ilk consider people. In one section, Pico describes a time period during which the indigenous population of San Diego dropped by 60 percent. The period coincides, of course, with the first of Didion's five generations. "A benefit of having got there early."

Nature Poem gives us the Californian pastoral as it is so

rarely depicted: a horror story, but not for the protagonists we usually expect, tremulous in their bonnets. A story about the West, but not told by its hardiest bullies and glummest settlers. Here we have no white main character to guide us, Virgil-like, into the wilderness; here no "Our Man in Kumeyaay Territory" to give us that spicy journalistic edge. "I am missing many cousins, have you seen them" is a refrain that echoes throughout *Nature Poem*, as Pico traces the outlines—not of two-hundred-year-old settler wagon wheels, not of white men's footsteps on the surface of the moon—but of the narrator's inherited intimacy with death and the dead: casualties to the psychic realities of contemporary indigenous life in America, bequeathed its oldest story.

Still, while *Nature Poem* pulls no punches, Pico's poetry crucially refuses the hardened, taciturn pose taken up by so many white and non-Native Californian artists like Didion or Steinbeck, who often valorize (and fetishize) an imagined working-class speechlessness and reserve (crackpot realism in a prairie schooner), to go hand in hand with their manipulated and manipulative vision of the West: everyone and everywhere, void as an abandoned town, mute as the grave, grim and grimy in their silence. In Pico's California, instead, we are invited to imagine something like abundance; something like connection; a long and lively conversation, full of grief and gossip, between this world and all its many cousins. We are invited to a place where not every road runs into the desert.

"What if I really do feel connected to the land," Pico wonders, in a line that feels at once open, and green, and raw; and also care-worn, lifetimes-old.

"STYLE IS CHARACTER," DIDION WROTE IN AN ESSAY ABOUT THE artist Georgia O'Keeffe, a line that *New Yorker* writer Nathan Heller, in a recent Didion profile, aptly identifies as one of many overused Didion psalms—as with, for instance, "We tell ourselves stories in order to live," truly one of my least favorite lines ever written in American or indeed any nation's literature (a line which, it must be said, Didion herself never proposed as the inspirational doormat it has since interminably been deployed as; the thing about Didion is that while clearly her writing is not altogether very good, it can truly never be as bad as the writing produced in her image, by her acolytes). "Every choice one made alone—every word chosen or rejected, every brush stroke laid or not laid down—betrayed one's character," pronounces Didion, thereafter frightening countless young writers into nervously curating their words to resemble desiccated little minimalist tablescapes. Heller elaborates: "Reducing the world, as on the canvas or the page, is a process of foreclosing on its fullness, choosing this way and not that one, and how you make those choices reveals everything about the person that you are."

Like reducing Hawai'i to its white oligarchs; like reducing California's story to the story of its white settlers; like reducing American masculinity to John Wayne and his over-many sons;

like reducing the Mojave to a ghost. Character, one finds, is also character.

In her O'Keeffe profile Didion relies once again on the language of Western romance, her favorite register, the chosen dialect of her rare praise: "She is simply hard," Didion commends. "A straight shooter, a woman clean of received wisdom, and open to what she sees."

Anyone worth anything in the Didion universe—just as in the American one—shares the same qualities: to believe that being "clean" of received wisdom (like a good pioneering homesteader, suspicious of fancy talk and filth) is the same thing as living in the complexity and clarity of learned wisdom. To boast that one is open to what one sees, without ever really having the humility or discernment to know or be known by what one sees. Most of all: to be hard. To shoot straight.

"IN THE SEEMINGLY BARREN MOJAVE DESERT, PAIUTES DEVELoped irrigation systems to grow food," Damon B. Akins and William J. Bauer Jr. tell us in *We Are the Land: A History of Native California*, showing us the California that writers like Didion could not, would not, see:

> At Pitana Patü, near the modern-day town of Bishop in eastern California's Owens Valley, Paiutes used irrigation ditches to increase the growth of plants, such as *nä'hävīta* (spike rush). In the spring, the town headman announced

the beginning of the irrigation season, usually when snow runoff from the southern Sierra Nevadas caused creeks to rise. Residents of Pitana Patü then elected a *tuvaijü'u* (irrigator) to lead twenty-five men in building a dam out of rocks, brush, sticks and mud. After people completed the dam, the tuvaijü'u directed the water into the ditch, which fed northern and southern fields in alternate years.

"REALITY IS ALL
WE HAVE TO LOVE"

———————————————

La Rabbia [Rage], I would say, is a film inspired by a fierce sense of endurance, not anger. Pasolini looks at what is happening in the world with unflinching lucidity. (There are angels drawn by Rembrandt who have the same gaze.) And he does so because reality is all we have to love. There's nothing else.

JOHN BERGER, "THE CHORUS IN OUR HEADS"

was once commissioned by a famous, well-regarded literary journal to write an introductory piece to a series of photographs by Stéphanie Borcard and Nicolas Métraux, two Swiss artists whom I hadn't heard of, and whose photographs I had never come across. Upon receipt of their photographs, I wrote a text in response, as commissioned.

After reading my piece, the journal politely requested that my—critique, shall we say—of the photo series be tempered. After this request was declined by myself and my agent, both the piece and the photo series were ultimately pulled from the issue. My original text is republished below, unrevised. The photographs from the series in question were on exhibition at the Story Institute, a digital storytelling site based out of Los Angeles, California, and Bath, England:

Dad is Gone is focuses [*sic*] on children born from sex tourism in the Philippines.

Angeles City, eighty kilometres north of Manila, is known for its red-light district. Until 1991, the city was the home of Clark Air base [sic], the largest US Air Base outside the United States of America. This favoured the raising of many brothels and Girlie Bars [sic], turning the city into one of the most popular sex tourism destination [sic]. Today, about 12,000 [sic] women are working in the bars which flank Fields Avenue. Unlike in Thailand, international customers in the Philippines seek a "girlfriend experience" that can last for several weeks or months.

Each year, thousands of children are born from these paid relationships. The fathers, whether American, Australian, British, German, Swiss, Korean or Japanese often abandon their offspring. In this very Catholic country, abortion is considered as a crime and punished by law.

Left behind, these children grow up in search of their own identity, where the father figure is still a question mark.

STÉPHANIE BORCARD AND NICOLAS MÉTRAUX, DAD IS GONE

[Colonial photographs] remind us, whoever "we" are, of the violence that underlay the production and distribution of such images. . . . Again and again, such approaches have demonstrated the tendentiousness of the eye that sees but remains unseen, resting on bodies that it both fixes and consumes for purposes alien to the lives of those it photographs.

VICENTE RAFAEL, "THE UNDEAD: NOTES
ON PHOTOGRAPHY IN THE PHILIPPINES, 1898–1920s"

The Clark Air Base was founded in 1903, a year after the end of the so-called Philippine-American War, which took place between 1899 and 1902—as with any war of colonial occupation and local resistance, the date of the conflict's end is disputable. The Proclamation of the U.S. Commission Towards Conciliation and the Establishment of Peace, issued to Manila in 1899 and also known as the Schurman Commission, makes no bones about the true costs of American empire-building. It informs the Philippine people of "certain regulative principles by which the United States will be guided in its relation with them ... deemed of cardinal importance." The first principle:

"The supremacy of the United States must and will be enforced throughout every part of the archipelago, and those who resist it can accomplish no end other than their own ruin."

There is no definitive historical record of the number of Filipinos killed as America became America. Some of the more conservative estimates by historians place the number at around 600,000 deaths in Luzon and Batangas towards the beginning of the conflict alone; more comprehensive anecdotal reports suggest a number close to 1.4 million. The water cure—now more commonly known as waterboarding—was first used by U.S. soldiers in the Philippines as a form of torture during this period.

What is definitive is that the war was crucial to the imperial project of early twentieth-century American statecraft, and its global, economic and human consequences continue to permeate Angeles City and places like it.

The past can show up in a photograph like a ghost. And like with any ghost, the first way to deal with its presence is to pay attention. But to which ghosts do Stephanie Borcard and Nicolas Metraux devote their attention in Dad is Gone, shot in 2014?

An abandoned military plane. Dog tags around the neck of someone whose head has been cropped out. Low-lit rooms, somber figures facing away from the camera. A tattered couch covered in black stains, no print from the last living ass to warm it. A people-dappled Angeles City street at dusk, taken from far away and at a height, the perspective akin to a sniper's.

If, like me, you belong to a large diaspora—especially one as large as the Filipino diaspora—you probably get sent a lot of pictures. Usually they come to me through Whatsapp or Viber, sometimes by email, often via my mom. Both the senders and the subjects are nearly always women—women in the Bay Area, in Las Vegas, in Jeddah, in the Philippines. Among the pictured are women who were left by their white dads when they were babies, women who've asked if I could hook them up with a Western boyfriend to get them out of Saudi Arabia, women who found a long-estranged parent on Facebook and didn't send a friend request. Most of the pictures are self-taken, and the subjects are rarely stoic or even alone: they're cheesing with a girlfriend, with a new bag, with something good they just ate, some fresh pleasure whose trace might still be shared with the loved and the loving. Captions abound: they liked the latest Bruno Mars; they miss their kids; they've been bleaching their skin; they just got bangs.

None of the liveliness, complexity, vulnerability and tenacity contained in those selfies is present in Borcard and Metraux's project—not least of all because the subject of Dad is Gone isn't the Filipina sex workers whose precarious and undervalued labor powers the economy of Angeles City. Nor is it (contrary to the photographers' own description) the children of those workers, inheritors of a centuries-long colonial haunting whose now-globalized grip on the archipelago has yet to slacken. At least, the subject isn't who the children are, or might be, beyond their parentage. Do they play basketball? Have they had their first or last crush? You don't know, and Dad is Gone won't tell you.

No, the object of Dad is Gone's melancholy gaze is named in the title. The two Bangkok-based white Swiss photographers have come to Angeles City to document and mourn a very specific loss: they want to know where dad went, and how awful it's been since he went away. The result of this preoccupation is that even in photographs that are purportedly about them, taken in their hometown, Angeles City's citizens are decentered, reduced to tragic ellipsis, or obscured from view altogether.

The photographs aren't about them, not really. But we could have figured that out from the very first photograph in the series: a home altar to the Virgin Mary and the Santo Niño, both white. The Santo Niño's arms are outstretched, awaiting his devotees. An international dad, circa 2014 or 1899. An old ghost, crowding the living out of the frame.

INSTEAD OF CONFRONTING THE ARTISTS OF THE PHOTO SERIES they'd accepted, and confronting the worldview they'd tacitly complied with by agreeing to run that series, the editors made an easier decision—the journal pulled the plug on the whole project entirely.

This is the kind of thing that happens when people don't want to do decolonial work, and would rather, instead, run away—throw a black cloth over the problem, put a potted plant in front of the problem; keep calm and carry on, as they say in London, where I was living when this exchange took place, and where this journal is based.

When I was in London, I attended a graduate writing program where I spent perhaps one of the unhappiest and yet, equally, one of the most unremarkable years of my life: unhappy because I was a person of color in an institutionally racist and intellectually incurious program; unremarkable because I was a person of color in an institutionally racist and intellectually incurious program. Such places are not in short supply. It was the kind of program in which any pointed discussion of politics interwoven with aesthetics gets you branded as the Angry Brown Girl; the kind of program that emphasizes *analysis at the sentence level* (Me: "Okay, so *on the sentence level*, your writing doesn't think Mexicans are human"), the kind of program in which it is not only white men who uphold this impoverished aesthetic standard, but equally incurious white women and men of color, happy to sing the terrible song they've been taught.

Years later, I still remember one assignment in particular: we were asked to read two works by Henry James, *The Turn of the Screw* and *Daisy Miller*. I'd never really read Henry James before—those weird gaps in my American canon making themselves known—so I felt neutral-to-meh about the assignment. But then, from the moment I started reading *The Turn of the Screw*, I felt that visceral jolt that goes through any reader when she encounters a story that will be part of her own—that magnetic pull, not unlike meeting someone who makes the hairs stand up on your neck, someone you know will become a friend, a lover, an enemy; that lightning bolt of knowledge: *this will matter to me*.

To this day it remains one of my favorite stories about what storytelling, trauma, and being believed have to do with each other. *The Turn of the Screw* is a horror story; a ghost story; a wild genre headfuck in its structure and its premise; a story about a mystery, that in its own telling restores and revives the mystery it is ostensibly about; and also one of the most wrenching and original narratives about child endangerment—and adult harm—I'd ever read. Original most of all for its categorical refusal to provide the kind of reliable answers and explanations that, in other stories, can: banish ghosts, close doors to the haunted attic, relegate the past to the past. Instead, so much of its eerie, dooming force is in accretion: the slow gathering together of facts, memories, stories, rumors, gossip, terrors, biases, like a puzzle you don't even realize you're putting together, until you start to see that distorted chopped-up puzzle face for what it is—even if you don't yet know *what it is*, or how to name it. The way the story builds its world, the burgeoning miasma of dread and terror the reader suddenly finds herself suffocated in, feels the way the best horror stories feel: like one is both touching the alien skin of another world while also, crucially, glimpsing a buried, unspoken truth of our own world. I came to class vibrating with the need, the passion really, to discuss it.

The first thing the instructor—a white woman—said to the class was something along the lines of, *So who did the reading?*

Before anyone in the class could respond with more than groans and eye rolls, she continued: *Oh, I know, I know, right? You know what*—conspiratorial giggle—*this week, it's totally fine if you haven't read the assignment. God, his sentences are so long and difficult, aren't they?* To the relieved agreement and laughter from everyone in the room, the tension swiftly deflated, like air from a popped balloon.

I remember sinking in my seat. This was the second semester of my program, and I'd already spent the entire first semester doing the thing that all kids of color are taught to do: work twice as hard, be twice as good. Besides doing the customary Angry Brown Girl labor, of course, I'd still spent every workshop poring through my classmates' writing and trying to provide the kind of close line reading I'd been diligently trained to do during my (far more rewarding and rigorous) undergraduate education at Berkeley, a practice which was almost entirely absent from the instruction here, directed as the program's pedagogy was toward mainly older middle-class white hobbyists uninterested in the art of reading so much as in the art of Being Famous Writers One Day. For nearly every assignment we were given, I metabolized the work like the knowledge was a fortification (and it was, really, the way every student of color who dares to criticize a canonical work feels compelled to be more educated about that canonical work than anyone else in the room, simply to justify their critique): I not only read assigned pieces multiple times, I brought in related research to bolster my interpretations. I was, in other words, a Virgo in a classroom.

Until that day. That day, I wanted to fight for *The Turn of the Screw*, for the importance of doing the work of reading it, but by then I was also bone-fucking-tired; tired of doing twice the work, and getting so little back. Tired of doing the shadow homework that is always assigned to marginalized students in settings like these: having to prepare for the class, and then *having to prepare for the class*—do that extracurricular emotional and intellectual labor of fighting the latent racism and sexism in these largely white liberal spaces, while also trying to be a student, in an institution. Something went dead in me then—that moment of being told, once and for all, that people here didn't care about reading. Not really. For the rest of the semester I barely said a word, and gave up on talking, sharing, or really, even hearing. When I turned in my graduate manuscript, I privately promised myself that I wouldn't turn in the novel I had begun working on the summer before the program began—a draft of the novel that would become *America Is Not the Heart*. I didn't trust the people at the institution with reading that book; they'd been crystal clear about the kind of critical reading they were capable of. Instead, for my graduating thesis I turned in a collection of old blog posts, mashed together, somehow, into an essay collection about London. It was a deliberately self-protective move—I knew that universities often kept copies of students' final theses in their archives, and I didn't want the work that would become my first novel to be owned by them in any capacity. I certainly don't feel I owe its creation to that program, except in the way that a whetstone sharpens a knife; my grim time there honed me for the work I knew I wanted to do, the kind of reading I wanted to practice, diametrically opposed to what I had experienced in its classrooms.

I also know that my experience is far from unique; I am not the only student of color to have been laughably underserved by an institution supposedly devoted to her education—multiple other writers of color who attended the same program have shared with me similarly depressing stories of both incidents of racism in their workshops, and institutional indifference and neglect when it came to addressing that racism in any substantial way. When I hear these stories, I think back on that failure to even lead a proper discussion about *The Turn of the Screw*: people who don't want to engage with the work of reading, who can't even bother to impart to their students why reading might be vital, who can't even bother to create the space for students to learn and grow and *do the work*—is this

what our reading instruction (let alone our writing instruction) should look like?

THE SCHOOL TO WHICH THAT WRITING PROGRAM BELONGS,
Goldsmiths, part of the University of London, has a global reputation as a left-leaning public institution; that reputation was
one of the things that most attracted me to it (the only graduate
writing program I've ever applied to). It boasted as its faculty
and alumni artists and thinkers who had been influential in my
own work, people like the writer Bernardine Evaristo, whose
decolonial classicist novel-in-verse *The Emperor's Babe* was one
of the first books I read and loved upon moving to England; or
the feminist philosopher Sara Ahmed, whose writing on "feminist killjoys" I devoured in 2011 during the two months I lived
in an ex-council flat in Govan, Glasgow, learning to make ex-
perimental films with Digital Desperados, a filmmaking workshop organized for and by largely queer women of color.

Not long after I graduated from the program, I learned
that Sara Ahmed had resigned from Goldsmiths in protest at
the university's utter failure to address the sexual harassment
of students by faculty members. In a post still available on her
website, Ahmed wrote:

> In the last three years many people both within my own
> college and at other universities have talked to me about

their experience of sexual harassment. I began to realize something through these conversations: that there have been many cases of sexual harassment in universities, but there is no public record of these cases. They have vanished without a trace. No one knows about them except for the people directly affected. How do these cases disappear without a trace? Almost always: because they are resolved with the use of confidentiality clauses. The clauses do something: they work to protect organisational reputation; no one gets to know about what happened. They most often protect the harassers: there is no blemish on their records; they can go on to other jobs. But they also leave those who experienced harassment even more isolated than they were before (harassment is already isolating). They leave silence. And silence can feel like another blow; a wall that is not experienced by those not directly affected (because silence is often not registered as silence unless you hear what is not being said).

Much of the intellectual inertia and readerly inattention that permeated the writing program I was part of was consistently, conspicuously located: inertia and inattention, especially, when it came to stories about marginalized people, and in particular victims of sexual assault. When we were assigned Teju Cole's *Open City*, we were encouraged by our male professor of color to focus only on the "use of language" (that vaguest and most widely used of phrases), and no room was given to discuss the disturbing—and yet markedly muted—scene in which a young woman confronts the novel's protagonist and reminds him that he sexually assaulted her when they were teenagers. When a white male professor assigned a passage from Rousseau's *Confessions* in which Rousseau describes sharing a young sex worker—described in the English translation as a "little girl who . . . remained at everyone's disposal"— between two of his other friends, writing, "we all three went in turn into the next room with the little girl, who did not know whether to laugh or cry," the brief discussion in class centered on narration style ("use of language" rearing its ugly head again). When that same professor assigned us a passage from Kathryn Harrison's 1997 memoir *The Kiss*, in which she describes a sexual affair with her father, whom she met at age twenty, we were asked to discuss the use of memory in nonfiction while commenting on a scene in which the narrator describes falling asleep at "the sight of [her father] naked. . . . In the years to come, I won't be able to remember even one instance of our lying together. I'll have a composite, generic memory. I'll know that he was always on top and that I always lay still, as still as if I had, in truth, fallen from a great height"— with the male professor's framing of the discussion bordering on the politely prurient, with no discussion of Harrison's passage being a textbook example of dissociation, a common PTSD symptom in particular for survivors of sexual abuse.

When we were assigned a piece about the Philippines, it was the infamous (at least to students of Philippine and Filipinx

American studies) tragedy-porn fluff piece by white journalist James Fenton, and during class it became patently obvious that this essay was a regular assignment by a white teacher who was not used to having Filipinx students in class (no thought for the unexpected reader, here). I responded the following class by bringing in a copy of "James Fenton's Slideshow," Benedict Anderson's equally famous, acerbic, anticolonial rebuttal to Fenton. (This, predictably, went over like a lead balloon.) Fenton famously wrote a defense of classical conductor Robert King, who in 2007 was convicted of sexually abusing five minors. King was sentenced to three years and nine months in prison; Fenton wrote of his relief at the fact that the judge's relatively lenient ruling meant King would not be forbidden from working with children in the future. "To be debarred for life from working with the male treble voice would have been a harsh fate," Fenton wrote. "I strongly believe that when our most distinguished artists are in such terrible situations—whether or not they brought it on themselves—we should offer them some kind of support, not because, as artists, they deserve a better treatment than anyone else, but simply because we have so much to thank them for."

THERE IS NOTHING WRONG, IN THEORY, WITH HAVING BEEN AS-signed any of these passages, or to have had the discussions we had about them—discussions about narration, about memory, about language. But when those discussions so clearly and repeatedly avoid any discussion of these works that does not fall under the umbrella of what passes for supposedly neutral (which is to say, determinedly apolitical) literary interpretation, then "literary interpretation" comes to seem like little more than a smokescreen—or more pertinently, it seems like the confidentiality clauses Ahmed criticizes in her resignation letter, which routinely protect abusers, leaving victims of abuse isolated and muzzled. A commitment to upholding a particular type of readerly silence, from a particular type of readerly perspective.

These silences are intersectional, following the term coined by leading Black feminist legal scholar Kimberlé Williams Crenshaw (another thinker whose work I would mention in class, to absolute crickets from fellow students, except for one white student who said, "I thought intersectionality came from queer theory")—the white supremacy, misogyny, and classism that characterized so much of what called itself literary interpretation in this program were inextricably intertwined; drank deeply from the same well, with each oppression generously feeding the next. It was the school of literary interpretation that says white neocolonial journalists can tell us more about the Philippines and its diaspora (let alone about essay writing) than writers like Gina Apostol or Dylan Rodríguez or Catherine Ceniza Choy; the school of literary interpretation that says our readerly focus should be trained on important men and their fine sentences, and not the women-shaped detritus left in their great wake. It was the tepid school of literary interpretation that valued things like *silence* and *mystery* and especially *indeterminacy* (that golden calf of contemporary, sometimes protofascist, sometimes neolibertarian, philosophy) when it came to selectively reading and protecting the work of certain authors, by not interrogating their self-servingly indeterminate descriptions (and tacit defenses) of sexual assault—yet would not think to ask students to engage with the complicated, devastating (and in many ways unresolvable) silences and mysteries and indeterminacies that a book like *The Turn of the Screw* asks us to bear witness to. It was the school of literary interpretation that, by its deliberate omissions, teaches us how not to read, *what* not to read—what we ought to let perish in silence.

"When there is no official word by an organisation," Ahmed wrote in her resignation post, "it is not just that no one knows what happened; no one has to know. You are giving individuals permission not to know."

And just as the photographs in *Dad Is Gone* aren't actually interested in the supposed subject of their photos, this school of interpretation isn't actually interested in interpretation at all—not in the true risks of engagement that harness our bodies, our intellects, and our souls when we leave ourselves open to a work of art. Certainly the teacher who let us off the hook about *The Turn of the Screw* wasn't interested in those risks, or that labor. It's a school of interpretation that ignores entirely what the Marxist writer John Berger—who left his native England for a small commune in the French Alps in the sixties, and gained notoriety for giving half of his 1972 Booker Prize win-

nings to the Black Panthers—once called in an essay about
the queer Italian filmmaker Pier Paolo Pasolini "the ubiquitous
demands of reality"; demands "far too precious and too tough
to abandon":

> *The demand in a way a shawl was worn. A young man's face.*
> *In a street full of people demanding less injustice. In the laugh-*
> *ter of their expectations and the recklessness of their jokes.*
> *From this came [Pasolini's] rage of endurance.*

"REALITY IS ALL WE HAVE TO LOVE" HAS ALWAYS BEEN A COM-
plicated line for me to live with—though live with it I have. I've
turned Berger's line around and around in my head for years,
the way one works a tough piece of gristle in the mouth. For
someone who loved and still loves fantasy, mystery, science
fiction, ghosts, monsters, dwende, diwatas, kapres, engkantos,
every syncretized demon and every major and minor god from
all my people's many otherworldly worlds—for someone who
grew up in a diasporic climate of silences and mysteries and
half-stories, and therefore has long protected and nurtured our
right to silences and mysteries and half-stories, our human
right to honor all the unspoken and unspeakable things in our
lives—it's a difficult line: reality is all we have to love.

Berger knew that the presumed binary between the real
and the imaginary was a false one; it was not reality *as opposed
to fantasy* that he was honoring in this line. And not real*ism*,

either, as a moral or as an artifice and aesthetic—but: reality. The reality of our lives, the material realness of them—in the world, and to ourselves. In this light, *The Turn of the Screw*, like every ghost story, is also a story about reality—"a reply to the vertigo of nothingness," as Berger describes the work of Vincent van Gogh in his 1983 essay "The Production of the World," which is also a line that could describe every horror story ever written, and any person who has ever tried to speak about their experience of sexual assault.

It becomes unsettlingly evident that in the absence of anything resembling justice, an artist's instinctive respect for silence, mystery, and indeterminacy—the parts of our lives that necessarily and often indefinitely remain diffuse, inexpressible, and elusive; indeed, indefinite—can be endlessly malleable, exploitable, to be subsumed in that "vertigo of nothingness," so that the intellectual and emotional recognition of and respect for, yes, silence, mystery, and indeterminacy can just as swiftly be manipulated to protect the powerful and estrange the vulnerable, keeping a cloud of unknowing around the former, and a cloud of unknowability around the latter, trapping them all in a mystery, a confidentiality clause, a *Turn of the Screw* for all times.

"Reality is not a given: it has to be continually sought out, held—I am tempted to say *salvaged*," Berger continued. "Reality is inimical to those with power."

There's a Berger short story, published in *The New Yorker* in 2001, called "Woven, Sir" that reminds me, in a way, of *The*

Turn of the Screw. It's a short story in which Berger's adult narrator describes being in Madrid, waiting for a friend at the Ritz Hotel (with classic Berger observations around the sensual realities of class and wealth, as in his impression, in the hotel, of "the deafness of money . . . not an empty silence, but a silence of seclusion—like that of the depth of an ocean. . . . The seclusion, here, prompts me to remember the clamor of shanty towns and the everlasting racket in prisons")—while also, simultaneously, recounting his own childhood memories of the outsize influence of an older man in his life: a man whose last name is Tyler, whom the adult narrator believes he is encountering, in the present, in the hotel. As a reader you're never entirely sure if he's truly seeing Tyler there in the lobby, in the present. Other hotel guests, too, get named after mythical figures—for isn't that who Tyler is, for Berger's narrator: a mythical figure?—one, Circe, another Pasiphaë, another Telegonus, but soon enough a reader realizes that the point isn't to know for sure whether or not Tyler is there, in Madrid, in the present. In every way that matters, *he is there, in Madrid, in the present.* The narrator remembers something his mother once told him: "The dead don't stay where they are buried. . . . You may meet the dead anywhere."

Woven, the story is, with the past and the present, so there is no divide, grammatically or structurally, between the two time-spaces, and the reader lives them both, sometimes in the same paragraph; the narrator waiting for his friend Juan as an adult and hearing Tyler's voice in the hotel lounge.

Tyler was the narrator's tutor in a place called the Green Hut, "roofed with corrugated iron that was painted green. It had a door that fitted badly and three small windows. There was no heating and no water. . . . This hut on the edge of a field was our school. Nobody, however, referred to it as such, because Tyler insisted that he was not a schoolmaster but a tutor."

It was here that Berger's narrator says he first learned to write. We are in a primal memory, of a primal place. But soon the picture of this makeshift classroom—in which the narrator is joined by five other pupils, all "coached . . . to get into what were considered good schools," "making it possible to pass me off as a gentleman boy"—starts to come into focus: it's also a place where the six young children suffer from the cold, where they get chilblains and red noses; where the narrator can't remember how or where they shat, but does remember "vomiting there once"; where they are subject to the terse, half-haughty, half-tender catechisms of an adult man whose power over the children in his care will mark the narrator's entire life. It's important to note that the asymmetrical dynamic between Tyler and the pupils is one defined not only by their teacher-student relation, but by the divide of class—these are not the children of the powerful, with their tickets to Eton already set in stone; Tyler's tutelage is their ticket to class mobility. His lessons are in essence a kind of ad hoc training center for families circumventing the British schooling system—which is to say, the British class system. He teaches them "writing," but writing according to Tyler also has everything to do with class propriety and order: "Writing involves spelling, straight lines, spacing, words leaning the right way, margins, size, legibility, keeping the nib clean, never making blots, and demonstrating on each page of the exercise book the value of good manners." Values clean as a priest's.

"You never stop being interested, that's where the trouble begins," Tyler scolds Berger's narrator, sounding like every white teacher I ever had growing up, before gruffly ordering the child to wrap the end of Tyler's scarf around himself to keep warm and keep quiet. Most of Berger's narrator's recollections of Tyler consist of the older man dressing him down for some fault or another, with the dressing-down its own form of gruff affection: his inability to pronounce Spanish properly, his inability to saw straight, his inability to spell. Berger's narrator says both he and Tyler knew "the hopelessness of the project"—getting the boy to one day pass for a gentleman—"and this was our secret, which made us, in a strange way, accomplices." Treated (as some adults do treat children) as if he is older than his years, Berger's narrator remembers, during a very cold winter, mending the adult Tyler's glasses with sticking plaster: "I was seven years old," he says simply. (In *Here Is Where We Meet*, published four years after "Woven, Sir," the short story appears again, slightly revised, this time under the title "Madrid"—and this time, the child-narrator says, "I was six years old.")

And when Berger's child-narrator lingers after class in Tyler's private rented rooms ("from where later I caught the bus to mine"), intimate enough to be looking at a photo by the older man's bedside, the child thinks: "Nobody can help him, I told myself, as I sat in the wicker chair before his gas fire, rubbing my chilblains and eating my toast and honey. He's too old and he has too many hairs growing out of his body."

Secrets and complicity; hopelessness and tenderness; an adult's body and a child's memory. Here is a grievous portrait, grievous most of all in its unforgetting attention; grievous most of all in its kindness. This is what a formative influence is, after all: to be influenced. To be formed.

Much like *The Turn of the Screw*, Berger's story never makes it clear if this tale of indelible adult influence, of an adult specter in a child's life looming, eternal, is also a story of abuse. We know that "Tyler demanded work and obedience; the smallest sign of what he called slackness would be punished by a rap over the knuckles with a knotted yew branch that hung on a hook beside the cupboard where he kept the rules and exercise books." Yet in Tyler's living quarters, where the child-narrator is invited after school, "lessons were out of the question . . . slackness was ignored and he demanded only quiet and company." There is throughout the narrator's portrait of Tyler a persistent entanglement of registers: a preternaturally lucid and seemingly objective recollection of facts that, nevertheless, begin to ring slightly off-key in their accumulation— along with a residual respect, and a lingering, loving, loyalty.

Of the circumstances surrounding Tyler's mysterious death, "a story about a gas fire, or a house burning down, or an accident with a car left running in a garage with the doors shut," Berger's adult narrator chooses to remain in ignorance: "I have forgotten the details because they suggested that the methodical, tidy, gruffly shy man, who believed that quality mattered more than anything else in the world, died—or even put an end to his days—through indifference or carelessness." In the later, "Madrid" version of the story, Berger adds one succinct line to this paragraph: "The details are better forgotten."

In a 2016 discussion about "Woven, Sir" in *The New Yorker*, author Ben Lerner and editor Deborah Treisman discuss the story at length, especially illuminating Berger's deft hand with loss, the unspoken, and its relation to storytelling. Lerner characterizes it movingly: "There's a real relationship between the communicable and the incommunicable, and that it's important for him that the person who teaches him how to write also teaches him that there are some things that can't be talked about, and can't be expressed, and can't be corrected . . . there's an opaque spot at the heart of a story."

Treisman eventually reveals that the book jacket for the collection in which the story appears describes Tyler as "a pedophile schoolteacher." Both Treisman and Lerner express genuine shock. "*Really*," Lerner says. "I didn't get that at all while reading the story," Treisman says. "That changes things," Lerner remarks. "Well, does it or doesn't it," Treisman replies. "Was it just someone who didn't know, who was writing the jacket copy? It's a very strange thing. . . . There's a lot that's unspoken here, but you don't get the sense"—who is the presumed "you" here?—"that it's abuse that's going unspoken." The two tentatively discuss the fact that the story does include scenes in which Berger's narrator is in Tyler's private rented rooms: "I mean there's a lonely man and a young boy—it's not a relationship that would exist now, for sure, without lots of suspicion," Lerner points out. "If it is a story about abuse . . . then it is an incredibly non-judgmental and impersonal depiction of that relationship. There's nothing in the prose that makes me think Berger wants to write about a psychic wound he suffered." "And you wouldn't imagine calling an abuser methodical or tidy or shy," Treisman reasons. "It certainly isn't a denunciation, whatever else is happening," Lerner adds.

Both are entirely right, of course. The opacity at the heart of Berger's story is one that refracts, a frosted pane through which things can—for those who may themselves intimately recognize (perhaps the better word is *remember*) their contours—be just as easily glimpsed, and just as easily missed. Both stories are the story. What does bear some questioning is the subtle implication that the only way to write about abuse or trauma is through the courtroom logic of testimonial and confession, through the sensational drama of exposing a psychic wound (not a particularly English practice, in any case), or through the finiteness and finality of judgment and denunciation. And not also, for example: art.

"HE HAD A GREAT GIFT FOR LOOKING AWAY AND AVOIDING questions," Berger's narrator says of Tyler, very early in the story.

A YEAR AFTER WRITING "WOVEN, SIR," BERGER WROTE IN HIS essay on Pasolini: "What we have chosen to forget . . . such things often begin in childhood. Pasolini forgot nothing from his childhood—hence the constant co-existence in what he seeks of pain and fun. We are made ashamed of our forgetting."

"Woven, Sir" is a short story about an adult man remembering a childhood tutor, which is also a time travel story, which is also a ghost story, which is also a horror story. Berger's narrator looks at (not necessarily *back* at) this part of his life with what Berger calls Pasolini's "unflinching lucidity," a compassion and clarity that come not out of the story's exonerating commitment to its own opacity or indeterminacy, but, rather, its vulnerable, capacious, moral attention to all of the, yes, *mysterious* and indeterminate elements that make a childhood a childhood; a teacher, a teacher—a life, a life: "experiences which both question and answer leave aside." Like *The Turn of the Screw*, it is a story in part about the ordinary opacity of childhood and memory—about the making of an adult, and most of all, the making of an artist—whose force, too, is in accretion:

the slow gathering together of facts, memories, stories, rumors, gossip, terrors, biases, like a puzzle one doesn't realize one is putting together, until one starts to see that distorted chopped-up puzzle face for what it is—even if one doesn't yet know *what it is*, or how to name it. A puzzle—or rather, a textile; the word *text*, after all, coming from the Latin *texere*, to weave: "woven, sir." It bears remembering, too, that the main feature of a screw is its thread. And like *The Turn of the Screw*, "Woven, Sir" is most of all a story about reality—or rather, it is many stories about reality: woven, threaded together.

"The man who taught me to write," Berger's child-narrator says of Tyler, "was the first person to make me aware of irreparable loss." The story, in a gesture of forgiveness I cannot quite believe we deserve—though what, in the end, does forgiveness have to do with the deserving—trusts us enough not to distinguish whose loss.

What is it, then, to love reality? Not just to love reality, but to know that reality is *all* we have to love? What does that reality, and the love it implores, have to do with art, reading, classrooms, confidentiality clauses, abusers, or, indeed, justice? What does reality have to do with paying attention to the way people who are not equally listened to—people who have less relational power, like the poor with the wealthy, like a child with an adult, like a student with a teacher—tell their story: the stuttered labor of it, the time skips and inconsistencies, the withheld or redacted details, the difficult, dissonant sound of someone trying to live with, and perhaps even bear, their past? What does reality have to do with coming to the labor of storytelling at all—and especially, of imagining a writing in which, contrary to Tyler's lessons, the nib does not remain clean; a writing where the author makes blots?

What does reality have to do, in turn, with pointing out the places where silence can also be silencing, mystery can also be deliberate mystification, and indeterminacy can also be a determined effort to keep specific parts of ourselves illiterate; to keep specific parts of our lives illegible? "[Pasolini's] dismissal of the hypocrisies, half-truths and pretenses of the greedy and powerful is total because they breed and foster ignorance, which is a form of blindness towards reality," Berger wrote. "Also because they shit on memory, including the memory of language itself, which is our first heritage."

What does reality have to do, in other words, with reading a story like this? Because the conservative literary presumption says that if we are to read "Woven, Sir" as a formally inventive story about formative adult influence *and also* about formative adult abuse, we are politicizing, and therefore intellectually *reducing*, the story: reducing it to a tawdry tale about "a pedophile schoolteacher"; reducing it to a mere psychodrama about British repression and pedagogy and hierarchy, philistinely effacing its intellectual subtleties and mythological references and poetic omissions and literary elegances to little more than the evening news. The way a student bringing up rape in a discussion of Rousseau supposedly reduces our analysis of Rousseau's language; the way bringing up Benedict

Anderson's rebuttal to James Fenton supposedly reduces our discussion of Fenton's journalism (if indeed that is the word for it). It's of a piece with the train of thought that thinks engaging with identity politics in art is necessarily a diminishment of its artistic quality, because our working concept of identity politics rarely ever includes those whose identities, politics, and pasts get to remain unmarked, and thus are never seen as potentially contaminating (or, indeed, contaminated). But why can't "Woven, Sir" vibrate, tautly, in the tension of all those things? It can; it does. *We* do.

I know there is a material difference between the politicized intellectual silence of a writing classroom or a literary reader and an institution's bureaucratic silence in the face of widespread sexual harassment of its students. They are not the same violence—but they are kindred. One silences the art; one silences the person who might make that art. And when the two are combined and given institutional power and status, those violences become environmental: they become a culture. Then it falls to us to live in that culture—which, it may come as a surprise to some, does not have to be a horror story, in which each silence engenders and deepens another; in which each reply-less nothing, vertiginously, circumscribes another.

"The voices speak out," Berger wrote of the voice-overs in Pasolini's *La Rabbia*, "not to cap an argument, but because it would be shameful, given the length of human experience and pain, if what they had to say was not said. Should it go unsaid, the capacity for being human would be slightly diminished."

It falls on us to live in that culture and (though for some select few, the more precise and indeed preferred word may still be *or*; those who are safe enough to have a choice in the matter) to dismantle it: to take it apart, piece by piece, and expose its carefully curated silences, concealments, and confidentiality clauses to light. To revoke that culture's too-long-enjoyed permission not to know. Most of all, to give up *our* permission not to know—not to know that reality, which is the enemy of the powerful, and which is all there is for us to love: there where loving is a kind of knowing, and knowing, a kind of loving.

AUTOBIOGRAPHY
IN ASIAN FILM,
OR WHAT WE
TALK ABOUT WHEN
WE TALK ABOUT
REPRESENTATION

After that I had a sleep-dream
in which I grew a bright-green face;
granny-smith hued, high polished.
And even though I was green,
I was The Most Beautiful Woman in the World.
I had the best hair
and even did humanitarian work.
I was interviewed
about both things,
each night, for TV.

RACHEL LONG, "APPLES"

Why do I watch movies? I want to feel in love.

ISABEL SANDOVAL

1.

The first and unfortunately not the last Wes Anderson film I ever saw was *The Life Aquatic*. It is, it seems to me, mostly about hapless white sons and hapless white dads and hapless white people having mostly hapless white feelings, an exceedingly popular genre deserving of more attenuated criticism than it enjoys, in particular by those who might resonate with its highly specific identity politics. Halfway through the film, cartoonish stock villains in the form of Filipino pirates suddenly appear, seizing control of the ship with machine guns and taking its crew hostage. In Mark Browning's book *Wes Anderson: Why His Movies Matter*, Browning writes that these "undistinguished"—his own wording—pirates provide "pure cannon fodder."

Bill Murray's character, the oceanographer Captain Zissou, a kind of fan fiction Jacques Cousteau, never refers to Tagalog by name, even when a "bond company stooge" aboard the ship, played by Bud Cort, speaks Tagalog, and begins to interpret between the pirates and the crew.

"Bill speaks *their language*," Zissou marvels to his cohorts, like he's witnessing interspecies contact. "What are they saying, Billy?" Tagalog is the third most widely spoken foreign language in the United States, after Spanish and Mandarin Chinese.

Bud Cort's character says: "Apparently they're taking a hostage. Obviously they've chosen [Owen Wilson's character] Ned." Then his face goes stricken.

"Uh, now that they've found out that I speak Filipino . . . they seem to be changing their minds."

Eventually, the Filipino pirates are killed off by Zissou, who heroically breaks out of restraints to save his crew, guns ablaze. I watched the DVD of the film back in California, back when you still rented DVDs, back before I knew the joy of the internet spoiler, and thought I was in for some gentle white comedy to wind down an otherwise pleasant but unremarkable evening. I hadn't been expecting to see Bill Murray gleefully push a Filipino boy off a boat, then turn to shoot another one in the neck, so that the pirate's machete, now held by a lifeless hand, would fall down to slice into his white captive's shoulder; collateral damage. The only creature among the Filipino pirates that Murray's character shows any affection to is one pirate's dog, whom he names Cody, and whom he is desolate to part with when the hostage scene draws to an end.

One dead Filipino pirate is left on the ship. "Wrap this stiff in a tablecloth," Bill Murray's character says in an unexpected moment of brusque naval honor. "We're gonna bury him at sea."

They begin an improvised ceremony for the dead pirate, with Willem Dafoe's character reading a passage from the Bible. Yet they're interrupted by the captain's nemesis, played by Jeff Goldblum, calling to them from an approaching ship, in response to a previously sent distress signal. Zissou hurriedly orders his crew to make the ship look presentable.

"What about this guy?" Willem Dafoe's character asks, pointing to the dead Filipino they're in the middle of burying.

Notions of naval honor forgotten, Zissou says: "Just throw him over the other side."

2.

I still remember watching Mira Nair's *Monsoon Wedding* when it came out. I must have been fourteen or fifteen. A landmark film in Asian American cinema, the film follows the drama of an extended family coming together on the occasion of an enormous wedding, following the various narrative arcs of Pimmi and Lalit, mother and father of the bride, anxious over the complexities of orchestrating such a huge family gathering; the bride, Aditi, contending with the uncertainties inherent in an arranged marriage; the bride's cousin Ria, struggling with the trauma that this family reunion has resurfaced; the tender, budding romance of wedding planner P.K. and family maid Alice.

A writer much more knowledgeable in the region than me can get into what might be problematic regarding class and power in that movie; I've thought about it but don't think I'm equipped to write about it myself, not being versed in the particularities of the community. What I'm thinking about here today happens around its side narrative (in this case, it's fitting that it's a side narrative, as that's also structurally how abuse often happens in a family—as a side narrative): specifically, the story of Tej, the family's wealthy benefactor, and his history of molestation, specifically with the family's adoptive daughter, Ria, and that abuse's radiating effect on the family. It's about the culture of silencing that crops up around this kind of abuse within a family, and especially how much that culture of silencing is perpetuated by women in collusion with patriarchy.

When the climactic confrontation with her abuser, Tej, happens, the adopted daughter/niece, Ria, says these words to her family, the family that doesn't want to believe her story: "You don't want to believe me? Then fine. I'm not a part of this." Her voice breaks. "I'm not part of you—"

Postconfrontation, her adoptive father/uncle, Lalit, begs Ria not to leave the family. "Everything will break without you," he pleads. Many of us know intimately the pressure of that plea; many women know that their silence is precisely what holds entire families and communities together. Many of us stay, and instead we're the ones who break; many of us leave, in lieu of speaking out. Ria's face during this scene, when Lalit cups her face, knows intimately the future of compromise, silence, and incomplete forgiveness that's being asked of her. It's on her face when they have to take family wedding photos, and the unknowing photographer asks her to sit at the knees of her abuser. The shutter of the camera catches each movement of Ria's face, from smiling performative compliance to deep pain and grief.

Ria wants to be a writer. Early in the film, before the abuse has been revealed, there's a scene at a prewedding get-together, in which Tej gets up, a little drunk, and announces with great paternal warmth that if Ria wants to go to study in America to be a writer, he'll fund her entire education. Ria's face collapses in on itself. She begins to cry, and Lalit mistakes her tears for some mixture of happiness, and melancholy at the absence of her dead father. But we can see that Ria knows what it means: that Tej's influence will follow her everywhere—that not even in the space of art she's claimed for herself can she be safe or free. And when Tej is finally, finally driven from the party, the house, and the family, it's also a case of removing his direct power as the benefactor—malefactor—in her budding life as a writer; pulling the stubborn tendrils of that abuse out, root by buried root.

Many of us know that it doesn't always work out the way it does in *Monsoon Wedding*; many of us have left people to whom we've said, "I'm not a part of you," and absolutely no one has called us back to say otherwise. Many of us have seen that our families rarely choose to break apart the community, just to save one woman from silence. There's that heartbreaking moment, so familiar, when an older woman (I think it's Tej's wife, if I remember correctly) in the family hastily suggests that unmarried women say all kinds of things, make up all kinds of fantasies. And later, when Lalit has finally made the decision to believe Ria and banish Tej from the family, that same woman murmurs, a conspirator's murmur, a turned-a-blind-eye-for-years murmur: "For such a small thing . . ."

3.

I was in a situation almost identical to Ria's when I was a very young girl, also with someone older and important and central in our family; someone who lived with us, and whose banishment would mean an essential and cataclysmic rupture in the fundament of our family. This person was not, however, a wealthy benefactor like Tej, but instead, deeply economically vulnerable and dependent on our shelter, someone who had for a long period of time been undocumented in America, which meant that to banish him would produce an intersectional devastation, one that would cut across multiple lifelines and lovelines of our family's hand. Many families like mine housed a revolving door of vulnerable relatives and almost relatives, and relied upon this distinctly nonnuclear family structure to build community, to create safety nets, to care for children when so many adults in the family worked sixteen-hour days and night shifts. It's a protective social structure that also sometimes functions to protect abusers, because to not do so would be to condemn already at-risk individuals to further precarity, whether homelessness, the prison system, or death.

But my mother and father kicked him out of the house. And for all the difficulties I have occasionally had with my mother, whose self-immolating work ethic and survival drive went hand in hand with a volcanic temper I once desperately feared and resented but now know to be due to the immense stress of her labor as a nurse with sixteen-hour (sometimes longer) work days, along with the PTSD and attendant scarcity trauma of her youth in poverty—I have never forgotten that she drove this decision, a decision that made my father, quite literally, choose between two of his children. And he drove this decision, too, and made it—with true conviction, and true grief. All this to say: when I wrote earlier that I was raised with a furnace of immutable and indestructible pride, I don't say those words lightly; I say them because destruction has a real face—and it has come for me, again and again, like an early reaper who will not take no for an answer.

Sometimes, that early reaper came very, very close; and yes, it took some things for itself, forever—and left some things, as Alexander Chee puts it in *How to Write an Autobiographical Novel*. I am changed. But I was not destroyed, because the people who loved me read my story, believed it, and changed the world I lived in because of it.

Things were not perfect: that person came back, slowly, into our lives, tramping through that weedy, high grass of redemption, and I spent a long, long time trying to forgive; trying even to forget. Trying to make restitution happen, because I do believe in it, and so, to their credit, did my parents. But three are not always enough, it turns out, to make restitution in a large family truly stick. The person who was banished, and who after almost a decade of absence returned, never truly atoned for what he did, or even really looked me in the eye to acknowledge that these acts, or the years of silence that followed them, even occurred—though their weight passed between us at every encounter: the ones where we were eating together at Applebee's or the local pho joint; laughing together at our kitchen table; smiling in pictures at his summer Tahoe wedding to the white Chicana woman I loved more than him and who eventually left him, like every other woman in his life (he never had children); even at his hospital bed, which I have only visited once, where he is being treated for stage 4 metastatic urothelial cancer as I write this.

And this is the gift I'm giving to myself now: to not be there. To not bear witness to his eventual death. To not console him, or be with those who would console him: my other brothers and sister, my nieces and nephews, my grandnephews. To not pray that our thousandfold gods, large and small, protect him and keep him here; to not send him off with goodwill into the path of our bygones; to not ask our ancestors to bless him, and carry him, and look upon him kindly. To refuse, in this knife-shining instance, to offer any form of succor, comfort, or indeed, love. To know that—unlike Antigone, perhaps myth's most famous younger sister—I do not owe it to him to unlock the house of the dead, there where our father will be waiting. To be, in other words, and finally, a bad sister.

There are people in my family who are currently wondering about my absence during this time of grief and mutual support in our clan, especially since at twenty-two I was famously the person who was at my father's hospital bed every single day until the day he died, a few months before he would have seen me graduate from college. I was also famously the person who demanded that everyone, *everyone* in our family be at his bedside; the person who raged against siblings and cousins—even, on occasion, my mother—when their absence felt palpable, when they didn't come to keep vigil, stand sentinel; when I, cruelly, found their emotional resilience not up to par with the standards I'd laid out. I was the person who had once been known to Do the Most, in the complete sense of the phrase, to keep our family together, while the blazing sun of it was about to go out forever—or so it felt at the time.

I have no resolutions, nor any half-conclusions that might help me close this chapter in my life; that's just not how any of this works. I do know that I feel freer, today, than I did before—freer (if not fully freed) to never again be any brother's keeper. Freer to abandon that role, and abandon the place that figure carved out in my person, in my life, in my story. This is not to erase that place; nothing I ever do in this life will accomplish that. But to simply leave the grave untended—something I will have to stumble on, every now and then: in the middle of a laugh with my cousins, or a movie about siblings, or having to safeword out of a kiss with a man I love who has never, ever hurt me. Like living near the field where a mine once went off;

having to learn by heart how to trace a daily route around that place's quieted craters. Living with it, in other words. In whatever words there are that day.

4.

My favorite Asian male character onscreen—played by my favorite male actor of all time—is the character Lai Yiu-fai, played by Tony Leung Chiu-wai, in Hong Kong director Wong Kar-wai's late nineties film *Happy Together*. I've long said that it's Wong Kar-wai's best film, if only because there are only male characters in it, and so we escape the director's sometimes fetishistically romantic portrayal of women (I love many of the women in Wong Kar-wai's films deeply, but as I get older I wonder if I love them as icons of particular moods, more than as women with particular autonomy or depth outside their relation to men; but then, working through questions like this is also what reading is for). *Happy Together* has been my most beloved film for, it seems, almost half my life, to the point that I once made an hour-long essay film, half of which consisted of looping a single scene from *Happy Together* over and over while I added subtitles of my own text and commentary over the screen.

In the film, Tony Leung and Leslie Cheung Kwok-wing play a pair of fighting lovers in Buenos Aires, having outrun their tourist visas, in the era just before the Hong Kong handover. Leslie Cheung, who identified as bisexual—one of the few openly queer Asian actors we had, and pretty much the only other bisexual Asian I knew of growing up—is volcanically alive in his role as Lai Yiu-fai's erstwhile boyfriend Ho Po-wing: selfish, charismatic, petty, the future Big Ex to end all Big Exes; like the Big Boss at the end of a video game, but for heartbreak. His is a character whose gravitational pull drags your gaze toward him during every scene he enters. Ho Po-wing stuns, staggers, seduces. But I always loved Lai Yiu-fai.

That's an understatement. The truth is that there were years where I often found myself becoming Lai Yiu-fai. Like his character, I, too, once had operatically huge ruptures in love and life, and ended up licking my wounds in a foreign country, hesitating to call my family, the way Lai Yiu-fai hovers in phone booths and not-calls his father. And I, too, was taken by the character who shows up in the last third of the film, played by the Taiwanese actor Chang Chen. Chang Chen's character, also named Chang, slowly and carefully forms a tentative and ultimately healing flirtation and friendship with Lai Yiu-fai, who's still reeling after being destroyed by his unhappy love affair with Ho Po-wing. Chang and Lai Yiu-fai work together in the kitchen of a Chinese restaurant in Buenos Aires. They're in similar situations: both of them are stuck in Buenos Aires, their tourist visas having expired. They've both found work as cooks, though throughout the film, Lai Yiu-fai holds down other jobs: assisting as a tour guide for Chinese tourists and later, working in an abattoir, which he says suits him fine. The hours mean he works all night and sleeps all day; he's back on Hong Kong time, he realizes at some point in the film.

People often say Wong Kar-wai is a romantic filmmaker, particularly attentive to mood, and that's obviously true, but I've always thought he was a great filmmaker of labor, and in particular undocumented labor, affective labor, and what's often incompletely called crime. Which is not to say that these two descriptions are mutually exclusive—to be romantic, and to be concerned deeply with the life of labor—only that it's rarer to see them discussed as being mutually constructive, at least in Wong Kar-wai's work. The writer I can think of who talks about this relationship best is probably John Berger, whose radically compassionate attention to the marriage of labor (in particular, precarious, working-class labor under neoliberal capitalism) and love (in particular, sensual, embodied, life-remaking love) still startles me with the force and tenderness of its conviction—and yes, romance, especially in books like *To the Wedding* and *Lilac and Flag*.

I've been watching Wong Kar-wai's films since I was fourteen or so, and one of my biggest frustrations is that I can't remember the first time I saw *Happy Together*. I remember when I saw it for the first second time, which is to say, the first time I remembered having already seen it. It was in college, when I was nineteen—a graduate student instructor, Luis Ramos, who later became a friend, showed the film in a class he was teaching. When I saw it then, I knew I'd seen it before, probably on one of those illegal VCDs I used to buy from the Filipino grocery in my hometown, where you could get Asian films for cheap that you couldn't rent at Blockbuster. When I was a kid the only Asian films you could rent at our local Blockbuster were martial arts films, even though the town was majority Southeast Asian. Occasionally you'd find something sexy and confusing, like *In the Realm of the Senses* or that other one, sort of based on the old Sei Shōnagon novel, *The Pillow Book*, where, if I remember correctly, Ewan McGregor's skin gets turned into a book for his older Japanese male lover.

Wong Kar-wai's films always felt romantic to me, specifically in that they never really try to pretend that people don't fall in love, eat food, or act weird, while also being inextricably part of the sociopolitical economy of their universes. Especially the falling-in-love part. You could be historical, without having to be Historical; you could be an Asian girlfriend without being an Asian Girlfriend. I'd never been to Hong Kong, I didn't understand any Cantonese; but I recognized the way Tony Leung made soup in that kitchen.

You never know for sure if Chang Chen's character is gay, either. What you know about his character is that he had eye problems in his youth, and therefore cultivated a practice of listening to people in a super-heightened, super-sensitive, practically supernatural way. Even after a surgical procedure restored his eyesight, he tells Tony Leung's character, he never lost the habit of listening.

Happy Together was one of Chang Chen's first films. Later, he plays a similar character in Ang Lee's *Crouching Tiger, Hidden Dragon*: a desert bandit whose fidelity and purity of motive both attract and weigh heavily on Zhang Ziyi's character, who isn't ready to be loved so completely. He plays the responsible scoundrel, the honorable thief—the kind of man who walks away singing while you're taking a bath, so you can be alone while also knowing where the wall of his body is. The Japanese Taiwanese actor Takeshi Kaneshiro does the same thing for another character played by Zhang Ziyi, in Zhang Yimou's *House of Flying Daggers*, a film that I didn't especially care for, except for the part that's similar to what Chang Chen does in *Crouching Tiger, Hidden Dragon*. Takeshi Kaneshiro's character doesn't sing, but he flicks his sword to make a clanging sound, and it's the sound that acts as the wall for Zhang Ziyi's aloneness in the bath in this film. In both those scenes, I was seeing something I didn't know yet that I'd always wanted, always needed, a yearning in me I had yet to name: the erotic tenderness of a lover who protects the space around which you can be vulnerable, and therefore safe, and therefore free.

Now that I think about it, Chang Chen played a similar character yet again in Hou Hsiao-hsien's *Three Times*. Especially in the contemporary section of the film, when he falls in love with a young epileptic woman, played by the Taiwanese actress Shu Qi, who already has a girlfriend, but who falls in love with him right back. Had I ever before seen a nonsensationalist depiction of a romantic relationship between a bisexual woman and a straight cis man, one in which I could recognize the contours of my own life? This film was perhaps the first one. Shu Qi is known for her work in the films of director Hou Hsiao-hsien: beginning with *Millennium Mambo* (yes, that opening scene to the tune of Lim Giong's "A Pure Person" is one of the greatest cinematic moments of all time, and it definitely lives in my memory bank under the category Bi Awakenings) to the aforementioned *Three Times*, to Hou Hsiao-hsien's 2015 wuxia epic, *The Assassin*. A film which—there is no other way for me to say this—fucked me *all the way up*.

5.

From what I remember, most of the reviews of *The Assassin* center on its visual beauty, on its truly staggering array of landscape shots, on the way Hou Hsiao-hsien masterfully films natural wonder. Those observations went hand in hand with a general conclusion that the plot itself was thin on the ground, overly slow, with a tendency toward the abstruse. Basically, it was just a pretty film, was I think one critic's assessment. Personally, I love weird films where "nothing" happens; one of my fave filmmakers of all time is Apichatpong Weerasethakul, a queer Thai director who beautifully, politically, and unspectacularly brings queer characters to life on his screens, and whose long, slow films full of careful, languorous takes are often described in just this way. So I wouldn't have been all that upset if those reviews were actually on the money.

But I don't think *The Assassin* is about the visual beauty of the ninth-century Chinese landscape at all. The function of the nature shots in *The Assassin* is to emphasize scale, the ethic—and effect—of which is to depict a particular type of wordly indifference: the indifference of a larger ecosystem to the machinations of the tiny human lives bustling within it, for example. Often when Hou shows a landscape, a character is also in the shot, looking impossibly dwarfed by the surrounding magnitude. What those shots (not to mention their sound; often the sound mixing in the film is such that the noise of the natural world—birds, rustling trees, wind—is accentuated, so that human conversation is not privileged but contextualized, making the voices occasionally sound muted, if not muffled) emphasize is how small, how literally physically and existentially vulnerable these characters are, which is especially provocative framing in a film that's also about significant political and court machinations at the end of a dynasty.

But most of all, most of all, the film is also about what it is to build a personal life for yourself after trauma. Shu Qi's character, Yinniang, is the titular assassin, kidnapped from her family at the age of ten to be raised and trained by her master and captor, Jiaxin, a powerful warrior nun. As a punishment for failing to complete a previous mission due to her own conscience (the assassin, upon seeing her target in the same room with his innocent son, cannot go in for the kill), Yinniang is ordered by her master to kill her cousin—and former betrothed—Tian (played by Chang Chen), who is the military governor of his province, Weibo. It's one of those primordial narrative structures: the departed child returns to her homeland as an adult to confront her past. Shu Qi shows this journey with a carefully banked intensity and restraint. During a scene where Yinniang is finally reunited with her long-estranged mother, Lady Nie Tian (who has dutifully endured the pain of her daughter's absence for years, nevertheless continuing to sew clothes for her, every spring and autumn), her mother recounts the emotional backstory of the circumstances that, we come to understand, led to her daughter's departure from home. (There is a way of thinking about *The Assassin* as not just a story about dynasty and personal agency, not just a thoughtful riff on a classic wuxia story, but also fundamentally a trafficking story, a story about different kinds of trapped women—entrapment and freedom being two of Hou Hsiao-hsien's most revisited subjects.) For much of the story, the camera lingers on Lady Nie Tian's face, her comportment at once stiff as a stranger, yet here and there staring helplessly, hungrily at her long-absent daughter, as if starved. The film cuts to Yinniang's reaction as she listens to the mother she barely knows, body frozen, head bowed. When the mother's story is finished, we cut to Yinniang using her top to cover her entire face, so that all we see is the convulsive shudder of someone hiding herself as she sobs.

As a cinematic choice, as a way of showing—and crucially, not showing—emotion, it's one of my most beloved scenes in any film. I don't think I can even express here how uniquely moving I found it then and still find it now: this showing, without showing. This grief that remains private, remains *someone's*—this acknowledgment that the role of the cinematic spectator is not to always see everything, but to also sometimes bear witness to that which cannot and will not be revealed; reminding us that seeing is a feeling—and that sometimes the only way to really see is to feel it. Who doesn't know what it feels like to hide your face while you cry?

Yinniang is deeply internal and reserved, someone who's lived much of her formative years outside of the context she was born into and under a system of strict daily control, and Shu Qi deftly plays the faint *weirdness* of her character, the way she's just slightly out of step with everyone else she meets, as a testament to her years of isolation and training. She also plays Yinniang as someone in the process of slowly realizing that it might be possible for her to break out of the structures she's beholden to, whether the authoritarian influence of Jiaxin or the larger dynastic politics of her work, assassinating select government officials deemed to be corrupt (by whom, and for what ends, becomes one of the self-actualizing questions Yinniang has to ask herself). So much of what gripped me in this film was the genuinely edge-of-your-seat experience of watching someone try to figure out what a good life, on her own terms, might look like. What her convictions might be if she honored them; what her desires might be if she followed them; what it might feel like to be decent, or loved, or known. It's a portrait of a woman coming into herself, trying that decent, knowable life on like a coat; minor, meaningful.

By the end of the film, she once again refuses to go through with her assignment, finally breaking free from Jiaxin's hold. Instead she keeps a promise, made earlier in the film, to be the traveling bodyguard of a young, decent, and kind mirror-polisher. It's in the culmination of this very personal journey that Hou's style of nature filming, the living allegory of it, becomes almost unbearably moving: the screen is filled with another epic landscape shot, and in it, the characters are small, small, small. The soundtrack shifts completely, to the distinctive, almost plaintive sound of a bagpipe—the song "Duc de Rohan," by Breton pipe band Bagad Men Ha Tan in collaboration with Doudou N'diaye Rose, famed Senegalese drummer and master of the country's traditional instrument, the sabar. Hou Hsiao-hsien describes his use of the song in an artist's entirely instinctive way: "When I heard it, for some reason, I just liked it." The song choice here is distinctive precisely because of how much it stands out from the rest of the film's restrained, naturalistic, and at times deliberately traditionalist use of diegetic sound and music. In contrast, "Duc de Rohan" sounds like the music from another land, another life; a different story. The bagpipes blare out with a defiance that feels alien to the inhibited world we've been living in, and as we watch the small figures moving across the screen, the drums kick in, engulfing; almost mutinous in their ecstatic, life-grasping warmth and joy—even triumph. That this could be a kind of mutiny: to grasp at one's life. Here the emotional weight of that defiance becomes clear: we *are* listening to the music from another life. A different story. The figures move slowly—with purpose, but not a mission. Yinniang is among them; minor, meaningful.

6.

I read once that the *In the Mood for Love* shoot alone lasted fifteen months. Wong Kar-wai is pretty famous for his epic, grueling film shoots—for shooting several films within a film and deciding how it will end up only during editing, jettisoning whole plots, characters; for the fiction of the film and the lived lives of the actors to bleed into each other. Tony Leung and Maggie Cheung were rumored to have had an affair during the shoot; Cheung announced the end of her marriage to French director Olivier Assayas shortly after filming ended. Yet despite the end of their marriage, they still ended up making another film together, another one of my favorite films: 2004's *Clean.*

In interviews, Cheung has compared the lacquered femininity of her character in *In the Mood for Love* (she's often talked about what a pain in the ass the hair and makeup were) with the makeup-free shagginess of her character in *Clean.* What I love is that Cheung frames both roles as artifices, equally; distinct visions of femininity by two very different male directors. Cheung's performance in *Clean* is a master class on grief, loss, addiction, and recovery: a woman struggling to kick her addiction and regain custody of her estranged son after her partner dies of an overdose, from heroin she gave him. We see her in scene after scene of banal moments of life-building: eating a hamburger with a subtly crushing father-in-law; figuring out how to rely on your friends (and which ones you can't really rely on); having a faintly mortifying meeting with a powerful ex-girlfriend (Cheung's character is unremarkably bi); trying to be a parent when it feels hard enough to just be a person.

The film is chock-full of so many formally stunning scenes: a gorgeously virtuosic long take of Emily in the Chinese restaurant where she works, going through withdrawal, to the tune of Brian Eno's "Spider and I"; a scene in Gare du Nord (the film largely takes place in Paris) where you watch Emily just about to run away from one of the hardest moments in her life—and then, crucially, not run away. We get to watch her shore herself up; watch her bring herself to shore. Throughout the film's dramatic arc, instead of going bigger, more dramatic, Cheung goes deeper; burrows down and in. She closes doors instead of busting them open. Like the Shu Qi weeping scene in *The Assassin*, she knows that privacy is something that belongs to the cinema, too. There are multiple moments in which you feel as though you're being treated to the radiant, palpable quiet of just watching a singularly internal and self-protective person think. And throughout the film Emily's triumphs are few and fragile: trying to rebuild her career as a singer, writing songs, being told they're just okay. Loss is nearby; that makes it feel like life.

What Cheung does in the film is so often devastating because she eschews the more obvious acting gestures that might be expected of a character recovering from heroin addiction—what the *New Yorker* film critic Richard Brody has sometimes criticized as "actorly self-transformation," and which has of late cannibalized Western cinema, such that every award-winning film nowadays seems to be a historical biopic, which is what happens when a moviegoing audience is conditioned to worship at the altar of mimicry, to produce awe at the technique of "disappearing" into a role (usually somebody already historically famous, so that the ouroboros is complete). It's the cinematic version of Didion's aerialist vision of writing: the actor's body and soul as vessels for faithful reproduction, the magician's tools for prolonging a spell of judgment—rather than the actor's soulful body bringing a singular, kinetic way of *being* to the screen, which, in the most thrilling performances, has nothing to do with "disappearing into a role," nothing to do with disappearance at all. Another word for this quality—which Cheung possesses more than perhaps any other actor on earth, right next to her habitual screen partner Tony Leung Chiu-wai—is presence.

7.

There's a documentary for *Happy Together* called *Buenos Aires Zero Degree* in which various crew members talk about the film's long, long shoot. The film was originally meant to take three weeks to shoot. It ended up taking five months. The grim joke of the documentary seemed to be that making a film about homesick migrants in Buenos Aires actually produced a bunch of homesick migrants in Buenos Aires. In the documentary,

Tony Leung remarks that maybe Wong Kar-wai did it deliberately. "Maybe he wanted us all to feel like we were dying," he says, a little wryly.

Tony Leung's character definitely looks like he's dying in *Happy Together*, like everyone else in the film. Nearly everyone in the film is miserable and poor and horny and lonely. Tony Leung looks like he hasn't slept in ages—not that this ever damages his beauty. Washing cow blood down with a hose, pushing carcasses around, welcoming wealthier tourists off a bus with a cheesy grin, sweating in a restaurant kitchen. Trying to eat or have a phone conversation while people scream in another language behind you. Winning petty cash with soccer games during breaks. Using the kitchen at work to make a little food for yourself because your own place is a shithole. Tangoing in a kitchen with the ex-boyfriend you really shouldn't let in again. Trying, failing, trying again, to visit known tourist spots. Not being able to figure out how to read a map. Getting fired from your demeaning job because you couldn't take it anymore, broke a bottle, and went fucking batshit.

According to the documentary, there were multiple other subplots in the film, to do with characters who were (and were played by, if I remember right) actual Chinese immigrants who had made their lives in Argentina. They weren't included in the final cut. I seem to remember once reading a criticism by Christopher Doyle, Wong Kar-wai's white Australian cinematographer, complaining that the film failed to really engage with the city, that Wong ended up abandoning the Manuel Puig novel that had inspired the film's original title, *The Buenos Aires Affair*. Despite filming in Buenos Aires, said Doyle, Wong's spatial preoccupations remained the same as all his previous films: same old bars, fast-food shops, and trains as ever.

But I love that: the film's coruscatingly obsessive interloper quality, how narrow the film's vision of Buenos Aires is, how claustrophobic (claustrophilic) the film feels. Most of all, how there's no real attempt to "engage" or "be part of" Buenos Aires in a facile touristic fashion, any more than the film shows—that there is no belief in a monolithic ideal of Buenos Aires that must be seen or shot; the Buenos Aires of Chinese restaurant kitchens, cramped immigrant apartments, and late-night tango bars and bathrooms where gay men go to cruise *is* Buenos Aires. And why shouldn't it be?

Wong Kar-wai's only concession to what we might consider a dominant-culture vision of Buenos Aires is in the fact that he shows, multiple times, with the same postcard-like shot, the obelisk at Plaza de la República. Every time it shows up in the film, it feels like looking at Big Ben, or the Eiffel Tower, or maybe the Empire State Building—a huge national monument that both imposes upon and organizes civic time and space. During the years of the Perón dictatorship, the words "El silencio es salud" were displayed on the obelisk. Silence is health; a dictator's proverb. The obelisk in the films hovers over, or lurks beneath, the film's own time and space: the Buenos Aires back alleys where Chinese kitchen workers play soccer, outdoor porn theaters, bars to get in a fight in, pizza

places to get a good margarita and endure some casually af-
fectionate racial profiling.

The film believes in the radiant force of a certain type of
showing, that looking at certain things critically, lovingly, and
banally has a force of its own—and there is something subversive about that determined attention to the peripheral, the
minor, and the vulnerable. The film shrinks down the official
watch-face of the city, scrambles its frequency with this immigrant time-space. The Buenos Aires in *Happy Together* is
small, small as a heart, and only lovesick migrants live in it.

The city that really haunts the screen in *Happy Together*,
the city that Wong Kar-wai traces over the shapes of Buenos
Aires in every frame, is of course Hong Kong. The film takes
place in 1997, the year of the Handover, or the Return, depend-
ing on whom you ask: the transfer of Hong Kong from British
rule to Chinese sovereignty. In the first few seconds of the film,
we see rapid shots of Lai Yiu-fai's and Ho Po-wing's passports
as they enter Argentina. Both passports identify them as "British nationals (overseas)."

When Lai Yiu-fai, Tony Leung's character, finally makes
it back to that part of the world, he stops over in Taipei first.
The news on the television in his hotel room the morning he
wakes up: "Chinese leader Deng Xiaoping died last night in a
Beijing hospital, aged ninety-three. PRC Central TV announced
early this morning . . ." Lai, in a voice-over, says, "It's afternoon
when I wake up in Taipei. I'm back on this side of the world on
February 20, 1997. I feel like I'm waking up from a long sleep."

The title *Happy Together* refracts like a prism: in one, light, optimistic; in another, ironic; in one light, a wish; in another light, a joke. In one vintage *Happy Together* poster I've owned for years and have carried like a grail from various apartments all over London to my home now in California, Lai Yiu-fai and Ho Po-wing are embracing desperately, desolately; the tagline reads: *a story about reunion.* Not a hard leap to imagine that a love story that's also a story about a dysfunctional relationship that's also a story about a breakup that's also a story about hope and renewal—might also be a story about decolonization, about the place where the private self and the civic self touch.

One of my favorite scenes in *Happy Together*, the one in which I'm most certain of having become Lai Yiu-fai, is the scene in which Chang is about to leave Buenos Aires. He's made enough money to buy his ticket back to Taiwan, and on the way he's going to visit Ushuaia, the southernmost city in the world—the end of the world. Chang always carries around a tape recorder, usually to document interesting sounds he hears around the city. This time, he hands it to Lai Yiu-fai and asks him to say something, anything. Something to remember him by, something to take with him on his travels. Lai, a little bashful and a little drunk, doesn't know what to say.

Chang says, "Anything from the heart."

He goes on to say he'll take it with him to the end of the world; the premise being that he'll leave the words there. He leaves Lai Yiu-fai alone with the tape recorder, saying he's going to go dance. It's yet another moment in which Chang

Chen plays someone who leaves a person alone to be safe; to create a perimeter of remove in which that person can at last be vulnerable.

On the dance floor, you see Chang dart a glance over at Lai Yiu-fai. Lai holds the tape recorder up to his mouth, looking hesitant and awkward. He tries to say something, but as he struggles to come up with something, his face collapses in grief. Slowly, he starts sobbing into the tape recorder.

Then he gathers himself, tries to shake himself out of it. Blinks away the tears. Looks around a little furtively, embarrassed.

Then he folds back into the tide of sorrow—can't help it, can't even begin to stop it—and mashes his face against the recorder to hide his eyes.

This is the scene I looped over and over again in the essay film I made, years and years and years ago. It's a scene that once looped over and over in some innermost, innersouled part of me, for years and years and years.

Wong Kar-wai has Tony Leung's character do something similar at the end of *In the Mood for Love*, when he goes to Cambodia, to Angkor Wat, after his love affair that isn't a love affair with Maggie Cheung's character ends. He speaks into a hole in a tree, then plugs up the hole with dirt and grass. We don't get to hear what he says. Only the tree records it. In *Happy Together*, when Chang finally reaches Ushuaia and plays the tape recorder, he says that all he hears are indistinct sounds. Something that sounds like a moan.

I think I read somewhere that Wong Kar-wai, like many directors, was a writer before he was a filmmaker. It's true that many of his characters are writers; words matter to them. More than that: unspoken and unspeakable things matter to them. His films always seem to know that in a life there are things you can't say, things that defy all the languages you live in, so sometimes you have to leave them in the world as murmurs and imprints: as a moan, in a tree. So many of the things I've written in my life—including the things I've written in this essay—are things I have never and will still never speak about, so that even the space of this page feels like that to me now: like a borrowed tape recorder, watched over by someone who's given me the space to be both safe and naked; like a whorl in a patch of bark, whose soft and small openness provides a kind of ear, a kind of mouth; where the secret whispered into it might also be, not quite a kiss, but a kind of mouth-to-mouth— a breath that brings you back to life.

8.

Being brought back to life is something that happens in two of my favorite Park Chan-wook films, *Sympathy for Lady Vengeance* and *The Handmaiden*. Two of my favorite films about how women, in particular, come back to life.

I once attended an event featuring Park Chan-wook at the BFI Southbank in London, where he talked about his writing process with his longtime female screenwriting partner, Chung

Seo-kyung. He described their collaborative writing process: how they sat across from each other, each with their own monitors and keyboards, but connected to the same program, so that they would see each other typing, and be able to edit each other in real time.

With a grin, he said that often he would write a line, see it appear on the screen—and then watch as that line would disappear, across from him the sound of someone pointedly deleting.

Like this:
Like this
Like thi
Like th
Like t
Like
Lik
Li
L

I remember loving it, loving his ease about it, this process of being edited and rewritten by a partner and by a woman; his apparent comfort with and delight in both collaboration and submission and revision—in being seen and reseen, read and reread. In an interview with *Interview*, Park was asked: "You said recently that you are a feminist, but you weren't when you made *Oldboy*. When did things change and why?" Park replied:

I couldn't say that I wasn't a feminist at all before *Oldboy*, because I had made *J.S.A.* [2000] and in *J.S.A.*, the investigator wasn't a female character in the original novel—I consciously turned her into a female character. So I did have a feminist side to me, just not in such a pronounced way. But the reason I said that was because after I made *Oldboy*, I realized that the only character who is not privy to the entire truth in that film was the female character; she was the only female character in the film, and she was excluded from the truth. That made me so uncomfortable in such a big way that it spurred me on to developing *Lady Vengeance*. That was the genesis from which I went on to make other films with strong female characters. So to simplify things, I said it like that, that *Oldboy* was the moment when I turned into a big feminist.

I admire the candor with which Park speaks about the slow and uneven journey of both his art and his politics, revealing the process of how artists come more deeply into the things they feel perhaps instinctively or subconsciously; in particular, how it takes concerted effort and self-examination to make art worthy of those instincts—how it's not enough to simply say, "I had a feminist side," or "I'm not a racist."

One of the things I love so much about *Sympathy for Lady Vengeance* and *The Handmaiden* is the ferocity with which the films believe in reparative justice. I say ferocity not just because the films are violent, which they are—Park's films are

often called extreme—or because they are wickedly and ir-
reverently comic, which they also are. But also because the
films' commitment to that idea—reparative justice, an idea
that can feel so bloodless and formal, so civic and responsible—
does feel *ferocious*; literally visceral, as many of Park's bloody
scenes will attest. In this they could be mistakenly believed to
share something of that classic American genre for the undis-
criminating libertarian, also known as the vigilante film—in
which, most often, a disgruntled and socially isolated person
(usually white, usually a man—except, thrillingly, in the case
of HBO's *Watchmen*) takes on a corrupt and oppressive world.

But *Sympathy for Lady Vengeance* and *The Handmaiden*
aren't vigilante films at all, in that they aren't primarily films
about the heroic individual on a mission against the rotten
world, taking the law into his own hands. They are, however,
vigilant films, by a vigilant filmmaker; they are painstakingly
attentive to what our damage does to us; most of all, what it
makes us want to do.

I say *want* because these films are also deeply curious
about where damage meets desire. The core of their moral conviction often feels steely, intractable (these are films that believe
that there are in this world people who wrong others, and people who avenge those wrongs, and sometimes they're the same
people—with *Mr. Vengeance, Oldboy*, and *Sympathy for Lady Vengeance* all part of what's called Park's vengeance trilogy)—and
yet they don't feel grimdark or didactic, the way so many moralizing works about the wrong that people do to each other

tend to be tediously grimdark and didactic (parts of *Game of Thrones* and *Westworld* spring to mind).

Park's cinematic concern is not whether or not the fact that humans can do evil and kill hope therefore means humanity is fundamentally evil, and thus hopeless. *Sympathy for Lady Vengeance* and *The Handmaiden* aren't films about humanity in the macro at all, but humans—particularly women—in the micro: about the painstaking work it takes to bring someone to justice, as in *Sympathy for Lady Vengeance*, in which a woman named Lee Geum-ja, framed by her serial killer older lover, is released from jail, and subsequently begins a mission of revenge and atonement, recruiting the help of a network of similarly wronged women along the way. It's about how long it takes to deprogram yourself from an abuser—whether a grooming elder, a religion, a patriarchy. It's about learning the painful fact that it isn't just trauma that takes a toll on us; *repair* takes a toll. It's about learning that justice is labor, and if we try to do it alone, that monumental burden—its loneliness, its weight, its corrosive rage and pain—will be crushing. It's about sobering to the adult realization that there are some things we cannot do alone—and there are also sometimes places in ourselves we cannot reach with community.

It's also about learning how to bake desserts, the way Lee Geum-ja does; how to make something beautiful and pleasurable, however ephemeral. About how small moments of intimacy, irritation, humor, and softness can restore us to ourselves—and how that work of restoration lasts a lifetime.

The violence in Park's films is always a revolving door, one that can open you out into the pasture of your new life, or just as easily spit you back into your old one. Park reminds us that justice and violence are temporary friends, and that what actually makes justice meaningful are the same things that make life meaningful: love, repair, intimacy, connection, solidarity, and the promise of the daily.

9.

I hate the idea of positive representation; always have. I get, grudgingly, where it's coming from; we need positive representation, or so the old argument goes, to provide a contrast to every other *Life Aquatic*, every Scarlett Johansson cast to play my mom (a joke past its expiration date, or evergreen, I can't quite decide). And in some basic way I know that this argument is not entirely morally bankrupt—though most days I wouldn't be able to muster up the strength or inclination to defend that somewhat annoying knowledge. It's the drive to *positive* representation that gives me pause; the way it so often delimits and waters down the art that gets to swim its way into the mainstream. Because when art gets made to check a box for positive representation, you feel it—you feel its intellectual limits, its political lassitude, its flat affect where a complex emotional life is supposed to be. "Representation matters"–type art is interested in people the same way Didion is interested in people, which is to say, not at all. People—the spiky, uneven feeling, striated with joy and boredom and grief and wonder, of being a living person in the world—don't matter to positive-representation art. Only representations matter, and representations in art perform a function not unlike monarchs in constitutional monarchies, or presidents in parliamentary republics: a figurehead function, meant as a living symbol, with no real power—except, of course, for the enormous and indelible "soft" power they wield as symbolic incarnations of everything their country supposedly means, values, and venerates. Representation Matters Art wants delegates, not people; a Crazy Rich Asian, an Asian Cowboy, an Asian Brad Pitt, an Asian Superhero, an Asian Joan of Arc, One Asian to Rule Them All. Representation Matters Art thinks we can save the settler colonial Western fantasy if we just make John Wayne Filipino this time.

On a 2018 episode of Netflix's *Ugly Delicious*, the food travel show hosted by chef David Chang, the artist David Choe praises actor Steven Yeun—admittedly, one of the biggest ongoing crushes of my li'l bisexual life—for his onscreen depiction of sex with a white woman in the show *Walking Dead*. In this intimate conversation between Korean American men, Choe cheers the scene with the hope of an entire nation—well, half a nation—with a kind of freely ribald violence that would be at home with Brett Kavanaugh or Trump's locker-room talk. Finally, a strong, virile, enthusiastically cis-hetero-heroic depiction of masculinity and sexual desirability in Asian men—who, as Choe in *Ugly Delicious* would have it, deserve reparations after years of being emasculated by white supremacist America, or so the soporific clichés go. But the thing is, these kinds of strong, virile, enthusiastically cis-hetero-heroic representations have nothing to do with dismantling the white supremacist heteropatriarchy that actually oppresses Asian people of all genders, because empowerment is not the same thing as emancipation. All those kinds of representations care for is a bigger piece of the poisoned pie. And none of it addresses the fact that the precise way white supremacist heteropatriarchy works is to pass oppression down, the way grief gets passed down, in Larkin's famous poem: from man to man, deepening like a coastal shelf—until its last station, women. But Larkin forgot to mention that part.

Representation Matters Art is late capitalism's wet dream, because it sublimates the immense hunger and desire for wide-ranging racial, sexual, gender, and economic justice into the Pepsi commercial of that justice. *Only the art that truly sees us will truly free us*, representational politics says, mistaking visibility for liberation. And too many of us buy into the capitalist remix of liberation politics, enough that I've been frustrated, time and time again, with how much Asian American (predominantly middle- and upper-middle-class East Asian American and South Asian American) antiracist politics *and* art rely on the tired narrative of supposed Asian cultural invisibility vs. supposed Black and Latinx hypervisibility—a stymied logic that would purport that the existence of Marvel's *Black Panther* somehow softens the edges of the anti-Black carceral state, or that the relative lack of mainstream Asian TV and film narratives as compared to their Black and Latinx counterparts in some way cancels out the fact that despite being the most economically divided racial or ethnic group in the United States, according to the Pew Research Center, Asians rank overall as the highest-earning racial and ethnic group in the country (not minority group—racial and ethnic group; this reality accompanied by the fact that income inequality in the US is greatest among Asians). But Representation Matters Art—and the extractive vision of the world it serves—absolutely relies on us mistaking visibility for things it is not: liberation, privilege, justice. That misguided focus keeps us from doing much more difficult work: locating not just the places where our struggles are conveniently shared, but where, even more crucially, they are messily entangled. Representation Matters Art loves for all of us to be uniformly and heroically oppressed, so as to more triumphantly be heroically liberated at the end of the story: it doesn't have time for us to parse the parts of our lives in which we are not just the oppressed but the oppressor, how intra-Asian racism and the desperate income inequality between Asian ethnic groups are fundamental to understanding the myriad, often conflicting, Asian American communities that make up that chimera I still have yet to truly encounter, "the Asian American community"; or how the nuances of class, power, and sexuality form and deform how we relate to the people who supposedly "represent" us.

I've often joked privately to friends that Wong Kar-wai is

secretly a Filipinx director. I remember reading that the prevalence of Latin music in all his films came out of something particular to the sonic landscape in Hong Kong, namely the numerous bars and cabarets where Filipinx immigrant singers entertained local audiences. In a 2001 interview with *IndieWire* about *In the Mood for Love*, the director is asked about the "Latin influence" in his films: "The suffering seems more Latin than Asian," the interviewer points out. "Does that come at all from your shooting in South America on *Happy Together*?"

"The Latin music in the film was very popular in Hong Kong at the time," Wong explains. "The music scene in HK was mainly from the Filipino musicians. All the nightclubs had Filipino musicians, so they have the Latin influences. It's very popular in restaurants at that time. So I decided to put this music in the film to capture—this is the sound of that period."

The Filipinx community makes up the largest ethnic minority in Hong Kong, mostly domestic workers, who are required to be "live in" workers, according to the country's employment laws. As of September 2020, approximately 200,000 domestic helpers came from the Philippines, with 155,000 coming from Indonesia. The notorious culture of discrimination and economic exploitation faced by Filipinx and other poor, usually darker-skinned Asian minorities in Hong Kong, particularly its migrant workers, is widely known. In an interview with *The Guardian* covering domestic worker protests in Hong Kong, Filipina domestic worker Annie confides: "[My employers] mistreat me and don't give me enough food. So on my day off, I have to stock up on snacks and canned goods to survive the week." Describing a life under constant CCTV surveillance by her employers, she says, "There's a camera in my bedroom. They monitor me all the time."

According to *The Guardian*, 84 percent of Filipino domestic workers "paid illegal fees to a recruitment agency, leaving them with debts that cut into their salaries for several months, with some reporting that their passports were confiscated as collateral. Those taking part in the survey worked on average 16 hours a day, with nearly half reporting food deprivation."

That knowledge informs and complicates my love of the Hong Kong that Wong depicts so attentively in his films—it means I can't just go to his films for the easy Representation Matters punch of liberation-through-visibility. And it would have been a surprise to my grandfather and uncle, both World War II survivors, the latter a survivor of the Bataan Death March, if I were ever to countenance the idea that my love for Japanese anime was somehow a representational win, or that to be a young Pinay American in Milpitas watching the very beloved and very blonde Sailor Moon was an uncomplicated win for Asian American solidarity, and not a source of pain and frustration for the older relatives who could not understand why I was so joyfully consuming the art of their conquerors and torturers. Seeing Maggie Cheung in Wong's films isn't some win for me because I'm an Asian woman (a point which, at least if I were to listen to the East Asian kids I knew in my youth and their strident opinions about whether Filipinx people count as

Asians—TLDR: no—remains ever in contention). When I see Maggie Cheung onscreen, I don't *see myself represented* when I look at her there; when I love her there. And so my relationship to those films can't ever be one of pure box-checking: Asian woman, Asian film, Asian representation.

But why on earth would I ever want that? How could I not prefer in every way this knottier, bristlier, more vital relationship, beyond the positive, beyond the representative? One where I myself am implicated; have to question myself; get to doubt myself; have to feel, like any true lover, at once joyous relief and unavoidable vulnerability—a relationship, in other words, where I am not spared the complexity of being a living person, in the world, having to deal with stories about living people, in the world? I cannot imagine ever wanting to trade that experience—the irreplaceable rush of *humanness* that blooms in us at every encounter with the art that matters to us—for something as tepid as positive representation.

When we talk about positive representation, we have to ask: positive representation for whom? Is Representation Matters Art made for us, the minority community being represented positively? Do we really want to see only the corporate hotel art version of ourselves? Or is that art only for the omnipresent gaze Morrison was pointing toward in her critique of Ellison's supposedly "invisible" man (invisible to whom?); the idea that says us seeing each other means nothing if white people don't see us, too; the idea that when our stories enter the mainstream, we must send the brightest of us, be on our best behavior, the way our parents turned on their "white people voice" when speaking to teachers and taxmen alike?

Representation Matters Art is still, ultimately, just another armed wing of the attritive arts of white supremacy: it's the kind of art you make when someone has told you to prove you're a human—and you agree. It's art that makes us stupider, the way white supremacy makes us stupider: it was bad enough to rob us of life, land, and language, but *style*, too, babe? It's the kind of art you make when every impulse you have is a conditioned fear response to some imaginary white specter in the audience, in the mirror.

Whoever the audience, Representation Matters Art accomplishes the singular feat of being both tailor-made for it and utterly unworthy of it. The point of positive representation is to give us visions of the world like an immigrant's sofa in the eighties: vacuum-sealed in plastic, guarded from the stain of living. That isn't the art we need; it's just the art we've been delegated.

10.

In 1984, when my mom was heavily pregnant, she was standing in line at a department store when an older woman violently shoved her to the ground. No one around helped. In Montreal in 2004, my aunt was once pushed by a young man into the way of a coming subway car, miraculously surviving by huddling between the rails, just beneath the train rushing above her. When at nineteen I lived on my own in Paris, I became afraid to leave my apartment because an older man who'd seen me in a neighborhood café had begun stalking me, not to mention the nearly endless stream of "wo ai ni" and "ni hao ma" from men that would greet me whenever I stepped foot outside. I even found a Facebook group, started by Asian French women, called « pour les filles qui en ont marre des wo ai ni et d'autres conneries dans la rue »: "For the girls who've had enough of the 'wo ai ni' and other bullshit in the street." A dear friend at the time, a Korean French girl who'd been adopted by white parents, was one of the few people I could talk to about the ugly vector of infantilization, fetishization, racism, and sexual violence that attends being an Asian woman in public, not just in France or America, but throughout the world. In the wake of Trump's anti-Asian coronavirus rhetoric, a spate of attacks have targeted the most visibly vulnerable Asian figures: lone Asian women, and lone Asian elders. And at the time of the 2021 Atlanta mass shooting, in which a young white man targeted several Asian-owned massage parlors, laying his racialized sexual frustrations at the victims' graves, famously excused by police as "having a bad day," many of the Asian women in my life, across generations, reached out to each other in private to offer love, support, and most of all a place to hold our shared abject terror and sorrow.

To mobilize any polity is difficult enough, and the politics mobilized around immediate tragedy have a historically understandable tendency toward triage: treating the life-threatening symptom before addressing the life-shaping cause. Political urgency becomes the justification for lapses in political memory, and as any comrade in any struggle knows (indeed any woman who has spent time in an anarchist squat with Žižek-worshipping dudebros, or any woman of color who has tried to organize with white feminists), the impulse to political unity "for the greater good" often ends up enforcing a politicized type of silence: to not speak about sexual assault in already beleaguered communities of color or activist circles, to not prioritize trans women in feminist liberation; to not speak about the racism, classicism, and sexual fetishization perpetrated upon certain Asian groups by other Asian groups (one only need to cast a scant eye on the online hate comments about Thai Swiss popstar Lisa Manobal, the K-pop group Blackpink's only non-Korean member, to know that intra-Asian racism is alive and well). Sometimes the silencing takes a soothing, paternalistic tone: minority groups within minority groups are told to "wait their turn," to save their niche concerns for later, and that their immediate political duty is to support, applaud, and identify with, effectively, their conquerors, employers, and bullies.

That there are major issues around how we critically analyze anti-Asian racism in both an American and a global context is clear: that this kind of scapegoating is not new, even in its latest Trumpian iteration; that there are also in our vast community both shared oppressions and profound historical rifts; that the economic privilege and cultural preeminence of middle- and upper-class East and South Asian Americans has for too long obscured the economic and cultural marginalization of poorer and more vulnerable Asian groups, like undocumented Asian migrant laborers and Asian sex workers; that even the acronym AAPI obscures the fact that Asian immigration has been a historical part of the settler colonial land dispossession of Pacific Islanders in places like Hawai'i and Guam; that the cultural perception that the growing Asian American voting bloc's main political preoccupation is whether or not its children are ensured their rightful places at elite educational institutions is endlessly frustrating for people from underrepresented Asian groups for whom the promises of meritocracy have always been specious; that these are only some of the many ways that white supremacy's simplification and commodification of these nuances drip poison into any substantial move toward political unity and liberation.

The way we reckon with our history has a bearing on how we reckon with each other, and how we reckon with our art— the kind of art we're able to imagine, the ability of our art to truly imagine us. In the wake of this contemporary political climate and the heightened awareness it has ushered in, the full-scale moral, aesthetic, and intellectual vacuity of Representation Matters Art—the crumbs that representation throws at us—only becomes more glaring.

I'm more interested in solidarity, even if I don't quite yet know myself what I mean by it, just the feeling I get from it— the startling, quenching relief of it; the force of its surprise, like being loved. What *does* solidarity mean, when it comes to art? Like empathy, solidarity is another one of those exceedingly boring, crusted-over oatmeal words—so easy to ring hollow, and signal vaguely. If anything, the particular cocktail of late capitalism and selfhood in the age of the internet makes solidity, not just solidarity, feel like a relic of the past. What's solidarity in the age of the hashtag and the protest selfie; what does art, of all things, have to do with it?

Most of us, if we are people of any kind, know that to be a person is to be patchworked: full of gaps and lacunae, leaking and seeping at every seam. Certainly modernity has taught us the beguiling story of our porousness; being full of gaps is also a way of being full of market opportunities. And that porousness isn't a lie. But we aren't just our pieces. It can't just be the realm of the reactionary and the fundamentalist to suggest that there might be something of worth in not being, forever, a honeycomb of hollows—in being, yes, solid: dense in places with meaning and purpose. We know this is true if we have ever met another person that we wanted to keep in our lives.

Because despite our natural human frangibility, there does come a time when we have to be solid for other people. When we have to not evade, obfuscate, be liminal, be of two minds or a thousand. When we have to try to be whole for other people—and face *their* messy, sewn-together wholeness—which is another way of holding other people, being held by other people; held together, usually.

Solidarity is not nothing. It is a labor—like building a person, a love, a body of knowledge. And that labor, its peopled dailiness, has a tangible, vibrating effect in the world, radiating liveliness like a furnace throws off heat in the cold. And the art that I truly love, the art that has saved me, never made me just feel represented. It did not speak to my vanity, my desperation to be seen positively at any cost. It made me feel—solid. It told me I was minor, and showed me my debts. It held me together. And a little like my mom, who went on to have the kid that white woman once wanted to kill: it gave me life. It brought me here. Hi.

THE CHILDREN
OF POLYPHEMUS

I would like it to be clear at the outset that I do not bring to these matters solely or even principally the tools of a literary critic. As a reader (before becoming a writer) I read as I had been taught to do. But books revealed themselves rather differently to me as a writer. In that capacity I have to place enormous trust in my ability to imagine others and my willingness to project consciously into the danger zones such others may represent for me. I am drawn to the ways all writers do this: the way Homer renders a heart-eating cyclops so that our hearts are wrenched with pity. . . .

TONI MORRISON, *PLAYING IN THE DARK:
WHITENESS AND THE LITERARY IMAGINATION*

One of my favorite stories growing up was "Cinderella." I read the storybook version as a child, then watched and loved the cartoon Disney version of it as a child; I remember not being particularly interested in Cinderella or Prince Charming, but being completely enamored with the brown worker mice that Cinderella essentially civilizes and clothes and names, eventually deploying them as her workers and native allies. Then, like many BIPOC girls who grew up in the nineties, I was so fanatically obsessed with the 1997 television film version of *Cinderella*, starring Brandy as the titular character, Whitney Houston as her fairy godmother, and Filipinx American actor Paolo Montalban as the Prince Charming, that not only can I still recite most of its song lyrics by heart, I'm alarmingly certain there is a photograph of me, somewhere in my childhood home, wearing a blue satin dress and a clumsy facsimile of the frosted blue eyeshadow Brandy made iconic in that film. Later, I was exposed to the "original" Cinderella tale, upon which the

Cinderella narrative as we know it was largely based, written by the French writer Charles Perrault.

Charles Perrault wrote his version of "Cinderella" in 1697. What was also happening in French society in 1697 was the signing of the Treaty of Ryswick, in which the Spanish empire ceded western Hispaniola, present-day Haiti, to French rule. The French named their new possession Saint-Domingue, and did what European colonizers of the period were in the habit of doing: they turned the colony into a sugar plantation, committed genocide against the indigenous Taíno population, and brought in enslaved African peoples to work the land.

I bring this up because Perrault's version is the first version of the Cinderella story to include mention of the famous pumpkin that becomes Cinderella's chariot, and takes her to the ball.

But pumpkin—and squash varieties, generally—are not native to France. They're not even native to Europe. They are, however, native to the Americas. They're a Taíno staple food.

In 1662, thirty-five years before Perrault's "Cendrillion" was published, Louis XIV commissioned a three-day festival to commemorate the assumption of his reign. The festival was called Le Carrousel, and its theme was a "Battle of Nations." The first and central nation was ancient Rome, which France itself was symbolically and iconographically fused with, in a kind of living metaphor of the French empire's ancient and thus practically divine roots. Louis XIV himself was portrayed as a kind of a Roman emperor and France's heroes were described as descendants of Homeric heroes like Achilles.

During this tournament festival, the divine and imperial team France-as-Rome symbolically battled four barbaric nations: America, Turkey, Persia, and India. They each corresponded to an area of France's major colonial interest. The Amerindian description is particularly graphic; while the other "barbarians" are dressed in silks and jewels, the Amerindian is described as dressed in animal skins, practically an animal himself. In short, the Battle of Nations festival amounted to a hodgepodge of fantasy history, an example of how to consolidate national identity through masturbatory self-aggrandizement and the willful demonization of the foreign and subjugated—something that the gilded shit show of Trump-era American politics might have looked upon as too subtle.

In terms of historical import, the festival is neither unique nor noteworthy. It is, however, noteworthy that the person who wrote France's officially commissioned report of the Carrousel / Battle of Nations festival in 1662 was none other than Charles Perrault. This is the context of the person who wrote the fairy tales many of us know and love today; this is the world that made him, and the world he helped make—the world we have now inherited.

In *The Story-Time of the British Empire*, scholar Sadhana Naithani investigates how the transmission of what we call folklore today was hugely dependent upon the colonial relationship between an empire and its subjugated peoples; folklore around the world was collected by European colonizers, and that collection was instrumental in creating what she calls the colonial archaeology of knowledge. Naithani writes:

> The importance of storytelling in the personal and public lives of individuals and societies cannot be overstated. . . . Cultures are formed, reformed, and destroyed in the process of storytelling. Political powers, too, are accompanied by storytelling in the process of their establishment and assertion. . . . How did this Empire create its identity? How did it communicate its identity? What stories did it tell about itself? How did it create those stories? What do those stories have to do with our perception of the world today?

When Naithani talks about the inextricable connection between empire-building, identity, and storytelling in *The Story-Time of the British Empire*, she's talking not just about the historicopolitics of how stories are written, but how stories are *found*, how they're collected—and principally, *by whom*: essentially, how they are read. She talks about the principles of what she calls "colonial folkloristics." Colonial story-collections in the British imperial era were created by one people (native storytellers), often transcribed and collected by different people (colonial administrators), and transmitted to yet different people (readers in the heart of empire back home).

Naithani points out that in Europe, European folklore was generally compiled and gathered by writers, poets, editors, scholars, and teachers. However, in the case of colonial folklore—which often remains the only records we have of native folklore at all—the stories were being compiled by administrators, missionaries, bureaucrats. In the former, European folklore was viewed by its compilers and readers as a form of cultural expression, as an aesthetic and historical treasure, as something that told them fundamental things about themselves; in short, as art.

Folklore that comes to us through colonial transmission, on the other hand, was compiled to provide, essentially, an entirely different sort of data—ethnographic data about a subjugated people, aimed specifically at the education and entertainment of their subjugators. It was data collected about a certain people, but not *for* those people.

Colonial folklore created a particular set of data outside the aesthetic or artistic—and the canon we inherit today bears the traces of that data gathering. Our mainstream literary discourse continues to read writers of color ethnographically—as if they provide crucial data about a certain subjugated group of people—and white writers universally, regardless of the particularities of their artwork. Not least of all because the primary literary gaze in American literature is still presumed to be white. As I've described earlier in these essays, even the incomplete politics of the idea that fiction builds empathy is an inheritor of this colonial practice; the idea that colonial whites back home could "learn" more about their subjugated peoples via the heavily biased data transmitted through their dubiously gathered folklore has a corollary in the contemporary practice of reading writers of color to "learn" more about whatever tragic slice of history has become most recently relevant to that readership; education and empathy become resources to mine, not ongoing practices to question and transform one's life, one's work, one's adjacency to power.

We know that the stories we inherit *and* erase, no different from the ones we produce or ignore, are never neutral or ahistorical, and the force they bring with them is one that influences, consciously or subconsciously, how we read our world, and consequently, how we write it. What we call our classics; what classics we condemn the world to never knowing. Charles Perrault's tale, this classic of the West, bears indelibly the trace of the world it circulated within. Such myths, folktales, and fairy tales are teeming with unnamed folk and fairies, without whose existence the tales would not be possible, yet whose material presence in these tales often goes unremarked or remains subterranean. In Perrault's hands, a pumpkin is just something to turn into a vehicle, a chariot to ferry around a would-be princess-wife, pale and glittering. But for yet others, a squash is an entire world—one Taíno creation myth about the birth of Puerto Rico (Borikén to its indigenous people), describes the entire ocean, and all its inhabitants, contained within a pumpkin.

When Naithani and Morrison (in *Playing in the Dark*) give us lessons on how to read stories, they're also giving us lessons on how to resurrect the history latent in them, so that those stories can be more fully manifest to us, who are the inheritors not just of these stories but the world that those stories have made. Or, as the contemporary Inuit and Haitian Taíno poet Siku Allooloo writes in the poem "Survivor's Guilt": "My ancestors say: / We have always been here // My job is to house the always / for a while / My job is to do this / despite you."

THERE ARE CONVENTIONS AROUND READING AND WRITING pedagogy that have been in popular circulation for so long that whenever you think about how to write or why you write, these conventions often flutter around the edge of your consciousness, with or without your permission. Things like, "Write what you know." Or: "Show, don't tell."

Growing up, that kid who was obsessed with Cinderella and Greek myth would have wanted to hear something else. Something more like, Write what you don't know, about what you supposedly know. Write what you haven't ever felt permitted to call knowledge, about what you see and feel and live. Show that which exceeds your ability to tell it. Tell that which exceeds your ability to show it.

When I think about reading and writing, I necessarily also think about silences, erasures, oblivions and misremembrances, pockets of inarticulacy; things that are nameless in me, which might touch or be touched by things that are nameless in others. Like many diasporic kids, that's how stories came to me, from the people around me, from the books I read, from my parents who were as much silence keepers as they were story-tellers: tales pockmarked with gaps, silences, unfinished business. That our lives are often incomprehensible to us is not just a human fact, part of the mystery of being alive, the mystery of being in the world—it's also a fundamental part of coloniality's legacy. Knowing that there are knowledges that are never counted, never mind recorded, as knowledges: this is really the beginning of a decolonial reading, let alone writing. No understanding of the classics—from the fairy tale to Greek myth—is complete without that reckoning. When we say we know what a monster is, when we say we know what a hero is, how do we come to know those things? What does that knowledge permit us to believe about our world, and how does that knowledge shape how we live in that world, let alone how we read and write in it? How can we think about storytelling not just as a wholly innocent or politically neutral act, but as something that carries within it the capacity for epistemic violence and erasure, a kind of power we're often reluctant to acknowledge when we want to unilaterally praise the moral good of reading and storytelling?

How do we hold ourselves accountable—the root of the word *accountable* meaning: how do we let the story of ourselves be told? How do we hold ourselves accountable to the things we've received and internalized: the knowledges and unknowledges, the narratives, silences, and violences, the particularities? To hold ourselves accountable—to truly *hold* ourselves, within the depth and vastness of our stories, and remain there, in their thrumming inconsolability—means that in our art, we bring to bear not our most powerful, authoritative, intelligent selves, but: our most particular, our most precarious, our most dependent selves.

If one of the great dubious bequests of coloniality is diaspora—from the Greek *diasparagmos*, being scattered and torn apart—then the act of decolonial re-membering might be about putting the splintered world back together. Not by erasing or rewinding what happened—neither storytelling, nor remembering, nor indeed living, works that easily.

But take, for example, the fact that my last name is Castillo. My family, and most Filipinx people I know, especially from Luzon in the North, would pronounce that name Cast-ILL-yo— and not the Spanish pronunciation, Cast-EE-yo. *Cast-ILL-yo* is a work of re-membering.

The concept of the surname in the Philippines is a young one. It begins only around 1849 with the Clavería Decree, a Spanish colonial law issued by the governor-general of the Philippines, Narciso Clavería y Zaldúa, requiring natives to adopt a name from the Catálogo Alfabético de Apellidos, or Alphabetic Catalogue of Surnames, for the Spanish empire's legal and civil use. The catalogue included both Spanish and indigenous surnames along with words from the animal, mineral, and vegetable kingdoms, geographical terms, and artistic terms (though the overwhelming majority of the words in the catalogue were indeed Spanish, and the indigenous words were of course transcribed by Spanish speakers, following Spanish phonetics and grammar). It was sent to different towns and settlements across the archipelago, with locals "free" to choose their own names, like picking out a shape in *Squid Game*'s Dalgona Honeycomb Challenge—trace these lines and hope you don't die.

Here was freedom and bondage, woven together: the illusory freedom of "choosing" one's own name, but only at the pleasure of the colonial state, for the convenience of its administrative efficiency. The lack of distinctive native family names in the archipelago made the daily practices of empire difficult, after all; how could one reliably collect the maximum amount of tax revenue from these diffuse social groups, whose connection to each other could not be codified according to European civil structures? Did tribespeople who shared children but did not share a name even count as a family? Certainly not a good Christian one. How could one be sure a birth or marriage was legitimate, at least according to the only authority that mattered, Shredded White Jesus? The only people exempt from choosing a name from the Catálogo were those who had either already adopted a name from the list at an earlier time or could prove that their own surname had been in use for at least four generations (which would likely mostly comprise the archipelago's mestizo, Spanish and Chinese middle class). Children whose fathers were dead were assigned their grandfather's surname or their uncle's surname; only children of unknown fathers were given their mother's surname. Some accounts have surnames being distributed according to town size, with *A* surnames given to provincial capitals, and *C* surnames to smaller towns. Natives who'd already converted to Christianity might choose a name like *de los Santos* (of the saints), while natives who revered local heroes might choose an indigenous name like *Agbayani* (heroic). According to the 1973 introduction to the catalogue written by Domingo Abella, then director of the Bureau of Records Management:

> In Oas, for example, the letter R is so prevalent that besides the Roas, Reburianos, Rebajantes, etc., some claim with tongue in cheek that the town also produced Romuáldez, Rizal and Roosevelt! The explanation is simple: in 1849 the provincial governor simply allocated to each town a number of pages from the Catálogo from which the people chose their surnames. Today, almost a century later, the effect of the Governor's will is still very much a part of Philippine life.

"The effect on Philippine historiography is . . . mixed," Abella adds, remarkably mildly, considering that what he's describing is state-sanctioned cultural genocide. "One obvious negative result is that genealogical studies, for families from the towns where the decree was enforced, are hopelessly handicapped; without the good fortune of stumbling on a document giving both old and new surnames, it is almost impossible to identify Filipino family trees beyond 1849." Which also means the practice that I've sometimes witnessed, of fellow Filipinx people—not limited to Filipinx Americans—using their names to trace a etymological path back to a hoped-for history, is shaky at best. I knew some people who thought that because their names were indigenous precolonial names, it meant that their ancestors fought the Spaniards better than others (the pick-me school of postcolonialism); I knew some people who thought that because their names belonged to a Spanish noble family in the Asturias, it meant that they too were descended from European aristocracy (often preening over this perceived link—one family I knew of even created a fake Spanish heraldic shield for themselves!—in the aspirational manner akin to the way some Filipinx celebrities identify themselves as "Spanish, Chinese, and Malay," because apparently identifying as Pinoy doesn't quite have the same cultural—which is to say, colonial—cachet). But the truth is, for many of us, neither an indigenous name nor a Spanish name actually indicates much of anything: because of the decree, both types of name were words put in a book by our colonizers, for our ancestors to choose from.

Then Abella concludes, in what feels like the kind of heavy, conflict-averse sigh that reminds me of some of my more resigned, post-Marcos relatives: "There is, in the last analysis, nothing a historian can do to change a decision made and carried out more than a century ago; whether they like it or not, Filipinos must go on living with the consequences of the Clavería decree."

So here we are, in the twenty-first century, whether we like it or not: living out the consequences of the Clavería Decree. Just as Abella predicted, I will likely never know what the many names of my ancestors were before their colonial governors sent them this grotesquely permanent multiple choice quiz. What I do know is that my name is itself the trace of a disaster—a disaster that repeats itself every time it is uttered. It's also an epic work of Spanish storytelling.

But our small, resistant act of repronunciation—of pronouncing that very Spanish name a distinctly *Filipinx* way, one that not even all Filipinx people agree upon, as I've learned to my delight when I tell people how to pronounce my name—gathers up the pieces. It makes something that isn't new, exactly, but isn't only what it was. Someone, somewhere, had to choose the name Castillo—whether they loved that name, hated that name, or didn't really give a shit, took it just to keep moving—I'll never really know. But pronouncing it my family's way, here and now, makes something of that enduring lacuna; shouts a punch line back to the void. It's a work of Filipinx storytelling: a work of decolonial reading, and re-membering.

And truth be told, the work of re-membering doesn't amount to much. It's minor, daily, humble, painstaking work, which has no end and no real reward: except in the world that it helps us build, and the lives it helps us bear—and bear witness to.

There's a verse I've loved for years by the Latin poet Horace. This verse also functions as a critique of a certain kind of writing—a certain kind of mythmaking. Horace says in an ode about another poet's work:

> You tell of the [lines of descent / genealogical tree] of Aeacus,
>
> and of the battles fought under the walls of sacred Troy.
>
> But you are silent about the price of a barrel of Chian wine;
>
> you do not tell who will heat the water for my bath,
>
> or when and where I shall be offered shelter from the Pelignian frosts.

Horace has something important to tell us about decolonial reading. As people contending with the legacy of what storytelling has done—what damage it can do, down to the destruction of our names—our task is not to just talk about the genealogical trees of our great heroes or the sacred battles of Troy. Decolonial reading means paying attention to the price of a barrel of Chian wine; paying attention to who heats the water for the bath. Decolonial reading shows us where to find shelter from the Pelignian frosts. Decolonial reading means rejecting the words "once upon a time" as a convenient and one-sided fiction. There was a place, there were people. They had names. They ate pumpkin.

ONE VERY OLD STORY GOES LIKE THIS:

Odysseus and the rest of his war buddies trample onto Polyphemus's island. They've just come from sacking the city of Ismarus on their way home from Troy, killing most of the men, dividing the women and wealth among themselves. It's only because they stayed too long at Ismarus, partying and raping, that the few survivors of the island, along with their allies, are able to return in greater numbers and chase them off, killing six of his crew.

And so it's in this mood, grumpy from their interrupted pillaging, that Odysseus and his men arrive on the island of the Cyclopes, a race of one-eyed giants. They've barely even looked at the place but they already know—they know it because it's their purview to know such things—that despite, or perhaps because of, its paradisical look, the island is a lawless place, full of cannibals. Anyone who doesn't eat yeasted wheat bread has to be a cannibal, they tell themselves. Someone not worth leaving untricked, uninjured—whole.

In the Homeric epic, it's Odysseus who is telling the story. He's telling the story to the Phaeacians, the most civilized people in the entire epic, who are the negative mirror image of the Cyclopes. (Anne Carson once called Nausikaa, the princess of the Phaeacians, "the cleanest girl in epic.") Odysseus says:

"We sailed hence, always in much distress, till we came to the land of the lawless and inhuman Cyclopes. Now the Cyclopes neither plant nor plough, but trust in providence, and live on such wheat, barley, and grapes as grow wild without any kind of tillage, and their wild grapes yield them wine as the sun and the rain may grow them. They have no laws nor assemblies of the people, but live in caves on the tops of high mountains; each is lord and master in his family and they take no account of their neighbors. Now off their harbour there lies a wooded and fertile island not quite close to the land of the Cyclopes, but still not far. It is overrun with wild goats that breed there in great numbers and are never disturbed by the foot of man; for sportmen—who as a rule will suffer so much hardship in forest or among mountain precipices—do not go there, nor yet again is it ever ploughed or fed down, but it lies a wilderness untilled and unsown from year to year, and has no living thing upon it but only goats.

"For the Cyclopes have no ships, nor yet shipwrights who could make ships for them; they cannot therefore go from city to city, or sail over the sea to one another's country as people who have ships can do; if they had these they would have colonized the island, for it is a very good one, and would yield everything in due season. There are some meadows that in some places come right down to the sea shore, well watered and full of luscious grass; grapes would do there excellently; there is level land for ploughing, and it would always yield heavily at harvest time, for the soil is deep. There is a good harbour where no cables are wanted, nor yet anchors, nor need a ship be moored, but all one has to do is beach one's vessel and stay there till the wind becomes fair for putting out to sea again. At the head of the harbour there is a spring of clear water coming out of a cave, and there are poplars growing all round it."

And here Odysseus takes a theatrical breath, adjusting his phantom pith helmet. Homer is showing Odysseus giving this speech because we're meant to understand that he's a civilized man: because where others might see wild nature, Odysseus sees the potential for agriculture. And one is further meant to understand that the Cyclopes are savages *precisely* because they have failed to do everything in their power to exploit all the land within their reach and beyond.

"They trust in providence," Odysseus sniffs—but trusting in providence, it seems, isn't enough to protect the Cyclopes from people with ships.

Odysseus and his armada land on the "unspoiled" island; kill the wild goats for food; get drunk like footballers at an away game. He says, "Heaven sent us excellent sport; I had twelve ships with me, and each ship got nine goats, while my own ship had ten; thus through the livelong day to the going down of the sun we ate and drank our fill."

The next day, Odysseus tells his men he's going to see what they're like, and chooses a few companions. "Stay here, my brave fellows . . . all the rest of you, while I go with my ship and exploit these people myself. I want to see if they are uncivilized savages, or a hospitable and humane race."

One can imagine the well-dressed, well-perfumed, well-fed Phaeacians leaning closer at every salacious detail. They, as the audience of this story, know which race of people they are.

Odysseus starts to ham it up: "This was the abode of a huge monster who was then away from home shepherding his flocks. He would have nothing to do with other people but led the life of an outlaw. He was a horrid creature, not like a human being at all, but resembling rather some crag that stands out boldly against the sky on the top of a high mountain."

And so, while Polyphemus is out shepherding his flocks—a labor, it must be noted, requiring constant care and attention, not the mindless thuggishness Odysseus attributes to him—Odysseus and his men enter Polyphemus's cave, filled with lambs in pens and racks of cheese, pails of whey. The savage Polyphemus, it turns out, is an artisanal cheese maker. In fact, according to Homer, Polyphemus is the first being on Earth to create cheese (feta, as it happens). The savage Polyphemus is the first being, literally, to create culture.

Odysseus's men urge their leader to make a quick escape,

to just take the cheese and lambs and go. But Odysseus is an explorer. He wants to meet the Cyclops. So they stay, light a fire, and keep eating the savage's handmade feta.

Polyphemus returns, and before he can spot the intruders, he begins his cheese-making work, which Homer describes in almost loving detail.

"He arrived bearing a huge weight of dry wood to burn at suppertime, and he flung it down inside the cave with a crash. Gripped by terror we shrank back into a deep corner. He drove his well-fed flocks into the wide cave, the ones he milked, leaving the rams and he-goats outside in the broad courtyard. Then he lifted his door, a huge stone, and set it in place. Twenty-two four-wheeled wagons could not have carried it, yet such was the great rocky mass he used for a door. Then he sat and milked the ewes, and bleating goats in order, putting her young to each. Next he curdled half of the white milk, and stored the whey in wicker baskets, leaving the rest in pails for him to drink for his supper."

Here is a radiantly quiet, private scene of a solitary man at work, right in the middle of all the tiny, daily tasks required to build a decent life: milking the flocks, curdling half of the milk, storing the whey, leaving a portion for himself to drink that evening. Each careful rite described brings us into a rare and almost unbearable privacy and homeliness. And it will, indeed, prove to be unbearable for Homer's heroic protagonists. The story will soon remind us that Polyphemus's minor, banal, painstakingly crafted life is not the stuff of epic.

Only when Polyphemus is done with his day's work does he light a fire, and see the men waiting there. Upon seeing the men, he asks:

"Strangers, who are you? Where do you sail from? Are you traders, or do you sail as the rovers, with your hands against every man, and every man's hand against you?"

Polyphemus wants to know if they are merchants, pirates, or mercenaries. For a supposed savage, he knows acutely the difference between friendship and enmity; between safety and death. Odysseus, with the taste of pilfered cheese still in his mouth, answers by demanding the customary hospitality and gifts accorded to visitors by the laws of the gods. The word for this in Greek is *xenia*.

People often say—certainly my old classics professors did—that the entire Homeric world, the entirety of classical antiquity, really, is founded upon this idea of hospitality, this practice of xenia. But that's not quite it. The Homeric world is founded not on hospitality but on the absolute limits of hospitality: who expects hospitality and never gives it, who deserves hospitality and never gets it. The idea of hospitality here is really an idea of civilization. Xenia is the way to describe what it meant, for the people within that civilization, to be a guest; what it meant to ask for favor from another; what it meant to enter into the home, and therefore world, of another. Xenia was also a type of enclosure; it was a way of understanding who *we* were, and who *they* were.

We know such enclosures very well today. Sometimes they take the form of a literal wall; sometimes a cage; sometimes the stripping of votes from a specific population; sometimes a red baseball cap.

The Cyclops, however, has a different culture; he doesn't believe in or observe any of those laws of xenia. He eats two of Odysseus's men, because to him, they are like sheep. But of course this act means that to Odysseus, Polyphemus's life is now forfeit. That Polyphemus might live outside of the practices Odysseus holds to be universal doesn't occur to Odysseus, son of Laertes, man of many minds. That in the eyes of Polyphemus, men the size of Odysseus and his comrades are as cows and lambs are to a human diet doesn't occur to Odysseus, son of Laertes, man of many resources. That Odysseus has asked for hospitality from a man whose home he's broken into and whose food and animals he has stolen doesn't occur to Odysseus, son of Laertes, man of many ways.

When the destined moment comes and Odysseus stabs Polyphemus in the eye, blinding him, he lies to the Cyclops and tells him that his name is Outis—Nobody, No Man—so that when the dirty deed is done, the Cyclops cries out in pain: "Nobody is killing me by fraud! Nobody is killing me by force!" This is the notoriously ironic scene of the Cyclops, which most of us know best.

This is also the genius of the trap Odysseus sets—a trap that is, fundamentally, a social structure. His impunity lies in his ability to dictate the terms of his visibility, his knowability. He makes Polyphemus blind not only physically but socially: for now he can no longer know, or even name, the one who has injured him. Odysseus shows us how to destroy a life without ever having to be accountable for it. Does the life of a savage even count as a life?

But Odysseus still isn't quite satisfied with the nameless safety of an escape. After he mutilates Polyphemus's eye, he can't resist revealing his true name after all. He says, "Cyclops, if any one asks you who it was that put your eye out and spoiled your beauty, say it was the valiant warrior Ulysses, son of Laertes, who lives in Ithaca."

The boast is like an identity card he throws at Polyphemus's feet; it pierces more keenly than any spear in the eye. City waster, valiant warrior, man of many resources, son of, citizen of. It's his confidence in his own context that is Odysseus's greatest strength, his greatest privilege, and his greatest cruelty. He may be traveling, but he's not a migrant. Man of many resources, worldly-wise, skilled in diplomacy, lover of stolen wealth and sadistic games—Odysseus always has a home to return to. Wherever he goes is civilization, to the despair of everyone else. Polyphemus remains at home, but he's been *made* foreign by Odysseus: a barbarian, a savage, someone whose entire world can be invaded, stripped for parts, then abandoned.

The rest of Homer's story could have well been finished thousands of years later, by a Spanish admiral, talking about

another island entirely—and yet the tale continues practically
without a hitch:

"Weapons they have none, nor are acquainted with them,
for I showed them swords which they grasped by the blades,
and cut themselves through ignorance. They have no iron, their
javelins being without it, and nothing more than sticks, though
some have fish-bones or other things at the ends. They are all
of a good size and stature, and handsomely formed. I saw some
with scars of wounds upon their bodies, and demanded by
signs the cause of them; they answered me in the same way,
that there came people from the other islands in the neighborhood who endeavored to make prisoners of them, and they
defended themselves. I thought then, and still believe, that
these were from the continent. It appears to me, that the people
are ingenious, and would be good servants and I am of opinion
that they would very readily become Christians, as they appear to have no religion. They very quickly learn such words as
are spoken to them. If it please our Lord, I intend at my return
to carry home six of them to your Highnesses, that they may
learn our language. I saw no beasts in the island, nor any sort
of animals except parrots."

That's Christopher Columbus—or Cristóbal Colón—talking.
He sounds a lot like his ancestor Odysseus, son of Laertes, man
of many resources. You'll notice it's only after Colón talks
about "carrying home" a few natives as souvenirs that he is
suddenly reminded of beasts and animals. As if to add, in a
cheerful tone: "While we're on the subject anyway!"

———

IT MUST ALSO BE SAID THAT HOMER DID NOT WRITE ANY OF this, of course—Samuel Butler, his English translator, did. Samuel Butler, author of *Erewhon* and *The Way of All Flesh*, was born in England and, like many middle-class whites of his generation, he immigrated to the new settler colony later known as New Zealand, in September 1859. The name of the ship he arrived on was called *Roman Emperor*.

MUCH HAS BEEN MADE OF THE MEANING OF THE NAME ODYS-seus: the verb *odussōmai* means to hate, to be wrathful against. It can also mean to suffer—encompassing both the one who inflicts *and* the one who undergoes the suffering. Homer in Book 19 of *The Odyssey* describes a scene in which Odysseus explains his own name, given to him by his grandfather Autolycus. Butler's translation has Autolycus proclaim: "Call the child thus: I am highly displeased with a large number of people in one place and another, both men and women; so name the child 'Ulysses,' or the child of anger."

In the most recent translation of *The Odyssey*, by Emily Wilson—the first woman to translate the epic into English—she translates Homer thus: "Name him this. I am / disliked by many, all across the world, / and I dislike them back. So name the child / 'Odysseus.'"

It's notable that Butler's colonial-era translation leaves out the implication that Autolycus is not only displeased by the world, but that *the world is displeased by him.* Wilson's translation, on the other hand, preserves that nuance.

Odysseus is a name that concatenates—anger, suffering, wrath, hate, pain; a name that intertwines both the pain one metes out to the world and the pain endured in the world. Most of all it's a name that emphasizes hate not just as an abstract emotion but as a *relation*, concrete, and as an *inheritance*, traceable. Autolycus is passing down a specific kind of generational wealth—namely, his own experience of being in the world: that of hating others, and being hated by others; that of causing pain to others, and of being pained by others. "Noble Autolycus," describes Wilson's *Odyssey*, "who was the best / of all mankind at telling lies and stealing."

No time is spent on the meaning of the name Polyphemus. We know that Polyphemus is the son of Poseidon—the great enemy of Odysseus, in the epic—but we don't get the generational origin myth of his name, its meaning, its weight; we don't know his grandfather, what he did, what he was known by; what pain he invited, what pain he dealt out; if he lived his life by pain at all, in the world before Odysseus darkened his grandson's door.

Polyphemus, in the most literal translation, means many-voiced. Usually translated as "abounding in songs and legends," "much-spoken-of," "many-rumored," or even "famous," it conveys the meaning of someone about whom many tales are told; someone whose myth reaches far beyond him. Whether there is here a kind of poetic irony (it is Odysseus, not Polyphemus, after all, who is abounding in songs and legends, both in his world and ours—which are, in the end, the same world) is unclear. But what is certain is that the name Polyphemus is a name that honors not the one voice—but the many. Not one story, but multiple; not one author, but a multitude.

I wonder what stories Polyphemus might have had to tell us; what the epic might have looked like from his vantage point; what any other one of those manifold voices, rumors, legends, and hymns may have had to sing to us. I wonder if they have anything to do with the knowledge Horace passed down, in that verse about heroes, and silences, and wine, and shelter.

I do know the stories smell of handmade feta; they taste of pumpkin. They give us shelter from the Pelignian frosts. They remember pain; they have names. They have always been here. They will be here tomorrow.

ACKNOWLEDGMENTS

Once again in the spirit of utang na loob, or unpayable debts of gratitude (which, incidentally, my father once called the most corrosive and corruptive part of Filipinx culture, which is a v Aquarius thing to say, only bested by the fact that he also used to tell me Jesus was an alien):

Thank you to both of my parents (Aquarius/Aquarius) for their ferocious, foundational love, and for being far cooler, weirder, and more radical than they ever had to be, given the circumstances. Thank you to my father, for teaching me how to be a reader, let alone a person; thank you to my mother, who taught me by example how to be a reader in the world, far beyond the scope of books. Thank you to both of them for being the kind of parents who were absolutely chill with a bi kid; premarital sex; leaving the country multiple times before the age of nineteen; eloping at twenty; but who also once told me: "If you ever pluck your eyebrows, we'll disown you." Iconic. 100/10 Aquarius parenting. I still haven't ever plucked them.

Thank you to my brilliant agent and beloved friend Emma Paterson (VIRGO), for lovingly and fiercely believing in these essays and their author from the earliest, wildest days of both; for your razor-sharp instincts, iconoclastic verve, and visionary commitment to effecting actionable change on our shelves (and so in our world); most of all, for the life-source of your friendship, which makes me laugh out loud every single day, and keeps me paying democracy-destabilizer Mark Zuckerberg's bills, because how could I delete WhatsApp with your messages waiting for me? Knowing with absolute certainty that you are the present and future of the publishing industry makes me, for once, actually joyfully celebrate that present and look forward to that future. Thank you also to Emma's assistant, Monica MacSwan, whose early, extremely perceptive reading, and ongoing support on multiple levels, brought much joy and clarity to the entire process. Thank you also to Lisa Baker and everyone on the Aitken Alexander translation rights team.

Thank you to my incredible US editor and fellow Earth sign, Laura Tisdel (Taurus), for your indefatigable faith in this book and its author, and for your awe-inspiring willingness to put everything on the line to fight for both; for your singularly incisive and generous editorial style, and for the deep joy and solace of your friendship. This entire editorial process of this book was Virgo/Taurus solidarity and thus, the Dream. With a special shout-out to my UK editor, James Roxburgh (Aquarius), whose editorial grace, moral clarity, poetry of vision, openness, and humility have set a powerful model not just for how to be better publishers, but, in particular, how to be better and more engaged publishers for authors of color. Thank you also to the entire Viking/Penguin Random House family, especially Andrea Schulz and Brian Tart, for their tireless championing. Thank you to Sara Leonard, publicist extraordinaire, and to Elda Rotor for being the Penguin Classics fairy-godmother-from-afar. Thank you to Jenn Houghton (Leo), Laura's assistant and all-around superhero, for much-appreciated support in keeping this whole ship afloat in a hundred different ways, and also for much-cherished affection and support for Xena—especially in making sure the dog stays in the (author) picture. Thank you also to the entire Atlantic team, including Felice McKeown, Dave Woodhouse, and Kirsty Doole, and especially former Atlantic legend Bobby Mostyn-Owen: I remain so very, very delighted for and proud of you (sorry to still be that Filipinx auntie!). And a very special thank-you to the rock star Nayon Cho for knocking the cover art out of the park on the first try—thank you for giving this collection such a tough, bold, and literally incendiary face; I couldn't have dreamed up a more perfect or more distinctive visual grammar. Thank you to Claire Vaccaro for your brilliance and enthusiasm in creating the book's interior design, and thank you to Lavina Lee and Tess Espinoza for frankly heroically patient production editing. Thank you also to fellow dog parent and speaking agent extraordinaire Leslie Shipman and the entire team at the Shipman Agency.

Thank you especially to everyone I met at the various

festivals mentioned throughout these essays, but especially both the participants and organizers of the Auckland Writers Festival and the Sydney Writers' Festival (where much of this book was birthed); Rome's International Literature Festival (for which parts of "The Children of Polyphemus" were delivered as a speech) and the incredible women of my Italian publishing house, Solferino; and my loves at Michigan State University's Women of Color Institute, where early versions of some of these essays were given as readings. Doing my best to name everyone in gratitude, but please forgive my poor memory if you don't find yourself here, it was probably due to all that bourbon: Anne O'Brien, Roger Christensen, Nicole Strawbridge, Tessa Yeoman, Penny Hartill, Michaela McGuire, Tamara Zimet, Daniela Baldry, Steve Abel, Dustin Schell, Alex Chee, David Chariandy, Fatima Bhutto, Roanna Gonsalves, Andrew Sean Greer, Enrico Rotelli, Tayi Tibble, Isa Pearl Ritchie, Sugar Magnolia, Kiran Dass, Louisa Kasza, Jenna Todd, Rosabel Tan, Noelle McCarthy, Emma Espiner, Vincent Silk, Maeve Marsden, Winnie Dunn (and all the incredible women of Sweatshop), Giovanna Canton, Chiara Di Domenico, Beatrice Minzioni, Yomaira Figueroa, Tamara Butler, Estrella Torrez, Olivia Furman, Chingbee Cruz, Adam David, Glenn Diaz, Kristine Ong Muslim, Kristian Sendon Cordero, Honey de Peralta, Don Jaucian, Deborah Nieto, James Abuan, Chad Dee (and everyone in Manila I'd rather be drinking Fundador and eating sisig with right now). And since I'm going to be recording the audio book of this collection, I apologize ahead of time to every sin-

gle person, place, or thing whose name I inevitably mispro-
nounce, and, on a related note, I promise to be less of a dickhead
in the future when my own name and cultural touchstones are
mispronounced. Let's all just do our best while we're alive on
this wet little apocalypse rock.

Thank you to the fam closer to home, Ingrid Rojas Contreras, Jeremiah Barber, Ismail Muhammad, Scott Nanos, for whom
I have eternal love and gratitude, not least of all gratitude that
we somehow survived that Hot Ones challenge. Thank you to
Gina Apostol and Jessica Hagedorn not only for being the un-
disputed GOATs, but for a depth of love, welcome, and generosity that still staggers me; to the scholars like Dylan Rodriguez
and Catherine Ceniza Choy and Bliss Cua Lim, to whom Filipinx writers like me owe so much. A long ovedue thank-you to
Roxane Gay and Tim Jones-Yelvington for a kindness from over
a decade ago: to the latter, for being the editor at *Pank* who chose
a story of mine for their Queer Issue in 2010, which was the
first story I'd written in the three years since my father's death;
and to the former, for inviting me to blog for *Pank* and thus
giving me a space where I could teach myself how to write again,
after those years of silence and mourning. Thank you to Harry
Cepka, for your love and friendship being the best thing to
come out of those very weird weeks up in the Alps in Saas-Fee.
Thank you to Yael Villafranca for a grace beyond my compre-
hension, and for a much cherished period of love and support
across oceans. Thank you to Josh Grant for a group chat about
coffee I still don't understand and for making the music that

bolsters my parties, my home, my life. Thank you to an email thread that got me through 2021 and is still getting me through, especially to the brilliant and generous R. O. Kwon for bringing me into its wondrous community: Indira Allegra, Behar Behbahani, Ingrid Rojas Contreras, Rachel Khong, Raven Leilani, Antoinette Nwandu, Jenny Odell—for all the poems, the prayers, the flowers, the art installations, the dog videos. Thank you to my siblings (blood and not blood) and cousins (blood and not blood) from the Bay Area to Vegas, whose barbecue, beers, beach days, art, Strong Anime Opinions, dogs, and nonstop shit-talking both keep me going, and keep me tethered.

To my girl, my love, my best friend and favorite poet, Rachel Long (Scorpio)—where to begin. First of all, a Scorpio: exquisite. Legendary power and mystery. Your restorative love and friendship is the light of my life, and I would go back to Goldsmiths a thousand times if it meant I could meet you there again every time; thank you.

Finally, to my small, infinitely beloved found family: Fabien (Aquarius) and Xena (Libra, according to Thulani Senior German Shepherd Rescue, to whom I also owe a lifelong debt of gratitude). You do nothing less than make this life worth living; make any of it matter at all. I love you. I live for you. Thank you.

WORKS CITED

Please consider this informal "works cited" section as another form of utang na loob, in the hopes that it will serve not just as a resource for the works literally cited, but also as a kind of literary land acknowledgment: recognizing the terrain upon which this book was built, in the spirit of the Kincaid epigraph—"how you got to be the way you are." Also: jokes. The citations appear roughly in the order in which the referenced works appear in the text.

EPIGRAPH

Kincaid, Jamaica. *Lucy*. Farrar, Straus & Giroux, 1990. Honestly, babes, every single book I write could have an epigraph from *Lucy*. On colonialism, sex, mothers, migration, affective labor, writing, skewering white feminism, and more, it's all bangers, no skips.

AUTHOR'S NOTE, OR A VIRGO CLARIFIES THINGS

Morrison, Toni. *Playing in the Dark*. Vintage Books, 1992. What more can be said? The blueprint.

Plato. *Symposium*. Translated by Tom Griffith. University of California Press, 1993. Or at least this is the translation my father and I found in our beloved Bookbuyers (RIP), the secondhand bookstore on Castro Street, in Mountain View. Also filed under "Bi Awakenings": the last scene, when Alcibiades swoops in late to the party, already wasted, covered in flowers, with a flute-girl in tow; chugs more wine, has a fit, then proceeds to spontaneously recite one of the greatest valentines in history, while also reading Socrates—the valentinee—and his entire life for filth? 100/10 iconic bi disaster. Alcibiades's Venus is in Leo.

Joyce, James. *Ulysses*. Vintage International, 1990. Honestly, shout-out to my father for believing I could read this at thirteen. Ditto the following four works.

Rizal, Jose. *Noli Me Tangere*. Translated by León Ma. Guerrero. The Norton Library, 1961.

Russell, Bertrand. *Bertrand Russell's Best*. Edited by Robert E. Egner, New American Library, 1971. Extremely funny to open up this old-ass edition of mine and see that teenage me folded over a page in which Russell writes: "Cruelty is in theory a perfectly adequate ground for divorce but it may be interpreted so as to become absurd. When the most eminent of all film stars was divorced by his wife for cruelty, one of the counts in the proof of cruelty was that he used to bring home friends who talked about Kant." Russell may have been on the side of the film star, but I say to the wife: fuck-everybody-else-i-respect-you.gif.

Kant, Immanuel. *Critique of Pure Reason*. Honestly who knows which edition I had. There is no way I read this book in its entirety at that age.

Woolf, Virginia. Especially *Orlando*, and *Mrs. Dalloway*.

Carson, Anne. Formative. In particular *Eros the Bittersweet: Essays* (Princeton University Press, 1986), *Autobiography of Red: A Novel in Verse* (Knopf, 1998), *The Beauty of the Husband: A Fictional Essay in 29 Tangos* (Vintage, 2001), *Decreation: Poetry, Essays, Opera* (Vintage, 2006). Also the reason why my bio was so short for *America Is Not the Heart*. "Anne Carson lives in Canada" still slaps.

Mann, Thomas. Especially *Tristan*, *Tonio Krüger*, *Death in Venice*. At some point will finish *Buddenbrooks*.

von Goethe, Johann Wolfgang. Especially *Faust* and *The Sorrows of Young Werther*, but tbh the thing I remember most is that we share the same birthday. Virgo solidarity, I guess.

Yoshimoto, Banana. *Kitchen*. Translated by Megan Backus. Grove Press, 1993. Formative short novel on grief, mourning, food, and love. Contains one of my favorite characters in literature, a trans mom who reminds me a lot of a beloved trans godparent of mine. But then the character is fridged to further the storyline of the two cis hetero main characters, who spend the rest of the novel grieving her. Let the queers grow old, damn.

Puig, Manuel. Formative, especially for *Kiss of the Spider Woman* and *Betrayed by Rita Hayworth*. Also, one of my favorite descriptions of Puig or indeed any author comes from Francisco Goldman's introduction to Puig's novel *Heartbreak Tango*, describing the way Puig arrived at a party held in Brooklyn: "Puig turned up dressed as a butterfly, with gauzy wings and little antennae, and it wasn't even a costume party."

READING TEACHES US EMPATHY, AND OTHER FICTIONS

Stephens, Bret. "The Scandal of a Nobel Laureate," *The New York Times*, October 17, 2019.

Handke, Peter. *Der Chinese des Schmerzes*. Suhrkam Verlag, Frankfurt am Main, 1983.

Handke, Peter. *Across*. Translated by Ralph Mannheim. Farrar, Straus & Giroux, 1986.

Handke, Peter. Other works of his I read in that very Austrian period of my life were *A Moment of True Feeling*, *The Left-Handed Woman* (both translated by Ralph Mannheim), and *Once Again for Thucydides*, translated by Tess Lewis, in which Handke, on a trip to northern Japan, expresses surprise to see snow on an apparently "undeveloped" field: "rare for the Japanese who let nothing go to waste." What.

Matthews, Patricia A. "On Teaching, But Not Loving, Jane Austen," *The Atlantic*, July 23, 2017.

Matthews, Patricia, A. "I Hope White Hands: Wedgwood, Abolition, and the Female Consumer," YouTube webinar, March 20, 2017. I highly recommend anyone interested in Austen, the Regency era, or aesthetic theory watch this webinar, which was one of the most fun historical deep-dives I've gone on in recent years. The whole analysis of Wedgwood, the performance of abolitionist politics, and the formation of white women's political subjecthood (contemporary white feminism's great ancestor): thrilling and well-argued. Did I go on Etsy to look at vintage Wedgwood teapots? Yes, I did. Did I eventually buy a very inexpensive vintage Churchill Blue Willow sugar bowl and creamer set for its very suspect chinoiserie theme that reminded me of some old furniture my parents used to have? Yes, I did. Did I then realize upon the set's arrival that these vintage tea services are usually full of lead and thus fucking poisonous to eat on, making the metaphor so obvious as to be a blunt force object? Also yes. Anyway, personally, in the teapot racket, I like the tetsubin, those black cast-iron Japanese teapots, also favored by a certain Reynolds Woodcock in *Phantom Thread*. Certain people in certain group chats are laughing at me right now.

Austen, Jane. One of the first things I watched upon moving to London in 2009 was the ITV teleplay of *Persuasion* starring Sally Hawkins. I just remember the pining being very breathless and molten but also, pale, damp—as in, rained on; as in, takes place in Bath. And then that very gasp-y, almost *Secretary*-esque final kiss. Actually a lot of the film is sort of like watching Anne Elliot go through subdrop.

Hawkins conveys this same quality—a state of being both solid and liquid at the same time, as scientists at the University of Edinburgh discovered certain atoms, like in potassium, can exist—in the film *Spencer*. She's the realest and most relieving thing in the film (certainly Kristen Stewart's Diana believes this), but even her brief interventions of human realness and relief are only Davids, against a much greater Goliath; and this time, Goliath wins. (Hawkins here also reminds me a little bit of Maribel Verdú's role as a resistance fighter against the Francoist regime in Guillermo del Toro's *Pan's Labyrinth*.) *Spencer* is a remarkable film, not quite so much for being a portrait of Diana Spencer Windsor as for being a film entirely about dictatorship. The aesthetics of dictatorship, the rhythms of living under dictatorship, a regime's terrors and compromises. The opening scene in the Sandringham House kitchens focuses on a sign that admonishes workers to KEEP NOISE TO A MINIMUM / THEY CAN HEAR YOU as a soldier sweeps his flashlight over the surfaces; it shares much with another dictatorial proverb mentioned in this essay collection, namely "El silencio es salud" in *Happy Together*'s Argentina. From the drone shot of the title sequence; to the landmine references; the physical and mental disintegration of Diana under the palace's totalitarian surveillance; actor Sean Harris as the chef/general (drawing on his previous work as another complicated state enforcer, Micheletto Corella in *The Borgias*); Timothy Spall as the equerry-cum-Stasi-chief Major Gregory; lines like "tried to escape; got captured"; the major/soldier interrogation scene between Diana and her children; the use of barbed wire as framing and front (as in, theater of war); and of course the final no-man's-land sequence in which Diana successfully wrests her sons away from their pheasant shoot to finally make a wild escape. The film's subtitle, "a fable about a true tragedy," is accurate; but the fable is about dictatorship as much as about Diana (or, more specifically, it is about the drama of personality—in this case Diana's—under dictatorship). The true tragedy it is based on, then, is monarchy. (The Chilean-born director, Pablo Larrain, had of course already made several films about the Pinochet dictatorship prior to helming *Spencer*; it seems odd to me that people would question, as some film critics did, whether or not he was the right person to tackle a royal story. But royalty is just a more gilded, and thus more enduring, form of dictatorship. Similarly, in his previous film *Jackie*—also not quite a portrait of Jackie Kennedy—the fable is about national mythmaking itself, the human, as much as political, act of fabulizing. The true tragedy, there, is America.

Hugo, Victor. *L'homme qui rit*, 1869. This is one of my favorite Hugo books, not to mention one of the best critiques of the English aristocracy ever written, and given the above digression on *Spencer*, worth mentioning here. Often in the film, Stewart's Diana bitterly receives the subtle and not-so-subtle cruelties of her in-laws with the words, "Oh, just a bit of fun." Here is Victor Hugo, on "fun" as it pertains to the English aristocracy: "*Fun* is like *cant*, like *humour*, a word which is untranslatable. Fun is to farce what pepper is to salt. To get into a house and break a valuable mirror, slash the family portraits, poison the dog, put the cat in the aviary, is called 'cutting a bit of fun.' To give bad news which is untrue, whereby people put on mourning by mistake, is fun. It was fun to cut a square hole in the Holbein at Hampton Court. Fun would have been proud to have broken the arm of the Venus de Milo. Under James II. a young millionaire lord who had during the night set fire to a thatched cottage—a feat which made all London burst with laughter—was proclaimed the King of Fun. The poor devils in the cottage were saved in their night clothes. . . . It was the rich who acted thus toward the poor. For this reason no complaint was possible. Those manners have not altogether disappeared. In many places in England and in English possessions—at Guernsey, for instance—your house is now and then somewhat damaged during the night, or a fence is broken, or the knocker twisted off your door. If it were poor people who did these things, they would be sent to jail; but they are done by pleasant young gentlemen."

Morrison, Toni. *Playing in the Dark*. Harvard University Press, 1992.

Hall, Rachel. "Record Numbers Join National Trust Despite Claims of 'Anti-woke' Critics," *The Guardian*, October 29, 2021. L-O-L.

Eliot, George. *The Mill on the Floss*. This was the first new book I read after sending off *America Is Not the Heart* to the printers. I thought, I'll read something totally outside the world I've been living in, nineties Filipinx family, Communist resistance, bisexual disasters, scrappy young girls, the suburbs, etc., and then it turned out that *The Mill on the Floss* made me feel more "seen" (that faintly dilapidated term/emotional cadence) than most other books I'd read up until then. The pining, the family relations, the debt, the landscape, the racial metaphors. The early scene where Maggie runs away from home and calls herself a "gypsy" (her use of the slur) and subsequently tries to live among an actual Traveller community—even tries to appoint herself their queen!—and they basically pull a "bless your heart" on this delusional little English girl is one of the funniest and most perspicacious literary passages I can think of.

Bernhard, Thomas. Especially *Correction*, translated by Sophie Wilkins (Vintage, 2003); *Three Novellas*, translated by Peter Jansen and Kenneth J. Northcott (University of Chicago Press, 2003); *The Lime Works*, translated by Sophie Wilkins (Vintage, 2010); *Frost*, translated by Michael Hoffman (Knopf, 2006). I haven't read him in a while; writing this has reminded me to go back and reread.

Wittgenstein, Ludwig. *On Certainty*. Edited by G. E. M. Anscombe and G. H. von Wright. Translated by Denis Paul and G. E. M. Anscombe. Harper Torchbooks, 1972. Wittgenstein was truly My Shit during a certain era. And then later as an adult I found the anthropologist and scholar Veena Das's writings on Wittgenstein, pain, and Partition, especially her book *Life and Words: Violence and the Descent into the Ordinary* (University of California Press, 2007), which became influential in my own thinking. Here's Das: "It is often considered the task of historiography to break the silences that announce the zones of taboo. There is even something heroic in the image of empowering women to speak and to give voice to the voiceless. I have myself found this a very complicated task, for when we use such imagery as breaking the silence, we may end by using our capacity to 'unearth' hidden facts as a weapon. Even the idea that we should recover the narratives of violence becomes problematic when we realize that such narratives cannot be told unless we see the relation between pain and language that a culture has evolved."

Lispector, Clarice. Especially *The Hour of the Star*. Translated by Giovanni Pontiero. Carcanet, 1986.

Bioy Casares, Adolfo. Especially *The Invention of Morel*. Translated by Ruth L. C. Simms. NYRB Classics, 2003.

Marshall, Alex, and Schuetze, Christopher F. "Genius, Genocide Denier, or Both?" *The New York Times*, December 18, 2019.

Seghal, Parul, "A Mother and Son, Fleeing for Their Lives Over Treacherous Terrain," *The New York Times*, January 17, 2020.

Coetzee, J. M. *Diary of a Bad Year*. Penguin Books, 2007. A pretty great comic novel.

Lopate, Philip. *Two Novellas*. Other Press, 2008.

Baldwin, James. "Why I Stopped Hating Shakespeare," *The Cross of Redemption*, Vintage, 2011.

Thoreau, Henry David. *Walden*. Empire Books, 2012. I have no idea where my childhood copy is or where it was from; this citation was chosen at random.

Larson, Shannon. "'We came here and created a blank slate.' Rick Santorum, CNN Under Fire Following Commentator's Dismissal of Native American Culture," *Boston Globe*, April 27, 2021.

HONOR THE TREATY

Tibble, Tayi. *Poūkahangatus*. Victoria University Press, Wellington, 2018.

The Piano, written and directed by Jane Campion. Film, 1993. Also just texted someone to say I felt very smug about figuring out the plot early on in *The Power of the Dog*, essentially screaming in my living room, "This li'l twink is gonna kill u, Phil!!!" and "This is what people get for misidentifying a dom top for a subby bottom and vice versa," which is why I can never be allowed into a movie theater again. Re: movie-related WhatsApp chats, I was also once texting with someone about why we liked the end of *The Piano Teacher* more than *The Lost Daughter*: "listen when a white woman goes about her day with a stab wound it has to be iconic!!!!!"

McClure, Tess. "From Outrage to No. 1 Hits: How Maori Musicians Conquered the Charts in Their Own Language," *The Guardian*, February 4, 2022.

Taylor, Rory. "6 Native Leaders on What It Would Look Like if the US Kept Its Promises," *Vox*, September 23, 2019.

McFall-Johnson, Morgan. "Over 1,500 California Fires in the Past 6 Years—Including the Deadliest Ever—Were Caused by One Company: PG&E. Here's What It Could Have Done but Didn't," *Business Insider*, November 3, 2019.

Pierre-Louis, Kendra. "Minorities Are Most Vulnerable When Wildfires Strike in the US, Study Finds," *The New York Times*, November 3, 2018.

Milman, Oliver. "European Colonization of Americas Killed So Many It Cooled Earth's Climate," *The Guardian*, January 31, 2019.

Rodríguez, Dylan. *Suspended Apocalypse: White Supremacy, Genocide, and the Filipino Condition*. University of Minnesota Press, 2009.

Department of Conservation, Te Papa Atawhai, New Zealand Government. "Te Mana o Te Taiao—Aotearoa New Zealand Biodiversity Strategy 2020." Promisingly, because this strategy has changed, evolved, and developed in the years since I quoted the passage from 2020–all signs of a living practice—the currently available documents for the biodiversity strategy may appear different.

Carson, Anne. *Decreation.* Jonathan Cape, 2006.

Treisman, Rachel. "Nearly 100 Confederate Monuments Removed in 2002, Report Says; More than 700 Remain," NPR, February 23, 2021.

Walker, Peter. "'We Cannot Edit Our Past: Boris Johnson's Statue Tweets Explained," *The Guardian*, June 12, 2020. Johnson is a fucking floor Lego.

Said-Moorhouse, Lauren. "Just 5% of UK Windrush scandal have received compensation, report says," CNN, November 24, 2021.

Warren, Kristy, "Who Are Monuments For? Considering Slavery Legacies in London's Public Statues," Museum of London, July 3, 2020.

Hyde, Marina. "What Drew William and Kate to the Negro Page Painting?" *The Guardian*, April 29, 2016. What indeed.

Hirst, Gabriella. *An English Garden.* Public sculpture: Rosa floribunda "Atom Bomb" (Kordes, 1955), Iris "Cliffs of Dover" (Fry, 1952), engraved brass plaques, park benches, 2021.

Public statement from the Old Waterworks Staff and Board of Trustees, "Censorship of *An English Garden*," July 12, 2021.

I can't now remember whose names I must have rattled off in the more-than-slightly unhinged moment created by that white interlocutor at the Auckland Writers Festival who imperiously demanded the names of Filipinx (she said "Filipino") writers for her students, but I at least hope I mentioned writers and thinkers like Gina Apostol, Jessica Hagedorn, R. Zamora Linmark, Lysley Tenorio, Dylan Rodriguez, Catherine Ceniza Choy, Bliss Cua Lim, Kristine Ong Muslim, Glenn Diaz, and so many, many, many more.

Merata: How Mum Decolonised the Screen, directed by Hepi Mita. Film, 2018.

Bastion Point: Day 507 (1980), *Patu!* (1983), directed by Merata Mita.

That Tessa Thompson scene in Taika Waititi's *Thor: Ragnarok*: still extremely valid. Also still valid: the back-and-forth in *Hunt for the Wilderpeople* between the incredible Rachel House and Julian Dennison, in which House's child welfare services officer, Paula, says, "I'll never stop chasing you—I'm relentless, I'm like the Terminator." Dennison's Ricky Baker: "I'm more like the Terminator than you!" Paula: "I said it first. You're more like Sarah Connor. And in the first movie, too, before she could do chin-ups." Always here for a Terminator reference; also as a fledgling powerlifter who still hasn't managed a full pull-up, always here for a Sarah Connor reference. I think I once texted my friend Harry that *Terminator: Dark Fate* was an important intergenerational queer film, so again, I shouldn't be allowed in movie theaters. (The HBO Max show *Our Flag Means Death*, starring Waititi and Rhys Darby, is also excellent, and another example of important intergenerational queer content. Also: pirates.)

Kaufman, Mark. "The Carbon Footprint Sham: A 'Successful, Deceptive' PR Campaign," *Mashable*, July 13, 2020.

Blevins, Juliette. "Some Comparative Notes on Proto-Oceanic *mana: Inside and Outside the Austronesian Family," *Oceanic Linguistics*, volume 47, no. 2, December 2008. University of Hawai'i Press.

THE LIMITS OF WHITE FANTASY

Rowling, J. K. Potterverse.

The X-Men universe: the 1975–1991 Chris Claremont runs, the 1992 animated series I watched at early morning daycare when my mom dropped me off at school before the school's daycare technically even started, because she had to get to her morning shift at the hospital—shout-out to teachers who go the extra mile to help working mothers—and the early aughts film series directed by Bryan Singer, credibly accused by multiple young men of sexual assault. X-Men. That old torch song.

Threadgill, Jacob. "X-Men's Rogue: From Mississippi and Proud of It," *Clarion Ledger*, June 23, 2016. No one who loves Rogue as a character—as I certainly did growing up—can hear this account and not wonder about what Rogue's story, as a powerful, complicated, untouchable girl from the South, would have been had her artist known, or at least looked up, what Grace Jones looked like. "Claremont's only advice to Golden was that the musician and actress Grace Jones should inspire Rogue and that she have white streaks in her hair. The only problem was that Golden had never heard of Jones—this was years before her appearance in the second 'Conan the Barbarian' movie or the James Bond film 'A View to Kill.'"

Atwood, Margaret. *The Handmaid's Tale*. Seal Press, 1988. Who knows where my old high school copy is. Not cited within this collection but have also long been thinking about the extremely flagrant Orientalism and dodgy portrayal of Asian women in Atwood's *Oryx and Crake* (Bloomsbury, 2003).

Get Out, written and directed by Jordan Peele. Film, 2017.

The Day After Tomorrow, directed by Roland Emmerich. Film, 2004.

The Hunger Games universe; novels by Suzanne Collins, films directed by Gary Ross (1) and Francis Lawrence (2-5).

Fessler, Pam. "Study Shows Racial Wealth Gap Grows Wider," NPR, July 26, 2011.

The Watchmen universe; 1986 comics series by Alan Moore and Dave Gibbons, 2019 HBO series created, executive produced, and written by Damon Lindelof.

Harris, Middleton A., and Morrison, Toni, with the assistance of Morris Levitt, Roger Furman, Ernest Smith. *The Black Book*. Random House, 2019.

Vuong, Ocean. "Notebook Fragments," *Night Sky with Exit Wounds*. Copper Canyon Press, 2016.

MAIN CHARACTER SYNDROME

"Anna May Wong: The First Asian American Movie Star." UNLADY-LIKE2020 (series), produced and directed by Charlotte Mangin. PBS, April 8, 2020.

Didion, Joan. *Democracy*. Simon and Schuster, 1984.

Steinbeck, John. *Grapes of Wrath*. Penguin Books, 2002. Probably somewhere in my mom's garage with the rest of the books I was assigned as a kid. Honestly, justice for Sanora Babb and James Wong Howe.

Didion, Joan. *Slouching Towards Bethlehem*. Farrar, Strauss & Giroux, 2008.

Prickett, Sarah Nicole. "The American Experiment: Joan Didion's 1970s Notes on a Journey South," *Bookforum*, April/May 2017.

Long, John Luther. "Madame Butterfly," *Century Magazine*, 1898.

Loti, Pierre. *Madame Chrysanthème*. Current Literature Publishing Company, 1910. I wish I could show you this copy of *Madame Chrysanthème*, a very old translation from the early twentieth century, which I bought in some used bookstore, probably around the time that French was slowly supplanting Tagalog and Pangasinan as my most frequently used—and most grammatically confident—second language. It's a strange fact of my life, but there it is. Anyway, very early on I discovered the French orientalists; exactly how, I can't remember now, probably through Edward Said, but I can't say exactly. And *Madame Chrysanthème*, along with another Loti, *Le désert*, were books I read during that time. They're crowning (I use this imperial word deliberately) examples of French orientalist impulse, and this description of Loti in the introduction to *Madame Chrysanthème* may just as well describe Didion: "He indulges in a dainty pessimism and is most of all an impressionist . . . the style is direct; the vocabulary exquisite; the moral situations familiar; the characters not complex."

McCarthy, Mary. "Love and Death in the Pacific," *The New York Times*, April 22, 1984.

Mills, C. Wright. *The Power Elite*. Oxford University Press, 1956.

Mills, C. Wright, *The Sociological Imagination*. Oxford University Press, 1959.

Duras, Marguerite. I've only read her in the original French (dubious flex), and so on my shelves now we've got *L'amant* (Les Éditions de Minuit, 1984); *La maladie de la mort* (Les Éditions de Minuit, 1982); *Emily L* (Les Éditions de Minuit, 1987); *L'homme atlantique* (Les Éditions de Minuit, 1982); *Yann Andréa Steiner* (Collections Folio, Gallimard, 1992); *Les Yeux Bleus, Cheveux Noir* (Les Éditions de Minuit, 1986); *Théâtre: La Bête dans la jungle, Les papiers d'aspern, La danse de mort* (Gallimard, 1984); *Hiroshima mon amour* (Collections Folio, Gallimard, 1960); *L'amour* (Collections Folio, Gallimard, 1971). In writing all of that out I now realize that whoa, I have a lot of Duras, so I definitely had a Duras period. I think part of this collection is also because of a class I once took in college with a queer professor where we ended up spending a lot of time being fascinated by Duras's romantic obsession and affair with a young gay man thirty years her junior. Which is truly the most "queer who went to Berkeley" thing I could ever write.

Wharton, Edith. *The Age of Innocence*. D. Appleton and Company, 1920. As with Henry James and George Eliot, I came very late to the Wharton party and thank god for it, that I might be somewhat hardy enough in life to withstand its force. Please don't ask my friends about the fully unhinged texts I sent about Countess Olenska and which current Hollywood stars and their romances best encapsulate the Archer-Olenska dynamic, or the pictures of my dog in Ellen Olenska–like poses I sent to one group chat. (Justified by the fact that Wharton was notoriously also an Extremely Extra Dog Mom.)

Hugo, Victor. *L'homme qui rit*, 1869. I know I don't cite it in the Didion essay, but a line from one character, the Duchess Josiana, reminds me slightly of the self-enriching self-loathing of the wealthy touched on in the piece: "I want to despise myself. That lends a zest to pride."

LeBlanc, Paul. "Warren Calls Klobuchar's Health Care Plan 'Like a Post-it Note' in Fiery Debate Moment," CNN, February 20, 2020.

Didion, Joan. "Letter from Paradise, 21° 19' N., 157° 52' W." *Slouching Towards Bethlehem.*

Theroux, Joseph. "A Short History of Hawaiian Executions, 1826–1947," *Hawaiian Journal of History*, vol. 25, 1991. Hawaiian Historical Society. "Filipinos used to be hanged in Hawai'i with great regularity, just as the 19th century saw an equal number of Hawaiians hanged. Out of 75 documented civilian hangings in Hawai'i, 48 have been Filipino and Hawaiian. This place has always enjoyed a good hanging . . . Stanley Porteus, author of the informal Hawaiian history *Calabashes and Kings* (1945), was also the coauthor of a perfectly disgusting volume called *Temperament and Race*. In it, he said Australian Aborigines were nearly on a par with 'the idiot or imbecile.' Filipinos had 'a list of racial defects,' Hawaiians were unstable and dimwitted, Portuguese were 'impulsive, irresolute and excitable,' and Puerto Ricans were 'largely selected from amongst the most undesirable strata of the population' and were 'probably the worst timber for citizenship.' He gave much advice on how to maintain 'Nordic strongholds in America and Australia . . .' His book came out in 1926, during a lull in executions. In the year following its appearance, there were four executions, all of them Filipinos, a race that Porteus wrote was 'in an adolescent phase of development' and generally 'unstable.'"

Lacy, Robert, "Daughter of Old California," *Sewanee Review*, vol. 122, no. 3, summer 2014. Johns Hopkins University Press.

Didion, Joan. "The Executioner's Song," *The New York Times*, October 7, 1979.

Morrison, Toni. *Playing in the Dark*. Harvard University Press, 1992.

Didion, Joan, "Some Dreamers of the Golden Dream," *Slouching Towards Bethlehem.*

Gurba, Myriam. "It's Time to Take California Back from Joan Didion," *Electric Literature*, May 12, 2020.

Strings, Sabina. *Fearing the Black Body: The Racial Origins of Fatphobia*. New York University Press, 2019.

Jordan, June. *Some of Us Did Not Die: New and Selected Essays*. Civitas Books, 2009.

Chayka, Kyle. *The Longing for Less: Living with Minimalism*, Bloomsbury Publishing, 2020. "Being in the Glass House," Chayka writes, "among the handful of high-design, high-art objects that Johnson deigned to allow, doesn't really feel like freedom but entrapment in someone else's vision. Its sparseness might seem luxurious, but it's also expensive and finicky—a façade of simplicity."

Didion, Joan. *The White Album*. Simon and Schuster, 1979.

War of the Wildcats, directed by Albert S. Rogell. Film, 1943.

Rose, Steve. "'I promised Brando I would not touch his Oscar': the secret life of Sacheen Littlefeather," *The Guardian*, June 3, 2021.

Pico, Tommy. *Nature Poem*. Tin House, 2017. Also everything else Pico has ever written, including *IRL* (Birds, 2016), *Junk* (Tin House, 2018), and *Feed* (Tin House, 2019). Whenever I feel like lying down in traffic, I go back to read these poems instead.

Didion, Joan. "Why I Write," *Let Me Tell You What I Mean*. Knopf, 2021.

Fantastic Mr. Fox, directed by Wes Anderson. Film, 2009. And the first and only of Anderson's movies that I ever got, probably because I watched it at the right place, right time: having just moved to London with my love, feeling out of sorts, still grieving my father's death, and taking the long walk out from our shitty basement apartment under the heavy rain to the Notting Hill Gate cinema to watch this movie. The scene where "Ol' Man River" plays over the shot of these displaced animals in their found apartments, making a fragile, hopeful home—reader, I cried. That scene when Mr. Fox does a very embarrassing white liberal ally Black Panther salute to the wolf though? This is why we can't ever have nice things.

Als, Hilton. "Native Son: Daniel Beaty Pays Tribute to the Actor and Activist Paul Robeson," *The New Yorker*, March 23, 2015.

Heller, Nathan. "What We Get Wrong About Joan Didion," *The New Yorker*, February 1, 2021.

"REALITY IS ALL WE HAVE TO LOVE"

Berger, John. "The Chorus in Our Heads or Pier Paolo Pasolini," *Hold Everything Dear: Dispatches on Survival and Resistance*. Verso, 2007.

Berger, John. "Francis Bacon and Walt Disney," *About Looking*. Vintage International, 1991. Okay, it's going to become clear that I love John Berger, but the essay "Francis Bacon and Walt Disney" from the collection *About Looking* is a virtuosic fave that I couldn't quite write about in the collection itself; also a great riposte to the great aesthetes of grimdark nihilism and/or crackpot realism: "Bacon's view of the absurd has nothing in common with existentialism, or with the work of an artist like Samuel Beckett. Beckett approaches despair as a result of questioning, as a result of trying to unravel the language of the conventionally given answers. Bacon questions nothing, unravels nothing. He accepts the worst has happened. His lack of alternatives, within his view of the human condition, is reflected in the lack of any thematic development in his life's work. His progress, during 30 years, is a technical one of getting the worst into sharper focus. He succeeds, but at the same time the reiteration makes the worst less credible. That is his paradox. As you walk through room after room it becomes clear that you can live with the worst, that you can go on painting it again and again, that you can turn it into more and more elegant art, that you can put velvet and gold frames around it, that other people will buy it to hang on the walls of the rooms where they eat. It begins to seem that Bacon is a charlatan. Yet he is not. And his fidelity to his own obsession ensures that the paradox of his art yields a consistent truth, though it may not be the truth he intends. Bacon's art is, in effect, conformist. It is not with Goya or the early Eisenstein that he should be compared, but with Walt Disney. Both men make propositions about the alienated behaviour of our societies; and both, in a different way, persuade the viewer to accept what is. Disney makes alienated behavior look funny and sentimental and therefore, acceptable. Bacon interprets such behavior in terms of the worst possible having already happened, and so proposes that both refusal and hope are pointless. . . . Bacon's paintings do not comment, as is often said, on any actual experience of loneliness, anguish, or metaphysical doubt; nor do they comment on social relations, bureaucracy, industrial society, or the history of the 20th century. To do any of these things they would have to be concerned with consciousness. What they do is to demonstrate how alienation may provoke a longing for its own absolute form—which is mindlessness. This is the consistent truth demonstrated, rather than expressed, in Bacon's work."

Borcard, Stéphanie, and Métraux, Nicolas. *Dad Is Gone*. Photo series. The Story Institute, 2016.

James, Henry. *Daisy Miller* and *The Turn of the Screw*. Penguin English Library, 2012.

Evaristo, Bernardine. *The Emperor's Babe*. Hamish Hamilton, 2001.

Ahmed, Sara. "Feminist Killjoys (And Other Willful Subjects)," *The Scholar and Feminist Online*, issue 8.3, summer 2010. The Barnard Center for Research on Women.

Ahmed, Sara. "Speaking Out," http://feministkilljoys.com, June 2, 2016.

Cole, Teju. *Open City*. Random House, 2011.

Rousseau, Jean-Jacques. *Confessions*. Translated by J. M. Cohen. Penguin Random House, 1953.

Harrison, Kathryn. *The Kiss*. Random House Trade Paperbacks, 2011.

Fenton, James. "The Snap Revolution," *Granta*, March 1985.

Anderson, Benedict, "James Fenton's Slideshow," *New Left Review*, July/August 1986.

Crenshaw, Kimberlé. "Demarginalizing the Intersection of Race and Sex: A Black Feminist Critique of Antidiscrimination Doctrine, Feminist Theory, and Antiracist Politics," *University of Chicago Legal Forum*, vol. 1989, issue 1, article 8.

La Rabbia, directed and written by Giovanni Guareschi and Pier Paolo Pasolini. Film, 1963.

Berger, John. "The Production of the World," *Selected Essays*. Edited by Geoff Dyer. Vintage International, 2003.

Berger, John. "Woven, Sir," *The New Yorker*, April 2, 2001.

Berger, John. *Here Is Where We Meet: A Story of Crossing Paths*. Vintage International, 2006.

Lerner, Ben, and Treisman, Deborah. "Ben Lerner Reads John Berger, with Deborah Treisman," *The New Yorker*, July 1, 2016.

Greek myth nerd time. So Berger mentions three characters. Number one is Circe, whose island—and person—Odysseus visits in *The Odyssey* and finds so enthralling he takes a gap year with her instead of going back home to his wife, Penelope. Then there's Pasiphaë: cursed to be a size queen because her husband, Minos, wouldn't sacrifice a particularly beautiful bull to Poseidon, who as punishment, gives Pasiphäe the uncontrollable urge to mate with said beautiful bull. She succeeds and gives birth to the Minotaur. Then there's Telegonus, youngest son of Odysseus and Circe (Telemachus, on the other hand, is Odysseus's son with his wife, Penelope). An epic about Telegonus's journey to reunite with his father—the *telegony*—has survived only through mentions in other works, in multiple variants. One variant has Telegonus killing Odysseus, who mistakes Telegonus for Telemachus. All this to say: woven, sir.

AUTOBIOGRAPHY IN ASIAN FILM, OR WHAT WE TALK ABOUT WHEN WE TALK ABOUT REPRESENTATION

Berger, John. "The Chorus in Our Heads or Pier Paolo Pasolini," *Hold Everything Dear: Dispatches on Survival and Resistance*. Verso, 2007.

Long, Rachel. "Apples," *My Darling from the Lions*. Picador, 2020.

Sandoval, Isabel, and Galatini, Alessia. "Romantic Ecstasy: In Conversation with Isabel Sandoval," *Girls on Tops*, October 20, 2021.

The Life Aquatic with Steve Zissou, directed by Wes Anderson. Film, 2004.

Browning, Mark. *Wes Anderson: Why His Movies Matter*. Praeger, 2011.

Monsoon Wedding, directed by Mira Nair. Film, 2002.

Chee, Alexander. *How to Write an Autobiographical Novel*. Mariner Books, 2018.

Happy Together, directed by Wong Kar-wai. Film, 1997. Sudden urge to get this citation tattooed.

Berger, John. *To the Wedding*. Vintage International, 1996. "Scrap isn't trash, Gino. Marry her." I'm not crying you're crying!!!!!!!!!!!!

Berger, John. *Lilac and Flag*. Vintage International, 1992. Contains, for my money, one of the most wondrous portrayals of the afterlife, and one of the most effective surprise endings in literature.

In the Realm of the Senses, directed by Nagisa Oshima. Film, 1976.

Sei Shōnagon. *The Pillow Book of Sei Shōnagon*. Translated and edited by Ivan Morris. Penguin Classics, 1967.

The Pillow Book, directed by Peter Greenaway. Film, 1996.

Crouching Tiger, Hidden Dragon, directed by Ang Lee. Film, 2000.

House of Flying Daggers, directed by Zhang Yimou. Film, 2004.

Three Times, directed by Hou Hsiao-hsien. Film, 2005.

Millennium Mambo, directed by Hou Hsiao-hsien. Film, 2001.

The Assassin, directed by Hou Hsiao-hsien. Film, 2015.

While we're here, another fave: Hou Hsiao-hsien's *Café Lumiere* (2003), an ode to the films of Yasujiro Ozu, shot in Japan and staring Tadanobu Asano and Yo Hitoto. I've been trying to find the soundtrack to this film for almost twenty years. One of my favorite films in one of my favorite genres—slow cinema—especially for the scene when Yo Hitoto's character falls asleep on the subway with Tadanobu Asano's character quietly looking over her. Also the domestic dining scene after the main character reveals she's pregnant, and her gruff, taciturn father starts giving her the food off his plate.

Bagad Men Ha Tan and Doudou N'Diaye Rose, "Duc de Rohan," *Dakar*, 2000.

In the Mood for Love, directed by Wong Kar-wai. Film, 2000.

Clean, directed by Olivier Assayas. Film, 2004.

Eno, Brian. "Spider and I," *Before and After Science*, 1977. There's an interview with Eno in the magazine *Apartamento*, where he talks about class and music: "I have to say there is a lot of amazing music out there now, especially in England. But there certainly are some differences from the old times. For me the biggest difference is really based in the social arrangements we have now, as opposed to the ones we had in the past. If you think of the period from the end of World War II until about 1975, economists call it 'the golden age of capitalism,' because women acquired more rights, as did ethnic minorities and disabled people, people of different classes were able to move through society, workers got better protection, unions were more powerful. All the things that socialist governments want. So in my opinion it shouldn't be called the golden age of capitalism. It should be called the golden age of socialism. This was a time during which some version of socialism really worked well. One of the things that resulted from that was a new level of social mobility. So kids like me, from a working-class background, got a decent education because it was free. That's disappearing. We got proper healthcare, because it was free. And that's disappearing, too. And most important of all, when you left college, as I did, and didn't get a job, because you wanted to do something creative, the government looked after you—somewhat reluctantly, but it did. So many good bands and good artists came out of that period. This is a big difference between the music business now and then—the absence of a working-class voice. There's a lot of fantastic music now, and it's nearly all from the middle-class voice. I have no problem with this; it's the voice of people who have an expectation of stability and increase. But it's just one voice. I want to hear voices with some anger in them, voices of people who live closer to the edge. Some struggle. Some desire to change the world. And that's what the working-class voice can offer. The middle-class voice is one of melancholy. The working-class voice is one of anger."

I tried to find the *New Yorker* article where Richard Brody talks about actorly self-transformation and only found a tweet from him about it: "Natalie Portman is similar to Tippi Hedren—neither has enormous technique, both have a distinctive manner and a powerful presence. But actorly self-transformation is wildly overvalued now; many filmmakers—mainly 'prestigious' ones—cater to (or, likely, share) that critical taste." @tnyfrontrow, 5:04pm, October 30, 2018. I didn't remember that he also contrasted the value of "transformation" with presence!

Buenos Aires Zero Degree: The Making of Happy Together, directed by Wong Kar-wai. Film, 1999.

Sympathy for Lady Vengeance, directed by Park Chan-wook. Film, 2006. This is up there with *Happy Together* and Hayao Miyazaki's *Princess Mononoke* for "films that built me." Fun fact: the song "The Angel" from the soundtrack is one of my dog's favorite songs for me to play on the piano; I think it's all the high notes. (Update: Her new favorite is "House of Woodcock" from the *Phantom Thread* soundtrack; she's less fond of "For the Hungry Boy.") There's dopamine, and then there's seeing your dog sleepily roll over to expose her belly while you play the piano. I love you, Xena.

The Handmaiden, directed by Park Chan-wook. Film, 2016. This! Film! Yes, I learned how to play "The Saviour Who Came to Tear My Life Apart" on the piano, too. Why? Because I like crying, I guess!! Tear my life apart, too, I guess!!!!!

Brown, Emma. "Park Chan-Wook's Humor and Heart," *Interview*, October 26, 2016.

Chang, David. "BBQ," *Ugly Delicious*, Netflix, February 23, 2018.

Kaufman, Anthony. "Interview: The 'Mood' of Wong Kar Wai; the Asian Master Does It Again," *IndieWire*, February 2, 2001.

Moss, Emma-Lee. "'That One Day Is All You Have': How Hong Kong's Domestic Workers Seized Sunday," *The Guardian*, March 10, 2017.

THE CHILDREN OF POLYPHEMUS

Morrison, Toni. *Playing in the Dark*. Harvard University Press, 1992.

Cinderella, directed by Clyde Geronimi, Wilfred Jackson, Hamilton Luske. Animated film, Disney, 1950.

Cinderella, directed by Robert Iscove. Television film, Disney and ABC, 1997. Actually, put this film up there with *Happy Together*, *Sympathy for Lady Vengeance*, and *Princess Mononoke* for me.

Perrault, Charles. "Cendrillon ou la petite pantoufle de verre," *Histoires ou contes du temps passés*, 1697.

Another name given to the Treaty of Ryswick, in which, among other things, France "received" the Spanish territories of Tortuga and Saint-Domingue: the Peace of Ryswick. Other world-forming treaties that went by the stage name of "Peace": the Treaty of Peace, also known as the Treaty of Paris of 1898, signed by Spain and the United States, ending the Spanish-American War, with Spain relinquishing sovereignty over Cuba and ceding Guam, Puerto Rico, and the Philippines to the United States, thus establishing the latter as a global imperial power; the treaty between Spain and America was signed on December 10, 1898. The Philippine-American War, also known as the Philippine Insurrection, began February 4, 1899.

Perrault, Charles. *Courses de testes et de bague faites par le roy et par les princes et seigneurs de sa cour en l'année 1662*. Paris: Imprimerie royale, Sébastien Mabre-Cramoisy, 1670. Apparently you can see an original

illustrated copy of Perrault's (along with writers Esprit Fléchier, Israel
Silvestre, François Chauveau, and Gilles Rousselet) account of the festival at Princeton, maybe also the Met? Also, I wish I had been able to
include this in the essay: the 2016 sports documentary *Les Bleus: une
autre histoire de la France 1996–2016* is a fantastic exploration of the
political history of the French national football team, colloquially
known as *Les Bleus*, or the Blues (for their customary blue jersey). The
documentary particularly lingers on the hopes—and hypocrisies—
attached to the multiracial late nineties football team (also the team
my own partner grew up on), the postracial fantasies of French society, and the undeniable racism faced by its football players. And the
reason I'm bringing it up here is because in that documentary, there is
a scene that features a Parisian parade, held in the late nineties, that
almost exactly mirrors the "festival of nations" held by Louis XIV and
documented by Perrault, down to the (neo)colonial ethnic fetishizing
and national self-aggrandizement. The first time I saw it I was stunned,
but when I went back to look for it so I could make the comparison, the
documentary had been removed from all streaming sites. I still very
much urge people to find it and watch it.

Naithani, Sadhana. *The Story-Time of the British Empire: Colonial and Postcolonial Folkloristics*. University Press of Mississippi, 2010.

Jaffe, Nina, and Sánchez, Enrique O. *The Golden Flower: A Taíno Myth
from Puerto Rico*. Piñata Books, 2005.

Allooloo, Siku. "Survivor's Guilt," *The New Quarterly*, 2017.

The fucking Clavería Decree of 1849 and the *Catálogo alfabético de apellidos*. Source: the Ayalas Museum's Filipinas Heritage Library Catalog.
Also source: my name, life.

There are so many terrible English translations of this Horace ode,
most of them typical of their era and class provenance, i.e., weird little
imperial meringues that have nothing to do with Horace. But my favorite translation, which I can no longer find, was a kind of translation
within a translation. I first read it in Michel de Montaigne's *Essais*, with
Montaigne transcribing the Latin (his first language), to then be
translated into his French text. Here is the passage that precedes Montaigne's quoting of the Horace ode, translated by William Carew Haz-
litt in 1877 and with us by way of Project Gutenberg, where Montaigne
deftly describes just why the Horace ode speaks to him: "I should com-
mend a soul of several stages, that knows both how to stretch and to
slacken itself; that finds itself at ease in all conditions whither fortune
leads it; that can discourse with a neighbour, of his building, his hunt-